Social Democracy in Manitoba

Social Democracy in Manitoba: A History of the CCF-NDP

NELSON WISEMAN

THE UNIVERSITY OF MANITOBA PRESS

Canadian Cataloguing in Publication Data

Wiseman, Nelson, 1946-
 Social Democracy in Manitoba

 Includes index.
 Bibliography: p.
 ISBN 0-88755-118-1

 1. New Democratic Party of Manitoba—History.
 2. Socialism—Manitoba—History. I. Title.
 JL299.A54W58   324.27127'07   C81-091375-5

C. 2

48,876

To my parents

Contents

Preface

This study began as a PH.D. dissertation in the Department of Political Economy at the University of Toronto. It was researched and written between 1971 and 1974 and defended at an oral examination in January, 1975. In attendance were Gad Horowitz who served as the thesis supervisor, Meyer Brownstone and Kenneth McNaught who acted as advisors, W. L. Morton who filled the role of external examiner, and Stephen Clarkson and Jack McLeod who were kind in their comments and took me to lunch at Hart House afterwards. I am grateful to all of them. This book has been published with the help of grants from the Canada Council and from the Social Science Federation of Canada, using funds provided by the Social Sciences and Humanities Research Council of Canada.

The version of the study presented here differs from the dissertation in a number of ways. One chapter has been added and one deleted. A highly abridged version of the chapter that was dropped—one that maintains its argumentation but forsakes its documentation—appeared in *Queen's Quarterly* (1981) as "The Pattern of Prairie Politics." The chapter that was added—the last one dealing with the NDP in power—was written in 1975 and rewritten in 1979. All the chapters were revised and pruned, some more than others, at various points. A version of Chapter 2, one that is more detailed and set in a slightly broader context, appeared in the *Canadian Historical Review* (1973). A slightly different version of Chapter 4 appeared in *Prairie Forum* (1979). Other changes to the original study include the addition of an Introduction and an Epilogue.

Some chapters focus on specific incidents in the party's history such as its entry into a wartime coalition government (Chapter 2), the expulsion of three MLAs in the 1940s (Chapter 3), and the transformation of the CCF into the NDP (Chapter 5). Other chapters are more general and devote attention to subjects that stretch beyond a single point or incident in time. They include topics such as the party's membership, organization, philosophy, strategy, leadership, its relations with the organized labour movement and farmers, and its connections with the municipal and national wings of the party.

The form and substance of the chapters were dictated by the material in the primary sources that were available. The largest single collection consulted—the CCF Papers at the Provincial Archives of Manitoba—have little in them, alas, dealing with the period before 1940. The missing party files, according to a few people I spoke to, were swept away in the Winnipeg flood of 1950. Some archival material on the 1930s, as well as later years, was gleaned from the four boxes of papers dealing with "Manitoba" in the CCF Records at the Public Archives of Canada in Ottawa. Other valuable sources included the files of various party officials such as Stanley Knowles, Magnus Eliason, and Lloyd Stinson. I am grateful to all who gave me access to their papers, corresponded with me, and agreed to be interviewed.

The problem in dealing with the NDP in the 1970s was not a lack of primary material, but the opposite. The challenge here was not a reconstruction of past events with little data to work with but of sifting and interpreting the party's much more substantial recent files and the huge volume of paper produced by the NDP government. I was granted generous access to the NDP's party files, current as well as old. I arranged a transfer of these files to the provincial archives and transported many of them there in my car.

A note may be in order here about my relationship to the NDP. Authors are often associated with their subjects. Does my subject matter not reveal something of my political inclinations? Why did I not write a history of Manitoba's Liberals or Conservatives, Social Crediters or Communists? My relationship to the NDP changed during the course of my research and participation in party affairs. In the 1960s I served as president of the University of Manitoba NDP Club and sat, for a time, on the party's provincial executive committee. In 1972, after being active in a left-wing faction within the party known as the Waffle, I left the NDP. I devoted less time to politics and more to political science and other pursuits. During the NDP's period in office in the 1970s I worked for brief periods as a consultant to various government agencies, including the Department of Industry and Commerce and the Manitoba Housing and Renewal Corporation.

John Queen (All photographs
courtesy Provincial Archives of
Manitoba)

Frederick Dixon

William Ivens

Marcus Hyman

Beatrice Brigden

John Bracken

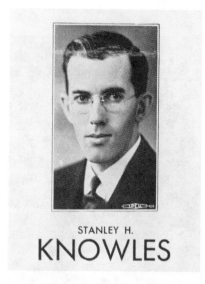

STANLEY H.
KNOWLES

S. J. Farmer

From a municipal campaign in the
1930s

KNOWLES WAS WOODSWORTH'S CHOICE- **HE MUST WIN**

THE NORTH CENTRE SEAT
House of Commons- Ottawa

VOTE CCF

The 1942 federal election

The coalition cabinet of 1942. From left to right: S.J. Farmer, J.S. McDiarmid, N. Turnbull, S. Marcoux, A.R. Welch, I. Schaltz, D.L. Campbell, W. Morton, J.O. McLenaghen, J. Bracken, E. Willis, S.S. Garson

What is the L.P.P. really after?

Look at the Record of Canadian Communists In Six Simple Stages

Can you trust people with such a record? . . . Can you have confidence in the spokesmen of the L.P.P.?

You can't, for you cannot know what their **real** aims are!

A CCF pamphlet in 1945

Berry Richards

D. L. Johnson

Wilbert Doneleyko

From the 1945 provincial election

BLAZING
THE TRAIL
TO

You Need the CCF — The CCF Needs You

The CCF caucus, 1945-49

VOTE CCF
SWAILES

FOR

MAYOR

VOTE
DON
SWAILES [1]

The 1952 Winnipeg mayoralty
campaign

CCF

HUMANITY FIRST **MEANS**

PROGRESS

Russ Paulley in the 1953 campaign

E. A. Hansford

Donovan Swailes

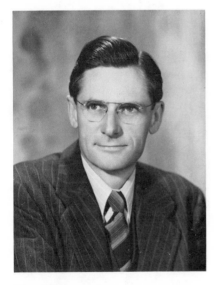

Lloyd Stinson

... When These Things Are Possible

USE YOUR BALLOT -- PREVENT POVERTY

1940s election pamphlet

1940s election pamphlets

1958 election pamphlet

Yiddish pamphlet, 1945. Top: S. J. Farmer and H. A. Gray;
Bottom: Donovan Swailes and Lloyd Stinson

ГОЛОСУЙТЕ НА

ССФ

І СТАВТЕ

ЛЮДСТВО ПЕРШИМ

STEWART, Alistair | X |

ПЕРЕВИБЕРІТЬ

STEWART, Alistair | X |

Ukrainian pamphlet, 1953

New Party pamphlets, 1959-60

From the *New Party Newsletter*,
vol. 1, no. 1.

Social Democracy in Manitoba

Introduction

In 1870, when Manitoba joined Confederation, it was an isolated settlement of some 12,000 people, almost evenly divided between French- and English-speaking, and mainly Metis. By the 1890s, the province had been remade in the image of Ontario.[1] Yet in 1919, the capital city of Winnipeg exhibited a level of class consciousness and class conflict that was decidedly more reflective of the European than the North American experience. Part of the explanation for these dramatic changes lies in the massive migration to the sparsely populated prairies. Between 1881 and 1921, the population of what are now the prairies grew from approximately 100,000 to 2,000,000. In 1911 over half of Winnipeg's population was foreign-born, and in 1913 Canada received one immigrant for every eighteen of its citizens. The United States, in contrast, received only one immigrant for every eighty citizens in 1914, the year of the greatest immigration to that country in the same decade. In Manitoba the three major sources of new settlers were Ontario, the British Isles, and continental Europe. These three distinct waves of settlers tended to settle in different areas and brought with them different political outlooks or ideologies.[2]

The first wave of settlers to Manitoba came from rural Ontario during the last quarter of the nineteenth century. They quickly occupied the best agricultural lands and secured homesteads along the new Canadian Pacific Railway. The Ontarians became Manitoba's charter group, and they settled in their greatest numbers in the rural southwest and in the fashionable areas of Winnipeg, especially south of the Assiniboine River.

The dominant ideological outlook of these Ontario settlers was what W.L. Morton called the "grit agrariansim" of rural Ontario. These settlers were essentially nineteenth-century laissez-faire liberals. Unlike their lib-

eral American cousins, however, they did exhibit some traces of tory influence, such as support for the monarchy, for parliamentary traditions, and
for public, community-wide institutions such as a national police force and
government-owned utilities. Canada's West, therefore, was less wild, less
woolly, and less liberal than the American West, and the state played a
greater role in its development. Ideologically, the Ontario group was essentially liberal, but "tory-touched."[3]

The transplanted Grits and Tories of Ontario became the early Grits
and Tories, and later Liberals and Conservatives, in Manitoba. Some of the
Ontarians were of United Empire Loyalist stock and reflected earlier,
American influences. Others were children of Ontario parents who had
emigrated from Britain in the early years of the nineteenth century, from
a society that was still relatively rural. It seemed both fitting, and telling,
that the Ontario-born son of Canada's first prime minister—Hugh John
Macdonald—became a premier of Manitoba late in the nineteenth century.

In a sense Manitoba was the Ontario of the prairie provinces. On the
issue of language rights it was more Orange than Ontario, as the bitter dispute over French and Catholic school rights revealed. Manitoba imported
its early American-modelled farm organizations—the Grange and the
Patrons of Industry—only after they had become established in Ontario.
Rural Manitoba, although dominated by Ontario's essentially liberal outlook, also reflected enough of Ontario's toryism, however, to reject reci-
procity with the United States, by both its legislature and electorate, an
act that bewildered liberal farmers farther west. In terms of popular vote,
in both Ontario and Manitoba the Conservatives won majorities in the 1911
federal election fought on the issue of free trade.

By dominating rural politics the Ontarians dominated provincial politics, since the overwhelming majority of legislative seats were rural. The
continuing influence of Ontarians in Manitoba politics in the twentieth
century was perhaps best reflected in the fact that every Manitoba premier
in the century, until Ed Schreyer in 1969, was either born in Ontario or was
of Ontario parentage.

A second wave of Manitoba settlers came directly from Britain.
Although Britain was the most advanced industrial state in the world, its
workers had had no real increase in wages between 1895 and 1913. Working-
class British immigrants came to Canada from an environment where trade
unions and labour politics were in the ascendancy, as the rise of Britain's
Independent Labour party in the 1890s reveals. Despite the wide cultural
and ideological differences between these two first groups of settlers—the
Ontario and the British—both were Anglo-Saxon pioneers and their status

in the West at the turn of the century was roughly equal. The newcomers were eagerly welcomed by the province's race-proud Canadian-born Anglo-Saxons. The British-born headed quickly for the cities to work in industry. With their experience in union organization, the British-born group became the backbone of Manitoba's nascent, organized labour movement, and in later years provided the leadership of the CCF–NDP.

The third wave of settlers in Manitoba came from continental Europe, and primarily from eastern Europe. These non–Anglo-Saxons were "alien" and suspect in the eyes of both the Ontario and British groups. At times their very presence was attacked and challenged; at best they were tolerated. The Winnipeg Trades Council in 1914, dominated by British-born immigrants, denounced eastern European immigrants as "half civilized people" and a threat to existing unionists. And when soldiers returning after the First World War beat suspected aliens and socialists in the streets, they were applauded by the *Manitoba Free Press* and middle and upper class opinion.

In Europe, these immigrants had been exposed to many of the radical political theories of the day. However, the Europeans did not play a leading role in early political developments in Manitoba. Rather, they yielded to the politics of the charter group. Large numbers of them were isolated in rural ethnic settlements on marginal farmlands. In response to their new opportunity and in their efforts to prove loyalty to their new country, these minorities generally voted Liberal (though in 1914 proof of loyalty expressed itself in a Conservative vote). However, those Europeans who settled in Winnipeg's traditional immigrant reception area, the North End, were sufficiently numerous, concentrated, and class-conscious to support radical and socialist causes and eventually to have a strong effect on the politics of north Winnipeg.

Labour-socialist politics in Manitoba were as much determined by the newly arrived Britons and Europeans as agrarian politics were determined by Ontarians. Before the mid-1890s the existing craft unions in Winnipeg had had much in common with their fraternal organizations in Ontario. Later, however, Winnipeg's labour movement was remade by British and European immigrants. In 1895 Winnipeg became the home of Canada's first Independent Labor Party, and in 1899 twenty-seven separate unions could be counted in the annual May Day parade. A year later, A.W. Puttee, the British-born printer and editor of Winnipeg's labour newspaper, *The Voice,* was elected to the House of Commons. Puttee's newspaper was a leading force in the propagation of British Labourist and Christian Socialist principles.

Although Winnipeg experienced an economic boom from the turn of the century to 1913, wage workers saw little benefit from this prosperity, and their conditions did not improve during the First World War. One of every five infants born in Winnipeg in 1912 died within a year; most of these deaths were in the North End. Real wages actually declined in Canada between 1910 and 1920. Conditions favourable to the rise of radicalism included an unstable and constantly changing work force, low wages, poor working conditions, and rapid industrialization. Under pressure from Winnipeg's business community, the Roblin Conservative government reduced the minimum wage for child labour and increased the maximum hours of work for women and children in 1914.

Many of the immigrant workers had known radical and reform movements in their mother countries. The British workers came from a society conscious of class divisions. They had some acquaintance with socialist and labourist ideas and many of them identified with British labour-socialist leaders such as Ramsay MacDonald and Kier Hardie who visited Winnipeg in 1906 and 1907 respectively. Some of the continental Europeans were familiar with various European radical movements including anarchism, Marxism, and syndicalism. In this fertile intellectual soil, several left-wing movements grew up during the first two decades of this century. In Winnipeg they included locals of the Canadian Socialist League, the Socialist Party of Canada, a Socialist Party of Manitoba, a Manitoba Labor Party, a Social Democratic Party, a Dominion Labor Party, a reformed Independent Labor Party (ILP), and a Labor Representation Committee. Most of these groups were led by and composed almost wholly of British-born immigrants, but some—like the SDP which was organized on the basis of language locals—had their largest base in the European community. Before the First World War, about a fifth of the SDP's national membership of 3500 lived in Winnipeg.

Ross McCormack's analysis of these movements has identified three distinct political tendencies or strains.[4] Winnipeg was a hotbed of radicalism in Canada and was a key centre for all three of them. On some issues, such as strengthening unions and improving social conditions, all three tendencies could agree. But there were profound differences among them as well as in their philosophies and strategies. The most moderate and the largest tendency was composed of British labourites. Drawing on the ideas of Christian ethics, Marxism, and Gladstonian radicalism, the leaders of this group worked for an immediate improvement of social conditions. These reformers believed in working within the established political system to effect social change. Parliament and the state's bureaucracy were seen as potential vehicles for social and economic change. This group modelled its politics and programs on the British Labour Party and mobilized many of the British trade unionists in Winnipeg. Many of its leaders, such as J.S. Woodsworth, Salem Bland, and Fred Tipping, were clergymen influenced by Methodism and the social gospel. They wanted to help man by improving his material conditions. This labourite, "reformist," tendency was strongly pragmatic and eschewed sophisticated ideological notions in favour of practical, specific legislative proposals.

A second strain of radical thinking in working-class circles was expressed by "rebels" who placed more stock in labour unions than in labour parties. This group were militant industrial unionists who believed that unions and the general strike held the best prospect for the advance of the working class. They saw industrial unions, as opposed to craft unions, as the only effective force to fight the increasing concentration of capital. This group included Winnipeg General Strike leader R.B. Russell and identified with the One Big Union (obu) and syndicalism, forces that were relatively strong on the west coast.

The third radical strain was made up of British Marxist revolutionaries and some eastern European workers who insisted that the capitalist system, by its very nature, was an exploitive system incapable of being reformed. Their goal was the abolition of the wage system, and their tactics were political action. To others on the left they were considered "impossiblists" because of their preoccupation with ideological purity and their insistence that capitalism could not be reformed. They were suspicious of Christian socialists and supported scientific socialism. Followers of this tendency considered the moderate labourite "reformers" to be counter-revolutionary because they were satisfied with securing piecemeal reforms rather than attacking the wage system directly. From this perspective, the labourites were hopelessly bourgeois. After 1920 many of this group of "impossiblists" would drift into the Communist Party.

In Manitoba, the influence of radical and syndicalist American labour —expressed in the United States in the Industrial Workers of the World— was not as great as it was in Alberta or British Columbia; nor was the influence of the British Columbia-based Socialist Party of Canada. Rather, the dominant political group on the left were the British-born labourites composed mainly of liberal-minded reformers, Christian socialists, and trade union leaders who were inclined to reform rather than revolution.

The dominant "reformist" strain that emerged in Winnipeg was class-oriented and imbued with reform rather than revolutionary ideas. It was neither doctrinaire nor sectarian. Its leaders spoke of the inevitable coming of a classless society and a Co-operative Commonwealth as the role of the state expanded, slowly but surely, in society. This tendency was represented by the Winnipeg Labor party in 1896, the Independent Labor Party in 1906, the Manitoba Labor Party in 1910, the Labor Representation Committee in 1912, and the Dominion Labor Party in 1918. It emphasized that its proposed reforms — direct legislation, the eight-hour day, public health regulations, a workmen's compensation law, a land tax, and public ownership of utilities and monopolies — would benefit all classes. The campaigns of these groups, however, were almost wholly dependent on working-class support. Because of their eagerness for publicly owned municipal enterprises, their leaders were often labelled, as in Britain, "gas and water socialists."

Beginning before the war, the Labor Representation Committee and the Social Democratic Party began to co-operate in their electoral efforts. In 1913, for example, they succeeded in electing SDP candidate Dick Rigg to Winnipeg City Council. Since then, Winnipeg has always had "labour" aldermen. Although the LRC and the SDP parted company in the 1914 provincial election over the issue of eastern European immigration, they combined their efforts again in north Winnipeg in the 1915 provincial election.

The Winnipeg General Strike of 1919, led by workers in the building and metals trades, reflected the social and political divisions between the established Anglo-Saxon and generally Ontario-born political elites on the one hand and the British-born and eastern European workers of all three radical tendencies on the other.[5] It also reflected the division between city and country. Every rural newspaper in Manitoba condemned the Strike, and labour issues such as the eight-hour day were ridiculed in the countryside. The Strike, which involved over 25,000 workers, was for some a struggle for collective bargaining rights; for others, it was part of a broader revolutionary class struggle, an anti-capitalist effort.

The Strike was defeated by vigorous action on the part of the federal government, including the arrest of the Strike leaders. In the aftermath, the radical and revolutionary tendencies, as expressed by the One Big Union, the Socialist Party of Canada, and the Social Democratic Party, lost most of their influence and were overshadowed by the reform tendency, which came out of the Strike relatively unscathed. When the SDP fell apart, some of its members, mainly Ukrainians and Finns, tended to support the new Communist Party, which drew upon their sympathy for the Russian Revolution. The British social democrats, however, drifted into the mainstream labourite camp. The British labourite reform tendency found expression in a once again reformed Independent Labor Party in 1920.

One of the far-reaching results of the Strike was the workers' growing aloofness from the general strike principle and revolutionary theory. The failure of the Strike undermined the influence of both the rebel and revolutionary tendencies, leaving the reformers, the labourites, to lead the majority of workers through the 1920s and beyond. The task was made easier by the heightened awareness of class interests that grew out of the Strike and the ruthless manner in which it was defeated.

The twenties and thirties:
the party's formation

1

The Winnipeg General Strike of 1919 left a lasting political legacy. Though the most radical and revolutionary elements of the leftist movements lost their influence, the more moderate reformers gained credibility. The increase in class consciousness fostered by the Strike helped the reformers gather support among the workers. Winnipeg's North End provided a secure base for reform and radical candidates at all levels of government, and in 1921 voters sent J.S. Woodsworth, a moderate whose political views were influenced by the social gospel movement, to represent them in the House of Commons.[1]

Labour and business interests, however, were further polarized by the Strike. Ideological divisions between the new British immigrant worker and the established Canadian farmer, both Anglo-Saxon, were represented by political factions and parties. Just as the Citizens' Committee of 1000 represented Winnipeg's economic elite and arose to challenge the Strike Committee,[2] the Independent Labor Party represented the largest bloc of Winnipeg's working class and arose to challenge the rural and business-oriented Liberal, Conservative, and Farmers' governments. The divisions were reflected over and over again after 1919 in municipal, provincial, and federal elections. It was not until fifty years later, with the election of the New Democratic Party in the provincial legislature, that a cabinet was drawn from the sons of the "aliens" as well as of the elite.

The first leader of the reorganized Independent Labor Party was Fred Dixon. The British-born Dixon, according to one of his political colleagues, "was without doubt the most popular man in public life that Winnipeg has ever had."[3] He was elected to the legislature as an Independent in 1914 and 1915; and in the 1920 election he topped a list of forty-one candidates in Winnipeg constituency, almost tripling the vote of his nearest rival. Dixon, a single-taxer, a pacifist, and a supporter of direct legislation, was a moderate and had received backing from the provincial Liberals before the First World War when his platform was identical to theirs. But after the War and the Strike, he broke with the Liberals. He remained a moderate, however, and at the ILP's founding convention he insisted that members of the Socialist Party of Canada and the newly formed Communist Party be excluded.[4]

Dixon's premature death in 1928 made way for the rise of two other ILP notables, S.J. Farmer and John Queen. Farmer came to Canada in 1900 from Wales and worked as a railway clerk. Like Dixon, he had been a supporter of direct legislation and had opposed conscription during the First World War. He traced his socialism not to the old country but to the results of the Strike and the formation of the ILP in 1920.[5] In the 1917 federal election he was the nominee of the Anti-Conscription League in Winnipeg Centre. He was elected mayor of Winnipeg for 1922 and 1923, and later became CCF leader and a provincial cabinet minister. John Queen, who had been nominated by the SDP in Winnipeg North in the 1917 federal election, followed Dixon as leader of the provincial ILP in the early 1920s and later became its municipal leader. He had immigrated to Canada from Scotland in 1906 and gained some popularity for sponsoring a bill in the legislature that permitted the operation of Sunday trains to Lake Winnipeg beaches, allowing workers' families a day at the lake.

By the mid-1920s the ILP was an established political force in Winnipeg with an electoral base in the central, western, eastern and northern districts of the city. Seventeen ILP branches, claiming a membership of between 800 and 1000, functioned in Winnipeg, Brandon, and northern Manitoba in the early 1930s. By this time the ILP could boast twenty-eight elected members at three levels of government. Between 1933 and 1937 ILP candidates for aldermanic and school board positions in Winnipeg received 20 to 35 per cent of the vote. If communist and independent labour candidates were added, the municipal leftist vote consistently exceeded 40 per cent. John Queen was elected to the mayoralty every year but one between 1935 and 1942, and ILP nominees also won the St. Boniface mayoralty and the chairmanship of the Winnipeg School Board.

The majority of the ILP's active membership was British-born and its socialism could be identified by its application form:

The Independent Labor Party of Manitoba is formed for the purpose of giving political, social and economic expression to the ideals and aspirations of all workers, regardless of industrial affiliation, who believe in the establishment of a Co-operative Commonwealth, based on the principles of *Social Ownership* of the means of production, distribution and exchange, for the supply of human needs instead of for profit-making. The old system of private ownership and profit-making now needs to be transformed. The conflict of interest between the worker and capitalist is a struggle for the control of government — the capitalist to retain and the worker to secure it by political struggle. This is the class struggle.[6]

The ILP's main political opposition during the 1920s and 1930s was the Bracken government. John Bracken represented the stability-oriented, established, Anglo-Saxon farmer. The older parties had been temporarily discredited, but their south Winnipeg elites quietly, and warmly, endorsed the United Farmers of Manitoba government of 1922 "because they hoped that a farmers' government would be a conservative and economical one."[7] And it was: keeping a tight rein on health, education, and welfare expenditures, one of its first acts was to reduce allowances for widowed and deserted mothers.[8] By the 1927 election the government referred to itself as the "Bracken party" and its prominent campaign slogan was "A Business (not a party) Government."

After the UFM withdrew from political activity in 1928, Bracken attempted to broaden, by co-option, his government's base. In 1931 he proposed a coalition, or what he termed a "non-partisan government," to his parliamentary opponents. The provincial Conservatives rebuffed his advances, and the ILP, led by Queen, rejected them as well. The Liberals, however, voted to join the government in return for three cabinet portfolios.[9] The merger proved mutually profitable as the new coalition partners, now entitled Liberal–Progressives, swept to a commanding majority in 1932. (see Table 1).

TABLE 1

Manitoba provincial election, 1932

Party	Seats	Percentage of popular vote
Conservative	10	36
Liberal–Progressive	38	40
Labour	5	17
Other	2	8
Total	55	101

In the same year, a new national party, the Co-operative Common-wealth Federation, was founded in Calgary at a convention of urban labour parties, radical farm organizations, and Christian socialists and intel-lectuals. The ILP provided the early leadership for the fledgling party in Manitoba, and for a brief time S.J. Farmer was chairman of both the ILP and the Manitoba CCF. The CCF, however, wanted to broaden its support, and to this end it embarked on a drive to find members outside the city. This new strategy—expansion beyond an urban labour base—was to lead to a fight with ILP diehards. Manitoba's farmers had certainly led something of an assault on the federal Liberals and Conservatives by forming the Progressive Party. But, as a member of the Brandon Labor Party put it, "It was not that old country Scotch socialism that the farmers were talking about."[10]

At the 1932 convention of the United Farmers of Manitoba, a few farmers sympathetic to the newly formed CCF tried unsuccessfully to enlist the support of the UFM for the programs of the new party.[11] The UFM, however, had adopted a "non-partisan" policy four years earlier and refused to give its support. The UFM continued to represent Manitoba's estab-lished Anglo-Saxon farmers who were largely from Ontario. These farmers, generally, were not in sympathy with social democracy nor with the prov-ince's ethnic minorities.[12] There were a few UFM members, however, who were disgruntled with Bracken and his new Liberal allies, some referring bitterly to the federal Progressive "betrayal" of the 1920s in which T.A. Crerar and his Manitoba MPs made peace with the Liberals. From this small amorphous group, critical of the UFM's leadership, came the nucleus of the Independent Farmer Party. It was a brief effort to establish a rural partner for the ILP.

The Independent Farmer Party grew out of a series of meetings orga-nized in the winter of 1931-32 by the Farmer–Labour Committee, which was composed of ILP representatives and a few socialist farmers. At the IFP's founding convention in April 1932, a radical, Marxist-influenced, anti-capitalist platform was adopted.[13] It called for the nationalization of util-ities, natural resources, grain elevators, creameries, and the milk distribu-tion system, as well as the "socialization" of currency and credit and the nationalization of land. But when the leaders of the IFP were quickly dis-owned and denounced by the UFM,[14] the party collapsed and disappeared without ever running a candidate for office.

The IFP and the Farmer–Labour Committee failed, but some of their rural leaders, including such future CCF officials as Mrs. T.W. McClelland and W.F. Gable, reappeared in another socialist-oriented agrarian organization soon after. The Manitoba Farmers' Section of the CCF represented a second small-scale effort to challenge the "no politics" position of the UFM. The new provincial party wanted desperately to create an agrarian affiliate for the CCF as a counterpart for the affiliation of the respective provincial farm organizations in Alberta, Saskatchewan, and Ontario. In keeping with the "labour-farmer-socialist" caption that the national party had adopted, it was hoped by the CCF leadership that the MFS could become part of the party's provincial council along with the ILP and a group known as the Manitoba Association of Social Reconstruction Clubs. These three groups together, CCF leaders thought, could present an image of a broad-based party capable of forming a truly representative government. Since there were some farmers who refused to have anything to do with the ILP but were willing to consider joining the CCF,[15] the MFS thus represented a bridge that could lead anti-ILP farmers into the CCF. But there were fewer such farmers in Manitoba than in either Saskatchewan or Alberta, and within two years the MFS was absorbed into the CCF Clubs of Manitoba.

Besides the Independent Labour Party and the Manitoba Farmers' Section, two other organizations were represented in the early CCF: the Manitoba Association of Social Reconstruction Clubs and the Co-operative Commonwealth Youth Movement (CCYM). There were twenty-five Recon-struction Clubs operating in nine of the seventeen federal constituencies, and they claimed over 600 members in 1933-34. They had very general objectives dealing mainly with the economic depression of the day.[16] They formally affiliated with the CCF in March 1934. The CCYM was formed in October 1934, and within three months had six branches and claimed approximately 500 members. It grew out of the Young Labour Association, the ILP youth group, an organization that included Russ Paulley, the NDP leader in the 1960s.

An influence at work on the early CCF was Christian socialism. In the 1920s this tradition was represented by William Ivens's Labour Church in Winnipeg. It was an influence that was first identified largely with Methodism and then, after church union in the 1920s, with the United Church. One CCF pamphlet in the 1930s, written by the president of the Selkirk CCF Association and entitled *Christianity, Socialism and the CCF,* made the connection between the three quite explicit. "The fact of the matter is that Socialism means a system of cooperative effort, whereby we all work for the good of all and it is hard for me to understand," he wrote, "why people 'professing' Christianity cannot, or probably will not, see such a system is in keeping with the principles of Nazareth."[17] Although they were an important contributing force to the CCF, Christian socialists as such did not have formal representation on the CCF council.

The League for Social Reconstruction gave the CCF intellectual content and leadership and the party's Britishness and cultural conservatism meant it did not appear alien in English Canada. *Pioneers in Poverty,* a book published by the Winnipeg branch of the League, reflected an eagerness to ameliorate the excesses of capitalism by controlling or transforming it, not by eradicating it. The thread of the arguments was in terms of "capitalism versus planning" rather than "capitalism versus socialism" (a word that is nowhere to be found in the book).

Each of the groups in the federated CCF was expected to accept the CCF program and to contribute a monthly grant to the provincial office which was situated in Winnipeg in the unlikely Chamber of Commerce Building. The Reconstruction Clubs and the MFS disappeared as distinct entities in July 1935, when the two were amalgamated to form the CCF Clubs of Manitoba with headquarters in Brandon.[18] This gave the CCF provincial council seven members from the ILP, seven from the CCF Clubs, and three from the CCYM.[19] The Clubs as a provincial organization, however, soon disappeared having gone the way of the MFS: nowhere. By 1937 membership in the CCF was direct, through centrally sanctioned CCF units rather than through federated groups.

In the attempt to strengthen and broaden its base of support, and to familiarize those in and out of the party with its philosophy and objectives, the CCF devoted a substantial measure of attention to educational activities. A party bookstore was established, weekly "people's forums" were held, study clubs were convened, and a debating union was formed. In addition there were the activities of the local branch of the League for Social Reconstruction, as well as weekend sessions dealing with party ideology and organization that were directed at local party officials, young people, and prospective candidates. Some effort was also made to communicate with those Manitobans who did not read or speak English.[20] Reprints of the Regina Manifesto, which outlined the party's manifesto, appeared in German, French, Hungarian, and Ukrainian in 1934-35. For a time, the *Manitoba Commonwealth* published a Ukrainian edition, and in 1936-37 the party hired a Ukrainian-speaking organizer. These efforts to attract supporters of European origins largely failed, however, both in Winnipeg and the countryside.

The party fared poorly among the rural Europeans because they continued to prefer the politics of deference. Virtually no Europeans were to be found in the higher echelons of the UFM or the older parties. "Canadian

Ukrainians do not have any influence," declared the *Canadian Farmer*, a Ukrainian paper, in 1932, the year of the CCF's birth. "We are poor and need political help. Ukrainian farmers and workers depend for their livelihood on the more powerful. This forces us to support a politically influential party. Affiliation with small radical parties brings us Ukrainians only discredit, and ruin." Another Ukrainian newspaper, the *Ukrainian Voice*, on the eve of the 1936 provincial election, put the logic of political deference this way: "All signs show that the Bracken government will remain in power. This means that we have to elect candidates put forward by the governing party. ... Candidates from parties making strange and impossible promises will bring us no advantage, only national dishonour."[21] Such deference did little for continental immigrants in the city. In the 1930s none of Winnipeg's banks, trust companies, or insurance firms would knowingly hire anyone with a Ukrainian, Jewish, or Polish name.[22] Those urban Europeans who did not defer to the established parties tended to support the Communists rather than the CCF.

Because the CCF espoused an ideology that differed from most people's values, attempts at internal education encountered some difficulty. Substantial confusion was generated in the minds of many, members and officials alike, about what exactly this new Co-operative Commonwealth Federation stood for. Writing to national secretary M.J. Coldwell in 1935, provincial secretary Farmer pleaded for a clarification and elucidation of CCF principles: "There is a very strong feeling in Manitoba that something more specific than that contained in the Manifesto is needed for the campaign, and I am afraid that the present position will not be very satisfactory to a lot of our people."[23] Problems along these lines were encountered by other party officials including the executive of the MFS.[24] Dozens of handwritten letters from new CCF units and members were directed to both national and provincial offices asking for more information.

The CCF identified with fraternal social democratic parties in Western Europe and the British Commonwealth. A typical party pamphlet, based almost wholly on the record of the New Zealand Labour government, noted that "today New Zealand is ruled by a government that is carrying out a policy and program such as the CCF advocates in Canada." The CCF also applauded Franklin Roosevelt's New Deal. Developments in the Soviet Union were usually commended in the party's weekly newspaper, but it tended to ignore the local communists, since CCF dealings with them were bitter. In the midst of the Depression, party literature emphasized economic welfare and the benefits of a planned economy; "security" was a common watchword. The *Manitoba Commonwealth,* in a typical editorial of that day, presented the image that the CCF tried to foster:

We cannot stress too much the guarantee of security which the C.C.F. plan offers you. Security destroys fear, security abolishes poverty, security smashes monopoly and builds economic democracy.

Security is the haven to which we all direct our courses. How many of us reach it? The wreckage of economic storms is cast abundantly over the waters these days. Watch the unemployed parades. Watch the border-line family with its perpetual and wracking battle against poverty and degradation. Watch the inevitable decay of morale in those young people who are unwanted.

The C.C.F. offers you pilotage through reefs and storms. The C.C.F. offers you no mere panacea, no superficial gloss over our real problems.

The C.C.F. offers you something which no other party has even mentioned. It offers you security through a planned economy and through sanity, efficiency and a waste-less administration.[25]

The 1936 ILP-CCF platform included some planks that were, between the 1930s and 1960s, to be implemented by the other parties. Other planks were pursued in the 1970s by an NDP government, and still others were dropped. The platform, like all those that followed it, promised a more planned economy, a larger public sector, and an improvement in social services:

1 Establishment of an economic council for planning private and co-operative ownership;

2 Public ownership of natural resources, utilities and major industries such as flour mills and packing plants;

3 Establishment of a provincial bank;

4 Government assistance to co-operative institutions;

5 Provincial construction program in housing, rural electrification, roads and hospitals to combat unemployment;

6 A provincial labour code;

7 Working toward an assured income for farmers;

8 A complete system of socialized health services;

9 State insurance covering sickness, accident, life and fire;

10 Improving child welfare legislation;

11 Increased old age pensions;

12 Adequate pensions for the blind;

13 Free education at all levels; and

14 Establishment of a public defender.[26]

Sometimes CCF speakers posited an explicit socialist policy. Other times they moderated the tone of the CCF's message in the belief that this made winning at the polls more possible. The debate within the party over these two approaches was heated. A series of articles arguing a variety of positions appeared in the *Manitoba Commonwealth*. A typical exchange was the following. It revealed the internal debate on strategy and tactics:

> In brief, the C.C.F. is a political party with Socialism as its objective. For example, we plan to socialize the banking system and the key industries of the country. This is no idle phrase or threat but the very cornerstone of the C.C.F. structure. Thus socialism is C.C.F. and conversely, the C.C.F. is socialism. But hush! some leaders advise. "Don't mention socialism. It may prejudice the people and they will not give us their vote at the next election." This type of opportunism is to my mind reprehensible and detrimental to the cause. Either we call a spade a spade and stand by our colours, or we shall find that our membership has deserted us for some second love.

In reply to this letter from Dr. D.L. Johnson, a vice-president of the CCF Clubs and a future MLA from Brandon, was a letter from Frank L. Taylor:

> The C.C.F. platform should have never mentioned Socialism. It should have called it public ownership. They are the same thing but why handicap ourselves by unpopular names. The Roman Catholic Church have already pronounced against us, which means we have no chance in at least eighty constituencies in Canada.... If we wait until we educate the people to Socialism we will have to wait as long as Methuselah. Study clubs are alright to educate leaders, but as vote getters they are an absolute failure. I know hundreds of people that voted C.C.F. and yet 90% of them never read the C.C.F. platform, never attended C.C.F. meetings, nor listened to radio speeches. They voted C.C.F. for some particular reason, something that interested them.... Winning an election is a business. Forget about idealism and sentiment. Get down to realities. Our opponents are unscrupulous. They will lie about us. But we have the goods, and all we have to do is show it to the people. But we must work. Are you willing to work?[27]

As with the national and sister CCF parties in the other provinces, the question of alliances with other anti-government parties kept cropping up. The two parties most often mentioned in this connection in the 1930s were the Communists and Social Credit. Immediately after the CCF's formation, social democrats were denounced by the Communists as traitors misleading the working class.[28] In 1935, however, Communist party strategy favoured a united front on the left for electoral purposes. A comradely appeal went out from the CP to national CCF leader, J.S. Woodsworth who on behalf of his party, rejected it.[29] This refusal led Tim Buck, national Communist Party leader, to contest Winnipeg North against ILP-CCF incumbent A.A. (Abe) Heaps in the 1935 federal election. Buck ran a fair third. Most members and supporters of the CCF desired a healthy distance between themselves and the Communists, but there was some sympathy in party ranks for a united front, including Communists, on the left.[30]

Others in the CCF touted Social Credit as a potential ally.[31] Although it had some influence, Social Credit was a divided, minor, and inconsistent force in Manitoba politics. Both it and the CCF appeared during the Depression of the 1930s as new movement-parties, appealing to anti-government, anti-establishment, sentiment.[32] Both characterized themselves as representing the little man against established, wealthy, interests. But Social Credit faded somewhat when its five MLAs supported the Bracken government after the 1936 election. That same year CCF leader Farmer wrote a little book condemning Social Credit theories as frauds in the struggle for reform.[33] Majority sentiment in the CCF was against Social Credit, and little talk of a CCF-Social Credit alliance was heard after 1936. Social Credit and CCF support were rooted in different constituencies in Manitoba: one was a minor, fleeting, force among farmers; the other was a major force among the urban working class with relatively little support among farmers. It was interesting to note, however, that there were enough Social Crediters in Winnipeg sympathetic to the CCF to put three CCFers, including Farmer, over the top with their transferable ballots in the 1936 provincial election. In the election, the CCF was left to rely on its urban strength, its traditional base, and it fared worse in terms of popular vote than the ILP had in 1932 (see Table 2).

TABLE 2

Manitoba provincial election, 1936

Party	Seats	Percentage of popular vote
Conservative	16	29
Liberal–Progressive	23	36
ILP–CCF	7	12
Social Credit	5	9
Other*	4	14
Total	55	100

* Includes two Independents, one Communist, and one Independent-Progressive

Paradoxically while the major rightist parties, the Liberal–Progressives and Conservatives, ran some Ukrainian and Jewish candidates in

Winnipeg in search of the European vote, the major leftist parties, the ILP–CCF and the Communists, often sought out Anglo-Saxon candidates to show that they were not alien parties. Even the ILP's sole provincial Jewish candidate in the 1930s, Marcus Hyman, was an Oxford-trained Briton. By running Anglo-Saxon candidates, the CCF and CP tried to make it possible for the European minorities, who harboured prejudices against each other, to rally behind a common and culturally acceptable candidate.[34] This pattern also operated at the municipal level. Between 1919 and 1945 not a single Labour alderman was of German, Polish, or Ukrainian origin. In the 1920s, 85 per cent of Labour aldermen came from Britain; in the 1930s, 70 per cent were British immigrants.[35]

A revealing episode in the CCF's early history was its running battle with elements in the ILP that favoured retention of the ILP banner. It may be suggested that this reflected the understandable desire on the part of a successful and functioning political organization not to be swallowed up by another.[36] But the wrangle also revealed the tension between the urban labour-socialist movement and the leftist Progressives in the agrarian movement that had come together in the CCF. It was, in effect, a debate over the "broadening out" strategy that the very creation of the CCF represented.

Shortly after the creation of the CCF, the Manitoba ILP had debated the advantages and disadvantages of formal affiliation. Objections raised by some members included fears that a federated CCF would be an invitation to opportunists who would join and dilute socialist principles. The ILPers were suspicious of rural "progressives" like Manitoba's federal Progressives who, they felt, had diverted farmers in the 1920s from forming a genuinely anti-Liberal party. For a long time the ILP excluded UFMers from its membership. Many ILPers argued that all socialists, if they were sincere and supported the national CCF movement, could join the provincial ILP without creating a separate party at the provincial level and without precipitating clashes over nominations and election slates.[37] Abe Heaps, the Jewish, British-born, ILP MP for Winnipeg North, had a fair measure of sympathy for this position.[38] However, supporters of this approach failed to appreciate that the CCF's creation was an attempt to reach beyond the urban voters the ILP could count on. The CCF, if it was to be successful, had to attract alienated farmers and former Progressives who could support a broadened out, anti-Liberal party, even though they might be suspicious of the CCF's ILP component, the major inheritor of the radical strike tradition. Led by Farmer, the executive of the ILP recommended in 1933 that, in the interests of the national CCF organization and the socialist movement in general, the ILP recognize and accept as allies the Social Reconstruction Clubs and support the skeletal provincial CCF council which contained ILP members as individuals. As long as the CCF did not meet in full convention, friction between various party elements was minimal. By 1936, however, when the first annual convention met in Portage la Prairie, the CCF had developed a clear identity of its own, one not dependent solely on the ILP. The MFS, the Social Reconstruction Clubs, the CCYM, and the CCF Clubs had all made contributions, however small relative to the established ILP, to building the CCF in those first three years. Farmer, furthermore, had taken over John Queen's role as house leader in 1935 while the latter devoted more time to his new position as mayor of Winnipeg. Farmer had done much as provincial secretary to try to expand and broaden the base of CCF support. This meant that many delegates at the initial convention in 1936 were new recruits and, having never attended an ILP meeting in the past, they closely identified with the new national party. They argued and voted for a straight CCF label when the discussion on the new constitution came to deal with elections and nominations. In order to avert a formal split with outraged ILPers, a compromise was reached that permitted one year's autonomy for the ILP in municipal affairs. The ILP was allowed to nominate its own candidates at this level and have them run under the ILP banner and program.[39]

In the 1936 provincial election, candidates in Winnipeg ran as ILP–CCF. Bitterness among ILPers over being forced to drop the successful ILP label at the provincial level and then at the municipal level led to a series of ILP meetings. Unable to reach a compromise with the CCF, the ILP voted at two of its conventions to disaffiliate until its demand for autonomy at all levels was met.[40]

When word of the split reached Ottawa, CCF MP M.J. Coldwell, national party secretary David Lewis, and national CCF leader J.S. Woodsworth sent personal appeals to Queen. The joint letter of Coldwell and Lewis mentioned the growth of reactionary and quasi-fascist movements in Quebec, Ontario, and abroad, and discussed the importance of a strongly organized socialist force to meet these challenges. They argued that a narrow "labour party" could never achieve its objectives through electoral politics if it were confined, as it must be by definition, to industrialized centres. They pointed to the importance of rural votes to the Socialist parties of Britain, Scandinavia, and New Zealand.[41] Queen was then shaken by a personal letter from Woodsworth stating that in light of these differences he might have to resign from the ILP. Queen protested that the differences had been exaggerated: he felt his position strengthened rather than weakened the national CCF.[42] With the impasse unresolved, the national council dispatched Coldwell and Heaps to Winnipeg to act as mediators. The various ILP branches were soon reaffiliated, but the rupture was resolved only after CCF loyalists gradually took over control of the ILP, from within, in the early 1940s. "The ILP still stinks of course but we've got them beaten," wrote Alistair Stewart, one such loyalist and future MP, to national secretary Lewis in 1942. "When the civic nominations come along we're going to put the skids on John Queen.... The main thing is that we control the I.L.P. and the whip is going to crack very gently from now on until we're ready for the show-down."[43] A year later, in 1943, the ILP disbanded.[44]

The ILP-CCF dispute seemed to reflect not much more than an internal squabble over a political label—both parties shared the same office and the same phone number during the periods of both affiliation and disaffiliation. But it also reflected a more substantive dispute within the labour-socialist movement. Many of the ILPers opposed the "broadening out" strategy that the CCF represented on the grounds that the Manitoba farmers who were to be courted were not socialist, and were not committed to a permanent break with non-socialist parties. Beatrice Brigden, a former CCF provincial secretary recalled that the feeling in ILP circles was that the "old English or British working class viewpoint was entirely different from our farmers' viewpoint in this country because the farmers' viewpoint and the people living in the city who hadn't come in with the British labour group were very, very, middle class in their outlook." This feeling by many in the urban labour-socialist movement, that "the ILP had been betrayed by going in with the farmers,"[45] kept some ILP aldermen in the city from ever really entering the CCF. ILP suspicions of agrarian participation in the new party were, in turn, resented by rural CCF sympathizers, making it all the more difficult to sign up new rural members.[46]

This debate within the labour-socialist movement was a reflection of the extent to which the antipathy between rural and urban Manitoba was reflected in the relations between urban socialists and progressive farmers. The tensions between country and city, rooted in different heritages, traditions, and histories, were not overcome even within the confines of a socialist party which posited reason as an electoral and economic alternative to sheer tradition.

As the 1930s drew to an end, the CCF, federal and provincial, became enmeshed in a divisive debate over conscription and the war. Many in

Manitoba, including Farmer, sided with Woodsworth's pacifist stance. Abe Heaps, however, Woodsworth's lone parliamentary colleague from Manitoba, was in the forefront of those urging all-out support for the war effort.[47] The irony of electoral politics was that Heaps was defeated in Winnipeg North in the 1940 federal election because of his association with Woodsworth and, in many voters' eyes therefore, with Woodsworth's pacifism. Woodsworth, however, was sufficiently popular, despite his personal views on the war, to win a narrow victory in Winnipeg North Centre. The provincial ILP ignored the official stand of the federal CCF (conscription of wealth rather than men) and came out, like Heaps, for full support of the war.[48] The ILP action was not helpful to the CCF, but the ILP was now in its last days, losing its influence as the CCF took on a life and tradition of its own.

In the 1930s the CCF played the role of the labour-socialist parliamentary opposition in Manitoba. The CCF was a movement, but it was always a party as well. It exhibited the characteristics of social democratic parties throughout the Western world. Because Manitoba did not suffer as badly as other parts of the prairies during the Depression,[49] and because its rural population was politically anchored by Ontario-origin Anglo-Saxon farmers with Conservative and Liberal sympathies, the CCF was not as popular in Manitoba as it was in Saskatchewan. In 1937 CCF membership in Manitoba was 600, largely concentrated in Winnipeg, while in Saskatchewan it was 3,400.[50] Membership in Manitoba was low in spite of a solid base of socialist support in working-class areas of Winnipeg and scattered support in some farm districts.

The leadership and ideology of the CCF was rooted in British labourism. Of the eleven CCF MLAs elected between the early 1930s and the early 1940s, seven were born in Britain, two in Canada, and two in Europe. While the CCF received support from some non-British immigrant groups, these groups, as in the older parties, exercised minimal influence on the party's direction and leadership. The "broadening out" strategy of the CCF failed to bring a significant number of new supporters to its banner. The CCF failed to expand successfully beyond its urban ILP base. This failure, combined with the desire to further an image of respectability, led the CCF to accept an offer to enter the provincial government as a junior partner in 1940. It was to be a unique coalition in Canadian history—the only one ever to include the CCF or NDP.

The "non-partisan" government of 1940

2

In 1931 and 1936, Premier John Bracken had approached the opposition parties to propose the formation of a "non-partisan" government. In 1940, he reiterated his proposal, this time arguing that a united front would help to impress upon the federal government the importance of speedy implementation of recommendations in the recently released report of the Royal Commission on Dominion-Provincial Relations. He also argued that with the crisis in agriculture and Canada's entry into the Second World War people would be in no mood for partisan politics — a lesson the opposition parties had learned during the last war. His final argument echoed his favourite theme: the legislature should function like a non-partisan city council.

S.J. Farmer, who had replaced John Queen as leader of the CCF caucus in the legislature, was immediately receptive to Bracken's proposal, but he could not act without the approval of his colleagues. He first approached the party's provincial chairman, Stanley Knowles.[1] "When Farmer first told me about it, not only was I horrified personally at the thought of it," recalls Knowles, "but I knew the party would never go for this. They'd throw Farmer out before this happened."[2] Knowles had ample basis for this opinion. The CCF leaders were determined that their party should persist as a political force and not wither as had its numerous agrarian and labour party antecedents. Thus they had a strong aversion to co-operation with other parties. This position was articulated in a resolution passed at the 1936 national convention: "The correct policy for the CCF remains that of increasing its mass support among farmers and workers throughout the country by an aggressive programme of socialist education, organization and participation in the daily struggle of our people for improved conditions. Therefore, no good purpose can be served by an attempt to weld together political organizations, the policies and working methods of which differ in principle and practice. The CCF, therefore, reaffirms its determination to maintain complete political independence." But the resolution also recognized the partial autonomy of the provincial CCF parties: "...Because of the diversity of conditions across Canada, the Convention declares that decisions regarding such co-operation shall rest with the provincial council concerned, subject to review by the National Council, if, in its opinion such co-operation conflicts with the platform and constitution of the CCF." The Manitoba party fully accepted the policy of the national party, and in 1936 rebuffed Premier Bracken's suggestion of a coalition.[3]

However, four years later, when Bracken again approached the leaders of the opposition parties and proposed the formation of a "non-partisan" government, the CCF did not reject the idea out of hand. Farmer described the proposal to members of the provincial executive, emphasizing the CCF's organizational weakness and Bracken's evident popularity. Gradually the idea gathered support from the executive: even Knowles was won over. The executive, however, insisted that any such arrangement leave the party free to run its own candidates at the next election.

Farmer wrote to David Lewis, the national secretary of the CCF, outlining the advantages and disadvantages of the proposal.[4] His arguments in favour of it revealed his preference. He expressed his fear that the CCF would be unable to gain strength and to discredit the government in the rural areas. He also said that a (non-partisan) coalition would postpone an expected election, which the CCF did not want, for a year. Farmer described Bracken as "very progressive." (Bracken had been an adamant foe of mild labour legislation in the 1920s and had fired civil servants in a show of government economy.) Farmer's arguments indicated his faith that gains would be made by associating with the government—a belief that was questioned by those in the party opposing any coalition[5] and that was to prove unfounded. He admitted that some problems could arise: the party in the other provinces and in Ottawa could be embarrassed; coalition could further hamper the Manitoba party's organizing efforts; and some would charge them "with selling out the movement (like the Progressives!)." Those who favoured a link with Bracken called the proposed arrangement "non-partisan" while those who opposed it called it a "coalition."

Upon receipt of Farmer's letter, Lewis, who strongly opposed coalition, polled members of the national executive. Angus MacInnis of British Columbia, E.B. Jolliffe of Ontario, party ideologue F.R. Scott, and party leader M.J. Coldwell all agreed with Lewis and opposed the proposal. Frank Scott, who either by accident or design insisted on referring to Bracken as an unhyphenated Liberal, suggested in his reply that there were three main questions to be considered:

The first is, will the CCF be sure of enough seats in the Cabinet to give it some real influence on policy? If it is simply going to be a lone voice, not affecting decisions and yet being held responsible for results, it should refuse. Without some real power it can do no good.

The second question is, what is the price of its collaboration? This should be agreed on in advance, and should include certain specific things that the CCF has advocated and which have not yet been adopted by the Liberals. These should be matters of immediate importance, capable of being enacted by the union government. Without this the collaboration will make the electorate think that the CCF leaders all along have just been seeking office and have not believed in their own program. On the other hand, if certain things of real value were accomplished just because the CCF agreed to sink its differences for the time being, the people would give all the credit to the CCF.

The third question depends on the political analysis of the actual situation. Bracken can win the next provincial election without the CCF. Why then does he seek its support? Can it be that he fears a post-war swing away from the old parties, and wants to compromise the CCF now? Does he aim at leading a new protest movement himself? He is the best Liberal leader in any province, and one whom the CCF ought to try to win over. But the best way to do this might be to make him feel that the CCF is going to emerge from the war greatly strengthened, and that his progressive ideas will get nowhere within the folds of official Liberalism.

On the whole I would be inclined to refuse this offer.[6]

These negative replies led Lewis to write a memorandum to Farmer and the Manitoba executive arguing that the CCF's influence in government would be minimal, since it would only get one or two cabinet posts; that any eventual credit due the government would go to Bracken, and discredit would go to all parties; that the arrangement would prevent the CCF from attracting new supporters; and that it would undermine the CCF's credibility in Parliament and the other provinces. Lewis suggested instead that the provincial party accept its temporary weakness in Manitoba, refuse the offer of coalition, but propose a truce to postpone an election. He also thought it should draft a program of specific policies which would leave the CCF uncompromised. *"All of us are unanimous in the conclusion that the proposal for coalition ought to be refused,"* wrote Lewis. Although he had not spoken to three executive members, including J.S. Woodsworth, "I have myself not the slightest doubt that all three would unhesitatingly support the position expressed in this letter and memorandum. In short," he continued, "both Mr. Coldwell and I believe that the National Executive would be unanimous."[7] Given the importance of the matter to the whole movement, he further suggested that he and Coldwell be invited to attend the next provincial council meeting.

If J.S. Woodsworth had in fact been strongly opposed to the coalition proposition it would have been difficult for Farmer to continue entertaining coalitionist ideas. Woodsworth's popularity and prestige in the Manitoba party was unrivalled, and his influence would have kept the rank and file from accepting the proposal. Knowles, who had been won over to Farmer's view, met privately with Woodsworth to ascertain his position. Woodsworth's attitude, Knowles discovered with surprise, "was one of wondering what was the best thing to do, but of complete confidence in S.J. [Farmer]'s integrity which included a willingness to trust his judgment."[8] This reaction encouraged Farmer and Knowles to continue their course. In defence of his own inclination to accept Bracken's bait (which was to be the Labour portfolio) and in reply to Lewis's memorandum, Farmer argued that he and Knowles felt that an electoral truce would be the poorest choice among their alternatives.[9]

When the provincial council convened on September 18, Lewis presented the case against accepting Bracken's offer. He pointed out that a decision to go ahead would undermine the CCF in Saskatchewan where it was now the official opposition; that no matter how few CCFers were returned in a provincial election, they would form the official opposition in Manitoba if the other parties accepted the government's offer. Furthermore, he was not as pessimistic as Farmer about CCF fortunes in an election campaign, arguing that an aggressive campaign could be launched which would secure some farm support. The party could maintain most of its seven seats if it were "ruthlessly to carry the fight into Bracken's camp and place upon him the onus of dulling the effectiveness of the western demand by tying himself [sic] to the parties representing and protecting the vested interests in the East against whom the struggle of the western farmers must be directed."[10] The council, however, was not as optimistic; it tried to impress upon Lewis that Bracken's personal popularity was at such a high point that he could sweep the province at will, particularly if the other parties joined his government. Members feared that the CCF would be completely wiped out if it refused to co-operate. "While Lewis's arguments for opposing it were very logical," recalls one participant in the meeting, "logic didn't seem to prevail at that particular time."[11]

Farmer then arranged a private meeting at Bracken's house, with Lewis, Coldwell, and Knowles also in attendance. The resistance of Lewis and Coldwell was slowly worn down. "When we came out I remember

Lewis and Coldwell saying 'It's not the right thing to do, I wish there were some way out... but I'm afraid you're stuck.' This of course," recollects Knowles, "had been my view.... They [Lewis and Coldwell] reached the point where they were resigned to it." After holding at least six joint executive-caucus meetings, the provincial council finally approved what appeared to them to be an inevitable decision. Party leaders were convinced that if the CCF refused to co-operate with Bracken, the other parties would accept his offer, and this would be effectively used against the CCF. "We accepted it not because of its merits, but because of the demerit, politically, if you will, of our not doing so."[12] The party newspaper's editor recalls that the sentiment for coalition was so strong among MLAs that they probably would have joined the Bracken government no matter what the executive or council decided.[13]

Despite the council's decision, Lewis's misgivings persisted. He persuaded the CCF provincial executives in the other western provinces to convey their views to the Manitoba people in the hope that the latter would reverse their decision, which had not yet been made public. But the Manitoba leaders were not swayed and plunged ahead. The annual provincial CCF convention, initially scheduled for July, then postponed to September, was further postponed to October 26, 1940, so that the still secret negotiations could be completed. Farmer arranged for Bracken to send a formal proposition of coalition on the eve of the convention. Bracken was now on the verge of accomplishing provincially what Mackenzie King had long sought and failed to achieve federally: the absorption of the parliamentary opposition on the left. Bracken's letter contained barely disguised threats, much flattery, and vague promises. It threatened an immediate election (which he knew the CCF feared), made an appeal to patriotic wartime non-partisanship, gave a vague and indirect promise of increased social services, and promised one cabinet post and one seat on the cabinet's Budget Committee. The last paragraph of Bracken's lengthy letter reflected his reasoning:

In whatever we may do in this connection, if anything, there is involved no sacrifice or compromise of principles on your part or our own. But in our judgment the differences of opinion which divide us in peacetime become of secondary importance in time of war. From war new and greater issues emerge. We suggest no abandonment of the peacetime principles of the co-operating groups but only that each should be united in the support of these new and paramount issues upon which fortunately there is common ground for agreement. If we did not think that without the least abandonment of principle you could support the above mentioned programme with respect to war, the Sirois Report and our western economy under war and post-war conditions, we would not be addressing this suggestion to you. We do so with the confidence that you will accept it because, like us we are sure, you do not in times like these believe in party first and the country last. We are not today only CCF, Labour or Liberal-Progressive or Conservative or Social Credit, but rather Canadians and democrats and free men. Our cause, even Manitoba's cause, is at this time greater than your party or our own.[14]

In essence, Bracken desired an all-party government which he preferred to call non-partisan. But Bracken's activities before 1940 (he merged his Progressives with the Liberals in the 1930s) and after 1940 (he continued to lead the strongly anti-CCF Liberal-Progressive caucus) were anything but non-partisan. Although he may well have been sincere in wanting the parties to unite in a co-operative effort during the war, he knew that it would be easier to ensure the success of his policies through a non-partisan government than by continuing on his own.[15]

Bracken's initial proposal to Farmer had specified that all parties would have their sitting MLAs returned by acclamation. But the CCF, though willing to coalesce for what it saw as immediate and pressing reasons, was unwilling to have its identity submerged. The compromise agreed to by Farmer and Bracken was that the various parties to the coalition would be permitted to retain their identities, platforms, and organizational work. In such an arrangement, the CCF would be free to introduce its own proposals, ask questions, call for information, and discuss and criticize government policy. The CCF for its part, however, agreed to contest only those seats in which candidates had already been nominated. Although no one could prevent the nomination of candidates by independent-minded constituency associations, such candidates were not to be officially endorsed by the CCF provincial council.

When Bracken's proposal to join a "non-partisan" government reached the convention floor, Stanley Knowles, as chairman, pointed out that the provincial council had endorsed the proposal. Farmer read Bracken's letter and then called on M.J. Coldwell to give the view of the National Council. Reversing his initial position, Coldwell went to lengths to endorse the proposal. The convention minutes record that: "He had discussed the matter widely with many in the Sask. movement and found most of them favored the proposal. He stated that Provincial Governments in relation to general economic policies are in a different position from the Federal Governments. Provincial Governments are merely enlarged city council meetings. In his conversation with Mr. J.S. Woodsworth, Mr. Woodsworth had expressed the hope that the proposal had merit and should be carefully considered."[16]

Coldwell's recorded comments give no hint of the real opposition to the proposal in the national and other provincial CCF parties, and they implicitly denied the value of the CCF's role at the provincial level. If provincial governments were no more than enlarged municipal councils, and if municipal councils were non-partisan, why had the CCF ever been formed at the provincial level? Moreover, Winnipeg's socialists had a long tradition of contesting municipal elections on a partisan basis. By citing Woodsworth—a man without equal at the time in the Manitoba CCF— Coldwell tempered potential criticism. Woodsworth's name had now been invoked by both Lewis and Coldwell to make opposing cases. Woodsworth did not speak publicly on the question and his position was probably somewhere in the middle: he had always personally rejected alliances with the old parties and, thus, frowned on this one; at the same time, he trusted his old friend, Farmer. Farmer's relationship with Woodsworth had always been close. Woodsworth had bought his membership card in the old Dominion Labor Party from Farmer, and both of them had been elected on Independent Labor Party tickets in 1921 and 1922—Woodsworth as MP for Winnipeg Centre and Farmer as ILP mayor of Winnipeg.

In the convention debate that followed, Coldwell and Farmer painted a much brighter picture of the proposal than was justifiable. Although it may be too severe to suggest that the convention was wilfully misled, it was, nonetheless, encouraged in a course of action based on Farmer's vague assurances. These assurances went beyond Bracken's guarantees. Excerpts from the convention minutes are revealing in showing the power of CCF leaders in swaying convention decisions:

R. Moore of Dauphin asked if Mr. Bracken could present a solid bloc of Western members, would it help get consideration at Ottawa. Mr. Coldwell replied in affirmative.

R.C. McCutchan stated that the Bracken Government had been hostile to organized labour. Mr. Farmer replied that in view of the fact that Mr. Bracken had slated the CCF group for the Labor portfolio, it was an indication that he was prepared to go in the direction of a more progressive labor policy....

J. Wilson asked what benefit would accrue to us from having a representative on the budget committee. Mr. Farmer replied that one of Mr. Bracken's proposals is to bring certain public utilities more directly under government control, and give us a voice in the management. To a further question Mr. Farmer replied that the Government would drop three of its present ministers to make room for the other groups.

S.H. Knowles asked if the CCF cabinet minister would be given a free rein in his department. Mr. Farmer replied that he would.[17]

It was not the old hard-core Independent Labor Party group from north and central Winnipeg which opposed the move, but a few radical farmers who may have had some bitter memories of the Progressive "sell-out" to Mackenzie King in the 1920s. A few of them argued that the object of the CCF should be to build socialism and not save capitalism by co-operating with the parties of big business. That the labour delegates to the convention endorsed the coalition was not completely surprising. The militancy of the strikers of the General Strike of twenty years before had largely evaporated; although Winnipeg Mayor and MLA John Queen and his ILP group had made protests about "diluting socialism" when the CCF was formed, they were cautious labourites themselves. And so, with only five delegates dissenting, none of them MLAs, the CCF voted to enter the Bracken coalition.

The real decision to enter the government had been effectively made more than a month before the convention. After the September 18 provincial council meeting Lewis resigned himself to the eventual outcome. He drafted a press release for the Manitoba CCF (dated September 23) accepting Bracken's proposal. When, in late October, the party officially accepted the offer, the press release it issued was, virtually word for word, a duplicate of the Lewis draft.[18] The statement itself unmistakably reflected Lewis's feelings if not his conclusion. It called for unity on the basis of the CCF policies of democratic socialism, yet endorsed the efforts of the Bracken government and pledged to support it. Lewis had earlier argued that these two points were in contradiction. Meeting in Winnipeg immediately after the provincial convention, the CCF national convention was presented with a fait accompli. Although the majority of delegates expressed strong disapproval of the Manitoba decision, there was little they could do.[19]

The decision to enter Bracken's government (which party officials refused at first to call a coalition, but called rather a non-partisan administration), brought numerous protests by rank and file members to the "letters" page of the *Manitoba Commonwealth.* A few protested on tactical grounds; the majority, however, protested on ideological grounds.[20] Stanley Knowles argued that "it is not a question of forsaking socialism; nor is it a question of trying to bring about socialism by co-operating with capitalist parties; nor are we trying to save capitalism."[21] Knowles denied that the arrangement with Bracken represented a coalition. He argued that it simply meant all-party representation on the Executive Council, just as there was all-party representation on other committees of the legislature. Knowles was sincere in that he, Farmer, and the caucus believed that Bracken would take a more open and less partisan approach in governing. In this, however, they were to be sadly mistaken. Knowles also mentioned the vague possibility that Bracken, apparently now to be considered a redeemed progressive, might join the CCF at some time in the future. He made no mention, however, of the agreement to contest only a limited number of seats. The only rebuttal that the editor of the party newspaper mustered to the letters of protest was that the decision, "whether wise or unwise," had been democratically arrived at in convention and should be accepted on that basis.[22]

On November 4, 1940, S.J. Farmer was sworn in as the Minister of Labour, the first CCF cabinet minister in any province. The other members of the Bracken ministry were eight Liberal-Progressives, three Conservatives, and one Social Crediter. The CCF leader, however, continued to sit on the left of the Speaker, and it was from that side of the house that he was to pilot through his departmental estimates. He was joined by the Social Credit minister and the CCF and Social Credit caucuses. Such a seating arrangement, it was felt, would give weight to the non-partisan notion of "round-table" government. The Conservatives, however, moved across the floor, and their link with the Liberal-Progressives also became more organic. (They continued together in coalition for a decade; in the 1943 by-elections, and more extensively in the 1945 general election, many riding associations held joint Liberal-Conservative nomination meetings which selected one "coalition" candidate.)

When the CCF joined the government, its leaders had hoped, in vain, that Bracken would break with his right-wing Liberals and look more sympathetically upon CCF proposals. Farmer, however, was frustrated in his attempt to change the direction of the government which kept its right-wing Liberals. Bracken, moreover, did not give Farmer a free rein in his department. On many proposals for legislation which Farmer brought forth, Bracken insisted on a free vote in the house. Predictably, free votes became party votes with the CCF always losing. The "non-partisan" experiment, which Farmer had accepted where he probably would have refused a "coalition," became a nightmare for the CCF. The party feared breaking with the government and precipitating an immediate election in which it felt certain to lose ground. "It was a fool arrangement," conceded Farmer several years later, "but we acted in good faith....[The] government was not what it appeared to be or what Bracken had promised it would be."[23] When Bracken led his Liberal-Progressives to defeat a CCF bill on the labour code, many felt that Farmer should have quit the government immediately. Farmer retorted that since he had entered the government with the advice and consent of the party he felt he should not resign without the party being again consulted.[24] This, in effect, postponed consideration of withdrawal almost a year, until the next convention.

When the 1941 provincial election took place, the CCF caucus was demoralized and attacked by many in the party. The party ran on a platform supporting the government and the caucus shrank from seven to three members. (see Table 3). In keeping with its earlier agreement with Bracken, the CCF contested only ten seats. "We ran" recalls candidate Stanley Knowles, "as 'CCF, supporting the Coalition,' the coalition that didn't exist."[25] Most party candidates and independents of various stripes referred to themselves as "supporting the Coalition" or "Anti-Coalition" and in sixteen constituencies MLAs were returned by acclamation. The campaign was far from being non-partisan. One Liberal-Progressive pamphlet, issued on behalf of the Bracken candidate in Glenwood constituency, asserted: "It is *impossible* for the C.C.F. to elect sufficient members to even attempt to form a Government. Likewise, it would be a miracle if the Conservatives could hope for the same. *Think!* Can you support the C.C.F. candidate? A stranger in our midst who has no interest in you or your community."[26] The CCF, unable to attack the government it was part of, contested the election on the issue of postwar planning. Only the CCF, argued its leaders, could be counted on to bring postwar security.[27]

TABLE 3

Manitoba provincial election, 1941

Party	Seats	Percentage of popular vote
Conservative	15	21
Liberal–Progressive	27	35
CCF	3	17
Other	10	27
Total	55	100

Although no record exists of the 1941 convention, the party decided to continue in government, despite the disappointments. With a caucus of only three and the party in poor organizational condition, it must have seemed that little could be achieved in or out of government. CCF fortunes, however, improved nationally in 1942. As support for the federal party began to rise dramatically, the national executive called on the provincial party to leave the coalition.[28] By this date, a number of constituency associations had also forwarded letters to the provincial secretary calling for the termination of the agreement with Bracken.[29] The provincial leadership had realized by this time the cost of continuing. "[T]he limitations placed upon us are now recognized by all our people and there is a growing desire to get out" wrote Stanley Knowles in March 1942. "Also, we are realizing that we are not going to be able to make an issue...Bracken will see to that, he will compromise, tell us to stay in a while and we will get what we want, etc., etc. The longer we stay, the worse matters will get. We are pretty well agreed, Farmer, Executive people, and I, that we will have to take a stand at the Provincial Convention...."[30] The 1942 convention proceeded on this count by authorizing the provincial executive to deal with any matter relating to the CCF's position in the legislature.[31] This would permit the party to act when an opportune occasion arose. When, later that year, Bracken decided to enter federal politics, the CCF decided to leave the government. Lloyd Stinson, one of the writers of Farmer's letter of resignation, termed it a "golden opportunity."[32]

Farmer's resignation from the cabinet in December 1942 precipitated a sharp exchange of letters between himself and the premier. Farmer attacked Bracken for pointing to his success in checking the growth of the CCF in Manitoba in his campaign for the national Conservative leadership. Bracken replied by charging Farmer with kowtowing to the national CCF by resigning.[33] The truth, of course, was simply that the Manitoba CCF was desperately looking for a way out. Bracken's intention to enter federal politics provided an excellent excuse. "The only value that I can see now in the coalition" commented one CCF executive member and a future provincial leader, "is that it gave Farmer a decent salary for two years."[34] Knowles concluded similarly: "Probably it was useful in our history in that it taught us a lesson."[35]

At the 1943 convention, Stanley Knowles introduced a motion that endorsed the action of the provincial executive and caucus in withdrawing from the government which was now led by Liberal Stuart Garson. The motion was carried unanimously. Like all future references to the sad experience, it used the term "coalition."[36]

Why did the Manitoba CCF enter the government when its national and other provincial CCF counterparts refused to consider such a proposal? One reason was Bracken: since he believed that provincial government was essentially a matter of administration, he was determined to form a government representing a number of parties. Another reason was the Manitoba CCF leadership: it was overtaken with a sense of defeatism. This did not occur in the other provinces where the CCF was an organized force. In British Columbia and Saskatchewan, CCF fortunes were on the rise and their leaders were adamantly opposed to coalescing with Liberals and Conservatives.[37] In Alberta and Ontario, CCF representation in the legislature was negligible, but their leaders saw no gains to be made in a coalition.[38] No government in any of these provinces, save Manitoba, cared for CCF participation. The national party, in a parliamentary position similar to that of the Manitoba CCF, was influenced by Lewis and Scott who, more astutely than the Manitobans, realized the inevitable failure of coalition government.

The Manitoba CCF leadership feared an irreversible isolation from public opinion if it alone, of all the parties in the legislature, refused to co-operate in what was lauded as a popular non-partisan undertaking. This fear was surprising since a refusal to accept would have elevated the party to the official opposition. Fear of a complete loss in an election was unrealistic since north and central Winnipeg could always be counted on for at least a couple of MLAs, and probably more. The leadership of the party was also in awe of Bracken's personal popularity, particularly in the countryside. But Liberal–Progressive support had always been in the rural areas where the CCF had no seats to lose. No matter how popular Bracken was, his party was disliked in most of Winnipeg and had never received more than a meagre 21 per cent of the vote there.[39] Why it was thought that the Conservative and Socialist voters of Winnipeg, more numerous than the Liberals, would desert their parties was never explained.

The coalition decision reflected the problems of pursuing a successful socialist strategy in Manitoba. The requirements of electoral and organizational activity in the 1930s had placed Farmer, party leader and secretary, in a difficult position. Socialist CCF principles were not stressed because they were considered a threat to the rural and cautious Liberal-Progressive voters the party was trying to attract. The educational work which was done was concentrated in north and central Winnipeg where, at forums and study clubs, leaders preached to the converted. Many party spokesmen canvassing rural districts that showed little sympathy for "socialism" had begun to argue that the CCF stood for platforms such as Bracken's, the only difference being that the CCF, as Farmer put it, simply wanted to go "farther and faster."[40] As CCF parliamentarians argued for quantitative and reformist changes, they developed no substantial alternative program to the government's. When Bracken's coalition proposal came along, there was little mettle within the leadership to resist on the grounds of violation of principle. The differences between the CCF and its opponents became those of degree and not of kind. The CCF leadership was convinced that the position of paramountcy that the Bracken government had attained after eighteen years in power was more or less permanent. They temporarily gave up trying to convert Manitoba's rural electorate, a group that held the key to provincial power. The CCF leaders wandered into the coalition, "a fool arrangement," because they saw it as the only way of ever gaining a voice in the government. They were resigned to a role of permanent minority.

During the war years, however, the party's hopes were raised again. Economic planning, the cornerstone of the CCF's thinking, was now accepted by more people as it became necessary for the war effort. Beginning in 1943, there was a surge in support for the CCF across Canada. In Manitoba, party membership, which had hovered between 600 and 800 during the two years of the coalition, jumped to 3,300 in 1943 and over 4,000 in 1944, with much of the new support coming from the developing mining centres of northern Manitoba.[41] This sudden popularity contributed to the success of Dr. D.L. Johnson and Berry R. Richards in two 1943 by-elections, increasing the CCF caucus to five. But the arrival of Johnson and Richards, two party mavericks, was to prove a mixed blessing.

The Communists and the expulsions

3

Riding on the crest of mid-war CCF popularity, Berry R. Richards and D.L. Johnson won legislative seats in two 1943 by-elections. Richards, campaigning on a program of New Zealand-type socialism,[1] won in The Pas, a seat vacated by Premier John Bracken when he went on to lead the federal Progressive Conservatives. Johnson won his seat in Brandon, in the rural southwest which the CCF had never penetrated before. CCF popularity was running high at the time (at one point in 1943 it was leading the national Gallup Poll), but these two victories were also, in large part, personal triumphs.

Both men were popular, competent, and committed to the party they represented. Johnson had been a member of the Brandon Reconstruction Club in the early 1930s, and in 1936 he became a vice-president of the CCF Clubs. Lloyd Stinson, the provincial secretary at the time, believed that Johnson could have gone on being perpetually elected in the riding.[2]

Richards, more magnetic than Johnson, and a more flamboyant debater and dresser, was elected to the CCF's national council and the provincial vice-presidency in 1943. He soon became the Manitoba party's chief organizer. As a result of his efforts, there were more CCF members in The Pas than in any other constituency.[3] In the legislature Johnson, a doctor, was the CCF's health and welfare critic, while Richards, a professional engineer, concentrated on natural resource development. They soon distinguished themselves as able and competent members of the small caucus. Richards, by several accounts, seemed headed for the party leadership.[4]

Despite their apparent popularity and commitment to the CCF, Richards and Johnson were to become embroiled in a dispute between the

CCF and the Communists—a controversy which, in the end, led to their expulsion from the party and the caucus. Initially, the dispute related to the question of the CCF's electoral role as the war drew to an end. The Richards–Johnson position, independently arrived at yet similar to that of the Communist-led Labour Progressive Party, left them vulnerable to criticism that they were collaborating with the Communists.

CCF–COMMUNIST RELATIONS

The Communist position on the CCF shifted several times over the years. Between the founding of the CCF in 1932 and 1935, the CP denounced the CCF as traitorous to the working class and a barrier to socialist revolution. From 1935 to 1939 the CP pursued a United Front policy aimed at fighting nascent fascism. In this struggle the CP characterized itself as the vanguard with the CCF a component part of the Front. From 1939 to 1941, in harmony with Stalin's line, the CP denounced the war as imperialistic and condemned CCF support of the war effort. From 1941, after the Soviet Union's entry into the war, to its conclusion in 1945, the Communists criticized the CCF for demanding "socialism now" and for wavering in support of the national war effort. By 1945 their literature had elevated Mackenzie King to the leadership of the progressive forces in the country. The Communists denounced the CCF for splintering the progressive vote and, thus, encouraging the rise of "Tory reaction." After the post-war spy scandals and increasing criticism of the Soviet Union by the federal Liberals, the CP turned around again and endorsed most CCF candidates for office by early 1948.

It was bitter irony for Canada's socialists to discover in the 1940s that CCF fortunes on occasion seemed more affected by changes in Soviet foreign policy than by the content of their own policies. It was, however, not altogether surprising. The public, influenced by the popular press and unable to distinguish between the often similar sounding objectives of the Communists and the democratic socialists, rewarded and penalized the CP and the CCF together. When the Soviets valiantly took on the Nazi forces after 1941, there was a revival of support for both the CP and the CCF. When the Cold War began after 1946 both of them suffered dearly. No formal study has been done, but it is almost certain that CP and CCF memberships in these years rose and fell together. In Manitoba, CCF membership rose dramatically during the war from less than 1,000 to about 5,000 in 1945.[5]

At the beginning of the war, both the national and Manitoba CCF parties were divided. J.S. Woodsworth appealed for pacifism at a national council meeting in 1939, but the appeal was rejected.[6] Isolationism, or pacifism, was rebuffed in Manitoba CCF circles too. While the Communists proclaimed the war effort an imperialistic undertaking, the Manitoba CCF endorsed it, "provided it be understood that the conscription of industry and finance should precede any further conscription of man-power...."[7] Some elements in the provincial party, such as the ILP, called for full support for an all-out war effort, but the CCF's war policy continued to be conscription of wealth and industry first, and manpower second.[8]

Throughout the 1930s the CCF had rejected Communist Party overtures. The reversal of Communist war policy after Germany's attack on the Soviet Union only heightened CCF suspicions of the CP. Now the CCF was being attacked by the CP for insufficient vigour in pursuing the war effort. Tim Buck, the national Communist leader, appealed to the CCF to co-operate and "not seek immediate party advantage in the situation created by the war." "It is entirely wrong," proclaimed the Communist *Canadian Tribune* "to suggest, as C.C.F. speakers and publications often do, that it must be 'Socialism or Nothing.'"[9] Public support for such a position was not insignificant, as the growth of the CP showed.[10] After the Communist Party was officially banned in 1939, Canada's Communists regrouped under the title of the Labour Progressive Party in August 1943. Almost immediately this "new" party applied for affiliation with the CCF in the interest of unity in wartime. W.A. Kardash, the newly elected Manitoba LPP leader, wrote to the 1943 Manitoba CCF convention: "We feel that our Party has a place to occupy in this movement. Any attempt to exclude those whose views of socialism differ from those of the CCF, is a shortsighted policy, for you must surely realize that our views about socialism are the product of our experience and thought as Canadians, and that we have the democratic right to hold these views. At the same time, this is not an obstacle to the firmest co-operation between our party and the CCF, on a program of Victory and Reconstruction."[11]

There may not have been an obstacle to unity on the left for Kardash but there was for the CCF delegates. They, like their national party earlier, turned down the LPP application. A few delegates, however, including old-time leftist Fred Tipping, who had been involved in the Winnipeg General Strike, and recently nominated CCF candidate D.L. Johnson, argued that unity on the left, although not always necessary or required, should be left an open question dependent on changing circumstances.[12] Johnson had been arguing in CCF circles for co-operation on the left throughout the 1930s with little success.[13]

Suspicion of LPP motives among CCFers was generated by the reversals and contradictions in LPP policy. Some CCFers, including potential LPP sympathizers, remembered and resented Communist attacks on the CCF in earlier years.[14] Others were downright confused by LPP intentions. For example, six months after Buck had denounced the CCF in February 1943 for demanding "socialism or nothing," Kardash denounced the CCF for misrepresenting what socialism was all about: "At the same time, he declared, the new party [the LPP] disagrees categorically with the C.C.F. when it points to New Zealand as an example of socialism. 'For an example of socialism we once again point to the only socialist power, the Union of Soviet Socialist Republics,' [he said]."[15] Thus, acording to the Communists, the CCF was to stop campaigning for "socialism now" while at the same time it was condemned for not calling for the "correct" type of socialism. The CCF, however, was being true to its reformist nature: the 1944 provincial convention passed resolutions calling for increased salaries for teachers, a new power development in the province, extension of unemployment insurance benefits, and the encouragement of co-operatives, credit unions and farm machinery pools.

The CP's call for unity usually meant, to the Communists, CCFers withdrawing in most labour strongholds (e.g., Winnipeg North, where an LPP candidate ran against the CCF's Alistair Stewart in 1945). In the 1944 Winnipeg municipal elections, the entry of a Communist candidate in Ward 1 kept future CCF leader Lloyd Stinson from being re-elected as an alderman. The unity-minded Communists also opposed the endorsation of CCF candidates by Winnipeg's two labour councils and applauded the defeat of CCFer John Queen's mayoralty bid in 1944.[16] The LPP's "unity line," therefore, was always a tactical ploy. The LPP's analysis—that without "Labour-Liberal" unity reactionary Toryism would come to power— did not correspond to the reality of the day. Between 1941 and 1944 there were nine provincial elections and the CCF gained votes or seats in all of them. Conservative popularity, on the other hand, was declining. The LPP's thinly veiled attacks on the CCF position of opposition to the Liberals eventually drew a response from the party. David Lewis recommended to the provincial secretary that the Communists be attacked in CCF platforms and in the constituencies.[17] Party pamphlets began to assail the LPP position, and an order went out to all constituency associations forbidding collaboration with the LPP.[18] Such rebuffs did not discourage the provincial Communists, however, and they called on their supporters to vote CCF as their second choice in Manitoba's preferential ballot system. They asked CCFers to respond similarly by voting LPP as their second choice. With such a history of conflict between the two parties, it is easy to see how disruptive it was for the CCF to have two of its most popular MLAs advocating a policy so similar to that of the Labour Progressive Party.

THE RICHARDS-JOHNSON AFFAIR OF 1945

The first indication of a falling out within CCF ranks came in a letter signed, "A Group of C.C.F. Members in Good Standing," which was mailed to many Manitoba party members in early 1945.[19] The letter accused CCF leaders of suppressing debate on the question of unity with other groups. It argued that two Ontario MPPs, Nelson Alles and Leslie Hancock, had been persecuted for their views on this question and were forced to resign from the party, and it concluded by claiming that the authors feared signing their names lest it encourage a witch hunt against them by the CCF leadership. The letter sparked a debate which, to a lesser extent, also rocked the Ontario and British Columbia wings of the party.

It soon became apparent that Berry Richards and D.L. Johnson, if not among the authors, were in sympathy with the thrust of the letter. A week later they wrote a letter to the party's executive committee, stating that the party leaders had been making many decisions on policies and tactics which were detrimental to the CCF movement; that, in the post-war world, "a positive and realistic policy, which at the present time our party appears to lack," will be necessary in dealings with the Soviet Union; that CCF electoral policy in the 1945 federal election should be reviewed in light of the Conservative victory over Liberal Defence Minister A.G.L. McNaughton in a by-election; and insisting that a special provincial convention be called within six weeks to deal with these various points.[20]

Predictably, these charges provoked a long debate at the executive committee meeting. According to the minutes of the meeting: "Knowles stated that now Dr. Johnson had put the cards on the table and we knew where we stood. It was the LPP line pure and simple. He asked Richards if he thought the CCF policy was wrong. Richards said 'yes.' He asked Richards if he thought the LPP policy was right, and he again replied in the affirmative."[21] Clearly outnumbered, Richards and Johnson declared that if the executive voted against holding a special convention, they would be obliged to dissociate themselves from the CCF and would issue a public statement of their position. They agreed, however, to inform the executive of their course of action.

Richards and Johnson then requested space in the *Manitoba Commonwealth* to state their position. Provincial secretary Donovan Swailes claimed that both the national and provincial CCF had already dealt with the unity question and had formulated clear positions. It was unstated but understood that the executive was not eager to open any divisive debate in the party newspaper in the midst of the upcoming federal election campaign. This refusal led Richards and Johnson to argue that the party was controlled from the top down. "The membership," they contended,

have never been faced with the thought that irresponsible political action on the part of the CCF at this time may lead to Fascism. Consequently they have never faced, discussed or decided any issue on this basis, either provincially or nationally. This issue has only become clear within the last short period, and this fact gives point to our original request for a special convention to discuss these issues. In other words we feel that the immediate job for the CCF will not be to establish Socialism, but to prevent Fascism. Through the defeat of Fascism in Canada, the proper basis for Socialism will be laid, and in no other way.

Whether or not Richards and Johnson were in league with the Communists, they were unmistakably stating the LPP position of the time. Eager to debate the question within the party, they informed the CCF office that they were going to issue a public statement and once again asked for space in the party newspaper. Swailes ignored the request and insisted on an advance copy of any public statement.[22]

On the day Swailes replied, Richards was in Portage la Prairie discussing with the local CCF executive the possibility of running a united front candidate. Provincial executive members were furious. Their distrust of the two maverick MLSs was shared by the national office which was convinced that, like the Alles–Hancock affair in Ontario, the Richards–Johnson arguments were "deliberately engineered to create embarrassment for us by creating the impression of [CCF] division in the country. It is obviously part of the L.P.P. strategy," wrote David Lewis, "to try to hurt the CCF."[23]

By this time, Richards and Johnson had been effectively isolated. Despite his being an executive member, Richards was not notified of the executive meetings which rejected his requests for use of the *Manitoba Commonwealth*. Determined to get a full-scale party debate on their ideas and repulsed in their attempts to use the party newspaper, Richards read a statement, signed by him and Johnson, in the provincial legislature. The two MLAs restated their views with respect to encroaching fascism, the need for a change in CCF electoral tactics, and the need for amicable relations with the Soviet Union after the war's end. They claimed that their views were being publicly expressed because the CCF leaders had stymied their attempts to appeal to CCF members within party channels.[24] The *Winnipeg Free Press* called the statement a "bombshell."

Reaction from the CCF was immediate. S.J. Farmer accused Richards and Johnson of making a statement "typical of Communist tactics, aimed at the disruption of the C.C.F."[25] David Lewis reiterated the charges in Ottawa. Adding to the CCF's anger was the fact that a number of Winnipeg's prominent Communists, as if forewarned, had been seated in the legislative gallery during the reading of the statement. The *Manitoba Commonwealth,* purposely held back from publication for two days in anticipation of the statement in the house, carried a full front-page headline entitled, "LPP Aims to destroy CCF."[26]

Neither side trusted the other. The executive was convinced that the rebels were either duped or outright Communist agents within the party. The two dissidents maintained that the executive was misleading and manipulating the rank and file. "Covertly," recalled Dr. Johnson, "we hoped that the publicity and shock from our actions might cause both membership and leadership to do some analytical soul searching and move back to socialism, not as a political football, but as the main essence of the movement."[27] But many CCFers took the Richards–Johnson position to mean a moving away from, rather than back to, socialism because it meant supporting the Liberals.

Political foes of the CCF tried to exploit this internal conflict. The only line of consistency running through *Winnipeg Free Press* editorials on the question was a fundamental anti-CCF bias. Perhaps for the first time in that newspaper's history it accused someone of red-baiting:

It is perfectly true that the statement issued by the two members has many points in common with the present Communist line, but the C.C.F. must remember, that, as a party, its own doctrine has no natural monopoly of the truth. What is important is whether the charges made against the C.C.F. line can be substantiated or not. One looks in vain for any refutation or even discussion of them in statements issued by C.C.F. officials.[28]

The *Free Press* editorial page—a reflection of Liberal party interests—did not attack the LPP line or Richards and Johnson, and never mentioned that the only beneficiary if the "Labour–Liberal" unity line was adopted would be the Liberals. Having argued for a dozen years that the CCF was not much more than a front for Bolshevism, the paper turned around and called, hypocritically, for a principled debate on the issues raised: "What will impress reasonable people about this episode is the vigor with which the c.c.f. seeks to suppress all dissent from the official line. The dissenting minority of today," commented the *Free Press* piously, "becomes the governing majority of tomorrow." The Winnipeg daily reasoned that the CCF had proven its Communist-like nature by exhibiting a vigorous anti-Communist position; "Indeed, the anomaly of the present situation is that, while the c.c.f. leadership remains as always religiously anti-Communist, the party itself has come closely to resemble the Communist party in basic form."[29] A few months later, when Richards supported a CCFer for election against a Liberal, the same *Free Press* argued that this proved that the CCF was tinged with Communism in content as well as form.

Free Press editorials were liberally quoted and complimented by W.A. Kardash in the Communist weekly, *Canadian Tribune*. Wrote Kardash:

Firstly, no political party will gain a clear majority of seats in the next federal elections to form a one-party government.

Secondly, and flowing out of the first, one of two things will happen: either a coalition government of the Tory reactionaries with right-wing Liberals, or a democratic coalition government including a progressive section of the Liberals, CCF, LPP and any other progressive candidates that may be elected.

If a reactionary coalition is formed it will mean the things which the people of Canada want to forget about rather than live through again — the Iron-Heel Bennett days of relief, slave-camps, mass unemployment, stifling of reforms and wrecking of national unity.

Kardash argued that the Richards–Johnson position (i.e., the LPP line) would command support from a clear majority of CCF members if "frank and democratic discussion" were permitted.[30] Both the *Free Press* and the *Canadian Tribune* had their own motives — the smashing of the CCF — to argue that the CCF was controlled from above. The Conservative *Winnipeg Tribune*, with little to applaud in the prospect of "Labour–Liberal" coalition, attacked Richards and Johnson and called on them to resign. It reasoned that the two were elected as CCFers and not as Communists or Liberals, and, if they could no longer support the party label that they carried, they should step down.[31]

In the midst of this gratuitous advice from its opponents, the CCF leadership tried to resolve the dispute internally. It was decided to debate and attack Richards and Johnson in their own constituencies. Stanley Knowles launched a series of bitter debates with Richards in northern

Manitoba. He accused Richards of open collusion with the LPP, of not first discussing his position with his own constituents, and of pursuing tactics designed simply to maximize publicity for his cause. Knowles's hint that Richards was a Communist agent or a pawn for the LPP did not go over well at the meetings. The Pas, Sherridon, and Cranberry Portage associations all sent letters to the provincial council attacking the executive's refusal to permit their MLA to state his views at a special convention or in the *Manitoba Commonwealth*. Richards was well-known and well-liked and to suggest he was a Trojan horse for others convinced few people in the north, an area where the LPP label was largely unfamiliar and irrelevant.

Support for Johnson in his Brandon constituency association was not as solid. J.H. Wood, provincial party chairman, and A.M. Israels, an executive member from south Winnipeg, were sent to debate him. After the long and stormy debate, a compromise resolution was passed calling on both sides to "smooth out their differences without so much publicity."[32]

The provincial council then met to deal with the dispute and to consider disciplinary action. Johnson spoke for an entire morning and Richards for the afternoon; Knowles played the role of prosecuting attorney for the executive in the evening. The debate offered little that was new. Johnson reiterated his position. Richards's analysis dealt more with the world situation. As a result of the war, he argued,

capitalism had received a new lease of life and could go on expanding for some years to come. Capitalism could provide social security. It was the duty of socialists in Canada to co-operate with capitalism; just as socialist Russia was co-operating with capitalist America. We could not elect a CCF government, and might have to decide on a coalition between one or other of the old parties. With Tories it was out of the question. He thought the Liberal government had been progressive, instancing family allowances, unemployment insurance, labor code, and old age pensions, as examples.[33]

This was LPP thinking—seeing coexistence with capitalist parties as a tactic, a temporary stage.

In recalling the meeting, Richards claimed his main concern was not so much pushing a "unity line" as it was dampening incipient adventurism in the CCF. In this, he feels, he was misrepresented. "The point there was that I was criticizing our irresponsible claims about socializing this and that without recognizing the nature of the Canadian constitution, and the limitations on provincial powers," he recalled. "My claim was that we were being dishonest in not coming clean with the electorate on the realities of the situation, in not indicating to them the struggles that would be ahead in building socialism in Canada. I made the point that raising unrealizable dreams among the people just for the purpose of getting elected would only result in their disillusionment in us, and our eventual defeat, and worse, our being characterized by the public as impractical dreamers, not to be trusted."[34] Such a claim, however, did not correspond to the facts: CCF policies were reformist and gradualist, hardly revolutionary. Richards himself had run on a platform stressing New Zealand-style socialism.

On the one hand Richards saw the CCF platform as the product of leftist "dreamers, not to be trusted." On the other hand he and Johnson took the attacks on them by the party as indications of the party moving right, not left. "The CCF leadership was showing growing evidence," Richards recalled, "that they were embarking on a right wing course, that they saw (in spite of their attacks upon liberals and conservatives at home) alignment with western capitalism as the choice they were going to make."[35] "I think," Johnson wrote later, "that fundamentally both of us wished to get the CCF back on the ignored, neglected or forgotten socialist path which was promised in the Regina Manifesto and which appeared to be taken seriously by a lot of people besides Richards and Johnson."[36] But it was Richards and Johnson at the meeting who, in the eyes of others, recommended co-operation with capitalism. "The collaboration of a working class party with capitalism, would be a betrayal of everything the CCF stood for," retorted council member Fred Tipping. He said that "there was no such thing as good capitalists and bad ones."[37] Arguing on behalf of the executive, Stanley Knowles tried to link Richards and Johnson with the LPP. He accused them of attacking the CCF leadership, as the LPP did, in an attempt to split the leaders from the rank and file, and cited the close co-operation between the two dissenters and Kardash in the legislature.

Richards and Johnson, therefore, were attacked from both sides. The leftists on the council interpreted their remarks as a capitulation to capitalism and attacked them on that basis. The more conservative members on the other hand, ever fearful of public identification with the Communists, attempted to associate them with the LPP. Richards insisted, in retrospect, that Knowles clouded the whole issue by introducing the Communist bogey in an effort to smear him. He claims his analysis was derived independently of the LPP and should have been dealt with on its own merits. "My personal agreement with this kind of politics grew out of my own way of thinking and my political background. I never was a believer in partisan politics..."[38]

Richards and Johnson were almost completely isolated within the provincial CCF. The council, after a full day's session, voted 33-5 to suspend their membership. The two mavericks could be expelled from the party only by a motion of the full convention, but as suspended members they were expelled from the caucus. All references to the two in the *Manitoba Commonwealth* ended, but their suspensions seriously weakened the party in their constituencies: membership in The Pas, over 500 in 1943, nearly 400 in 1944, plummeted to 141 by mid-1945. Similarly, in Brandon membership dropped from 289 to 145.[39] To the party these losses, although regrettable, were acceptable. Stanley Knowles was so determined to nip in the bud those pushing the "unity line" that he recommended the provincial council exercise its constitutional right to refuse endorsation of any candidate uttering it, no matter what the cost in terms of disaffecting the constituencies involved.[40] Outside of The Pas and Brandon, however, few dropped out of the CCF on the basis of the suspensions.

Determined to stay in the party and be vindicated by a party convention, Richards, with some embarrassment to the leadership, played an active role in the 1945 federal election as campaign manager for Ronald Moore, CCF candidate in Churchill. He correctly reasoned that Moore, and not the Liberal candidate, was in the best position to defeat the Conservative candidate.[41] The *Free Press,* which had only two months before attacked the CCF for not permitting dissenting viewpoints such as Richards's, reversed its position on learning that Richards was campaigning for Moore and demanded to know how the CCF could permit an alleged Communist to campaign for them.[42]

Amid these intra-party disputes, preparations began for the 1945 provincial election. Although the expected major gains in that year's federal election did not materialize, and the Ontario CCF suffered a dramatic setback that same year—dropping from thirty-four to seven seats—the Manitoba CCF, for the first time, had a credible chance of forming a government. Membership was high, Saskatchewan had voted CCF a year before, the party was the official opposition, and a near-full slate was to be entered. Optimistic about its electoral chances, the CCF sent executive members A.M. Israels and Lloyd Stinson to Regina to study CCF legislation and to report on the practical difficulties of implementing a CCF provincial platform.[43]

Desiring to avoid any adverse publicity during this period, the CCF executive decided to ignore, rather than openly fight, Richards and Johnson. They, in turn, declared that they would run in the elections under an Independent CCF label. In The Pas, Richards courted the support of CCF members, and the various CCF units in the riding refused to nominate an official CCF candidate against him. In the face of such support the provincial office could do little. In Brandon, however, Johnson's opponents in the local CCF association nominated an official candidate to run against him.

The results of the 1945 provincial election were both encouraging and disappointing for the CCF. The CCF led the polls with 35 per cent of the total vote, yet returned only nine MLAs. For their 33 per cent of the vote, the Liberal–Progressives returned twenty-five MLAs. Even the Conservatives, with 39,000 votes compared to the CCF's 74,000, won more seats than the CCF and ensured a Coalition majority. The CCF's electoral performance was penalized because most of the party's strength was in Winnipeg, a city dramatically under-represented with only ten seats in a house of fifty-five. (Richards's narrow victory in The Pas gave the party a tenth member if he stayed with them. Johnson ran a poor third, losing to a Coalitionist and trailing the official CCF candidate.)

After the election the party turned toward resolving the Richards–Johnson affair. Don Swailes wrote them insisting that they formally appeal the council's suspensions if the matter was to be dealt with in convention. Richards's appeal was conciliatory. Johnson's, on the other hand, was critical. Unlike Richards, for whom a successful appeal meant readmission to the caucus, Johnson had been defeated and a successful appeal meant much less. The appeals, however, were not well received by the leadership. "As for Johnson, I do not see how he can expect any consideration whatsoever," wrote Stanley Knowles from Ottawa to a caucus member. "I realize that Richards has been able to persuade a number of our people that he is a nice boy, etc. But when it comes down to the final question of readmitting him that would involve his re-entry into your caucus. Frankly," continued Knowles, "I do not see how that can be considered at all. In my view—and every last one of our M.P.'s here shares it—he cannot be trusted...I certainly hope that the convention will stand on its own hind legs in connection with this matter and will not be fooled by any 'lovey-dovey let's get together sort of talk.'"[44] But when the convention met in December, Knowles was away in England.

The convention, the largest in the party's history to that point, sustained the council's decision to suspend Richards and Johnson by a vote of ninety-six to twenty-five. This opened the way for a debate on whether the two should then be expelled—a power only the convention could exercise. After a prolonged and heated debate, both appeals against suspension were read and motions for their reinstatement were entertained. Each was permitted to speak, with A.M. Israels responding for the council. The debate pointed out differences between Richards and Johnson. Although both reiterated and defended their positions vis-à-vis the LPP and the CCF's attitude to the Soviet Union, Richards, unlike Johnson, stressed his desire to be reinstated and to abide by the party's constitution. Johnson, on the other hand, faced a convention that had been given evidence that he had actively worked against CCF candidates. The vote, taken by secret ballot after a lengthy debate that went past midnight, was 80-35 in favour of Richards's reinstatement and 30-80 against Johnson's.[45] Had he been there, Knowles would no doubt have put up a stronger fight against Richards's appeal.

When the convention re-convened in the morning, Richards's ideas were once again rejected. A letter to the convention from Kardash, calling for joint LPP–CCF discussions on electoral co-operation[46] was not even read, having been summarily dismissed by the executive earlier. A resolution from the Sherridon Unit calling on the CCF not to contest seats where the party had little chance of winning and instead to "support the most progressive candidate" was rejected by both the resolutions committee and the convention. A resolution from The Pas — "That the CCF Party should at all times adopt policies that will prevent splitting of the progressive forces" — was accorded similar treatment. In response to constitutional amendments requiring a constituency, and not the council, to initiate expulsion procedures, S.J. Farmer succeeded in changing this to a requirement that only notice of the alleged offence need be given to the constituency. Richards was kept in the party but his attitudes were in a minority. Sensing the mood of the convention, Richards declined to stand for nomination to the CCF's national council.

Immediately after the convention both Richards and Johnson went to Brandon and issued a joint statement. They declared that their views had not changed, although to keep his pledge to the convention Richards made no criticism of the CCF leadership. Their statement claimed to be "still critical of the C.C.F. in the matters of unity and attitude toward the Soviet Union,"[47] but it was a relatively muted declaration. Hesitant about reopening the debate, the provincial executive decided to ignore the statement.[48]

What were the motives, the thinking, of Richards and Johnson in 1945? The former was naive and confused while the latter's sympathies lay elsewhere. Richards's thinking was, like the LPP position of the day, untenable and illogical to the CCF. Johnson, although not an LPP member at the time, was a self-avowed Marxist. He had come to the conclusion that social democrats like the CCF had deserted the interests of the working class and had made their peace with capitalism. Writing to Knowles in

1949, in the midst of the day's Cold War hysteria and the CCF's endorsation of a Western military alliance, Johnson's deeper feelings were revealed:

I deplore and will continue to deplore the role of social democracy in the changing scene of history. You are, of course, sufficiently aware to realize I include the CCF in this group. The ambition ridden leaders of Social Democracy must — I am afraid — play their historic role in betraying the interests of the working people — but ... true Marxists must eventually realize the nature of their [the CCFers'] Judas role and be prepared....

... Not only do they [CCF leaders] appear to have forgotten the evils of capitalism; they appear to be cooperating with capitalism in its vicious fight — against the only real alternative — true communistic socialism.

The CCF — I am convinced — will follow the historic path of all social democrats and end up as one of the last hopes of Capitalism. But it seems to me that true Marxists should recognize this fact and be prepared to act...

History of course will judge them [the CCF] as it will judge all public people. The time is getting short. Sooner or later, we will have to decide on which side we stand — *the people's* side or the side of the unscrupulous exploiters and warmongers and profiteers. Politics makes queer bedfellows, but there is no need to persist in error. Sooner or later the CCF will be torn in two and a segment of true socialists will stand up for "Unity of the Working Class" and this will be a political development of major importance in Canada. The other group, will of course, go down the inglorious road of traitorism to the working class. The choice may not remain for any length of time. It appears to me that those who have ears to hear — might be well to ponder and condition their minds to the probabilities which lie ahead, otherwise the CCF will eventually turn out to be a leadership without a following.[49]

A few years after his expulsion Johnson joined the Communist Party[50] and ran as an Independent against former Conservative leader John Bracken in Brandon in the 1949 federal election. The Communist *Canadian Tribune,* which had given prominent sympathetic play to Richards and Johnson in 1945, was silent after the CCF convention expelled Johnson and took back Richards.

The difference between Richards and Johnson was that Richards never broke completely with social democracy, but Johnson did. Richards believed that the party reinstated him in 1945 because he was still a potential party leader and a good public speaker — assets that Johnson did not share.[51] He believed that he was not at variance with Johnson's political outlook, but he was. Although Richards was expelled from the CCF in 1949, as Johnson was in 1945, Richards rejoined the party in the 1950s and continued as a member into the 1970s. Johnson, in contrast, was never comfortable in the social democratic CCF. He always believed that old Brandon ILPers and the CCF leadership wanted him out of the party, even before his election to the legislature in 1943.[52] Johnson, unlike Richards, clearly left the realm of social democratic politics after his expulsion.

COLD WAR POLITICS

As the Cold War took hold in 1946–49 the position of social democratic parties everywhere was shaken. Despite a Labour Party victory and early pronouncements of Anglo-Soviet friendship, Britain, like the other states in Western Europe, moved inexorably, and often uncritically, into a military alliance dominated by the United States. The stated objective was to contain Soviet military expansion. The pressure on the CCF to support this policy was strong. The CCF's position in the immediate post-war period was weakened on two accounts. One was that the party's prediction throughout the war of post-war depression did not materialize. Another problem was that large numbers of Canadians vaguely identified the CCF with other leftist forces, including the Soviet Union, and Soviet troops at this time dictated the character of Eastern European governments. In this political climate, the CCF did not challenge Liberal foreign policy, which was headed in the direction of NATO. In its determination to dissociate itself from the Communists, the CCF stopped criticizing Canadian foreign policy and began attacking the Soviet Union. Opponents of these developments within the CCF were often turned on by the party with the zeal of a repenting sinner.

Having returned to the party fold, Berry Richards abided by his promise not to criticize the CCF publicly. He did, however, begin to attack what he saw as the growth of post-war American imperialism in Europe and Canada. To many CCF leaders, this was an attack on the party. Their suspicions of Richards, despite his popularity with many rank and file members, resulted in his being denied any executive or other influential position within the party. In spite of such rebuffs, his views commanded attention at conventions, and on occasion, as at the 1948 convention, they carried the day.

Friction between Coldwell and Richards quickly appeared. Richards criticized the national leader's speeches for making continuous reference to "the totalitarianism inherent in modern communism." Coldwell defended his comments by citing the Regina Manifesto's clause dealing with civil liberties which, he asserted, were being suppressed in the USSR.[53] Replying on behalf of her husband, Mabel Richards asked why, if the CCF was so committed to democracy, it made no similar strong statements regarding the suppression of civil liberties in Greece, Indonesia, and Spain. "One would expect," replied Coldwell, "that persons who are so critical of all the c.c.f. does, and who apparently give their loyalty elsewhere should be honest with themselves and go where their loyalty directs them."[54]

Such attacks on Richards did nothing to dampen his protests. At the 1946 provincial convention he argued against anti-Soviet warmongering in Canada and urged the party to fight any attempts to integrate US — Canada defence efforts.[55] In March 1947, he spoke at an LPP rally in north Winnipeg, condemning the presence of American troops in northern Manitoba on a defence exercise, and chiding the Canadian government for its dependence on American capital to develop the north. Richards had felt stymied by the CCF's silence on these issues. "Had the CCF been taking a position that recognized the threat of American capitalism," he recalled, "it would not have been necessary for me to seek other auspices."[56] Richards attacked American foreign policy on the floor of the house. S.J. Farmer, as always, was quick to dissociate the caucus and the party from these views.[57] A critical stand on American foreign policy, however, was not unpopular with the rank and file. The 1947 provincial convention agreed with Richards and voted to condemn the Truman Doctrine.[58]

Richards was given warm applause in the local Communist weekly, *The Westerner*, and gained more prominent notice there than in the *Manitoba Commonwealth*. Although not working in harmony with him, the LPP used Richards in their contention that the CCF leadership was suppressing rank and file support for Richards's position.[59] While on occasion in 1947 Richards did give voice to the "unity line,"[60] the LPP had begun to change its own position on this question. By 1948 "Labour-Liberal" unity was a thing of the past. Richards was speaking for a policy which was attacked as the LPP line but was, in fact, no longer supported by the LPP.

The Communist position of 1945 had been undermined by Canada's Cold War episodes. Fred Rose, the LPP member of Parliament from Montreal, was arrested and convicted on charges of espionage for the Soviet Union. Added to this were the related revelations about a Soviet spy network made by Igor Gouzenko, a clerk at the Soviet Embassy. The LPP was put further on the defensive when the Liberals, the so-called "progressives" of 1945, began supporting the Marshall Plan—a plan termed anti-Soviet by the LPP. These developments could hardly encourage "Labour-Liberal" unity, and the LPP changed its line. Photographs of leading Liberal politicians were quietly dropped from the pages of the *Canadian Tribune*. S.J. Farmer, a villain six months before, was applauded in 1946 for defending civil liberties.[61] Coldwell, scolded in 1945 for being adventurist in demanding "socialism now," was in the summer of 1946 condemned for not attacking vigorously enough the forces of monopoly capital.[62] By early 1948 the LPP turnabout had come full circle. The "Labour-Liberal" unity slogan of 1945 was replaced by "Unite at the Polls, vote CCF." Realizing that its position was weak during the Cold War and that only the CCF was a potentially viable force in fighting Liberal foreign policy, the LPP decided to contest only a few seats in the 1949 federal election. In those it did not contest, it endorsed the CCF, not the Liberals. Kardash went so far as to recommend not running a Communist in Winnipeg North[63] where the LPP had come quite close to winning in 1945.

The CCF was never enthusiastic about unsolicited Communist support. This was particularly true in the late 1940s when anti-Communism was becoming a national religion. The LPP endorsation of the CCF was a major threat to success at the polls. "Our worst problem with them [the Communists] was when they wanted us to join with them. It never bothered us when they were against us," claimed Stanley Knowles, "and if they wanted to support Mackenzie King we had good fun out of that, but when they wanted united fronts on this issue or the other or... when they issued literature supporting us we found this something we had to oppose."[64] The CCF's fear of identification with the Communists was not unjustified. After contesting Minnedosa in 1948, the party chairman, R.G. Frith, described "a whispering campaign carried on during the last few days of the contest, to the effect that the CCF was in alliance with the Communists, and that there was no difference between the policy of the CCF and that of the Communist party."[65]

A leading force in Manitoba in associating the CCF with Communism was the *Winnipeg Free Press*. Richards, who in 1945 had been depicted by the *Free Press* as a dissenter unfairly persecuted by the CCF became, by 1948, a central figure for the *Free Press* in its red-baiting attacks on the CCF. The paper denounced Richards as a stooge for the Soviets; they suggested he emigrate to Russia; and later, called him the "chief bus driver for the travellers."[66] By blackening the name of Richards, the paper also tarred the CCF. The *Free Press* was committed to fighting socialism and to a Western collective security pact anchored by the United States. The foreign policy debate within the CCF conveniently permitted the *Free Press* to tie these two topics closely together.

Developments at the 1948 convention must have confirmed the *Free Press's* view of the CCF. Led by Richards, The Pas CCF Association successfully introduced a resolution condemning the European Recovery Program (commonly referred to as the Marshall Plan) as imperialist and reactionary.[67] The resolution proposed instead an international aid program under United Nations auspices. Attempts to water down the resolution by deleting references to "capitalism" or the Marshall Plan were defeated and it was carried as proposed. Predictably the *Free Press* and the *Winnipeg Tribune* were outraged, while the Communist *Westerner* was delighted. The CCF leadership was opposed to the resolution, feeling that it too closely resembled the LPP policy on European affairs and would only contribute to unfavourable publicity for the CCF. An unsigned editorial, reflecting the executive's viewpoint, appeared in the *Manitoba Commonwealth* and argued that national, not provincial, CCF policy on the Marshall Plan was paramount. The Manitoba resolution, according to the editorial, was no more than a matter of opinion.[68]

In spite of opposition to the Marshall Plan in Manitoba and elsewhere (particularly British Columbia), Coldwell repudiated the Manitoba convention's action. Supporting him, the 1948 national convention, held after the provincial one, endorsed the European Recovery Program.[69] With the CCF now firmly behind this pro-American policy, the LPP modified its "vote CCF" line and decided to contest as many provincial and federal seats as possible, supporting only certain "progressive" CCFers where LPPers did not run.[70] This also meant entering Joe Zuken against Alistair Stewart in Winnipeg North.

Plaguing the CCF at this time was a form of political schizophrenia which understandably confused the public. Although successive provincial conventions attacked the Truman Doctrine and the Marshall Plan, the *Manitoba Commonwealth* still ran large photographs of President Truman. One issue carried a banner headline referring to him as the "Determined Fighter for New Deal Policies." Immediately next to this favourable story on the president of the world's largest capitalist state was a story reporting a speech of a local CCF candidate for Parliament. "Capitalism has outlived its time," he was quoted with the approval of the paper. "The present economic problems we are confronted with cannot be solved unless we change to a socialist economy."[71] Only a most flexible, or confused, mind could reconcile criticism of Truman's foreign policy, support for his domestic policy, and a call for the replacement of capitalism.

THE RICHARDS-DONELEYKO EXPULSIONS OF 1949

After the war, CCF fortunes tumbled. From 1945 through 1949 membership steadily dropped: a provincial membership of 5,000 in 1944 fell to 1,200 by 1950. Cold War hysteria and the CCF's public row over foreign policy had taken their toll. The largest CCF constituency association, outside of Winnipeg, continued to be Berry Richards's, The Pas. The second largest association was Wilbert Doneleyko's, St. Clements. Doneleyko, first elected an MLA in 1945 and appointed as a party organizer in 1946, became increasingly critical, like Richards, of CCF endorsation of American and Canadian foreign policies. He was, however, less articulate and had a smaller following than Richards.

The first public indication of Doneleyko's disenchantment came in a radio broadcast in March 1949. Speaking on behalf of the CCF in a series of free-time political broadcasts, Doneleyko began by reiterating the CCF's reformist platform on such issues as health care, education, and highway construction; but he ended the broadcast by denouncing the Marshall Plan as "nothing but a clever device to maintain and perpetuate in Europe the *status quo* and thereby slowly and cautiously expand American Imperialism."[72] He also referred to negotiations respecting the North Atlantic Treaty Organization and called them a scheme to perpetuate capitalism, at all costs, by the expansion of American imperial hegemony.

Although such comments were in keeping with the 1948 provincial convention resolution on this issue, the CCF leadership did not take kindly to them. The provincial executive and eight of ten caucus members (Doneleyko and Richards excluded) quickly repudiated the remarks in the broadcast.[73] Doneleyko was rebuked, and he issued a statement saying that the opinions expressed were personal.[74] The national CCF's position was held to be paramount over the provincial one. Stanley Knowles, ever watchful in Ottawa of developments back home, was still not completely satisfied. Certain of more trouble, he wrote the new provincial leader, E.A. Hansford, with some advice: "Do try to avoid a resolution against the [Atlantic] Pact being presented in the Legislature by Wilbert, Berry, or anyone else. You can argue rightly that this is a federal matter. If either of them insists on doing this—or if Kardash does it, you had better be ready to make our position clear by proposing an amendment. Indeed, if Wilbert or Berry were to insist on putting an anti-Pact resolution on, you might have to counter with a pro-Pact resolution. Better still, none at all."[75]

A few days later Knowles's thinking hardened. He suggested that if either of the two received constituency nominations, the provincial council, as entitled, should refuse them official CCF endorsation.[76] The option of suspension, which was always open and was employed in 1945, was not argued this time. "Frankly, I cannot fail to see the parallel between what happened in 1945, just prior to the elections of that year and the tactic being employed now," wrote Knowles to a caucus member. "It looks for all the world like an attempt to cause confusion and division just at a time when it might hurt us the most. I do not think," he continued, "we should give these monkeys the satisfaction of suspension, or martyr-dom in any way. But I do feel that we have to stand very firm in connection with the whole matter."[77] The only immediate support Doneleyko received for his comments was from The Pas. Writing on behalf of the association there, Mabel Richards denied that any CCF convention had ever endorsed the Atlantic Pact, in light of the fact that most information about it had just been released and had not yet been considered. She felt that Hansford had no right to criticize Doneleyko and that the national council should not have endorsed NATO until it was debated in convention.[78]

With NATO becoming a major political question in 1949, an unofficial CCF committee was formed in Manitoba to propagandize against it and the Marshall Plan. Berry Richards, as a member of the committee, asked the provincial secretary for the CCF's mailing list and was refused. Determined to express its views, the anti-NATO committee sent letters to whatever CCF names it could secure. The letter was signed by eleven CCF members including MLAs Richards and Doneleyko. It claimed that Ottawa's policies were fashioned after Washington's, termed the Marshall Plan a plot to re-establish capitalism, and asked if increased production of armaments was really for security or simply to ward off an economic depression. The letter went on to name some of the various elected CCFers who opposed the national council's stand on NATO.[79] (At this time the British Columbia CCF convention, led by some MLAs, refused to endorse the national CCF position.)[80] Concluding, the authors of the letter asked the opinion of members on NATO, on the Marshall Plan, and on the CCF's endorsement of these plans.

Aware of the circulation of the latter, the executive decided to ignore it, lest it only bring about more adverse publicity for the party. A month later, however, Winnipeg's newspapers printed a copy of the letter. By this time the party was in the midst of a federal election campaign and the executive took swift action, prompted by Knowles and David Lewis. Meeting to con-sider the letter, the executive rejected it, endorsed the national council's position, and referred the matter to the next provincial convention. David Lewis wired Swailes, pointing out how CCF opponents everywhere were making political capital of the letter during the election campaign and demanding a more vigorous public repudiation of it.[81] "Please note that we did not issue merely a statement of repudiation," wrote Knowles to soothe Lewis. "We are being charged with putting on a stage play in simply doing that every time this sort of thing happens. So we've cast the die for stronger action, namely expulsion by the convention."[82] In keeping with this new tough approach, Knowles and Swailes publicly attacked unnamed members—clearly Richards and Doneleyko—as "mischief makers... who had repeatedly adopted the disruptive tactics of Communism to embarrass the C.C.F."[83]

As in 1945, these strong feelings were prompted by press reaction and the CCF's fear of a bad image during an election campaign. Hysteria ran rampant in the editorial pages of the local press. The *Free Press* demanded expulsions of all anti-NATO elements in the CCF, and insisted that if such expulsions were not immediately forthcoming, the CCF should not cry foul when accused of being communist-tinged. When CCF executive members repeatedly informed that paper that expulsions could only be effected by a convention, the *Free Press* ignored their protestations and argued that the CCF leadership was impotent in dealing with its dissenters. To prove its point that a communist takeover of the CCF was at hand the *Free Press* claimed, falsely, that Richards was campaign manager for the CCF candidate in Churchill constituency.[84] The *Winnipeg Tribune* confidently predicted no one would be expelled in light of the 1948 convention's endorsement of what it thought was the LPP line.[85] Such dramatizations and misrepresentations in the press gave the impression that the CCF was dominated by its foreign policy dissenters and that these dissenters were, if not Communists, fellow travellers.

At the subsequent 1949 provincial convention three resolutions were proposed naming Richards and Doneleyko and calling for their expulsion. Two of the resolutions were from the Winnipeg North and the municipal Ward Two (roughly corresponding to Winnipeg North Centre) associations. Both of these areas were represented in the House of Commons by executive members—Knowles and Alistair Stewart—both of whom were personally determined to have the rebels purged. Richards had become too big a thorn, and Knowles, who thought the party had erred in 1945 by letting Richards stay in,[86] was determined not to let it happen again. Knowles, on behalf of the resolutions committee, formally moved and argued for the expulsions.

The convention clearly favoured Knowles's position. This time however, unlike 1945, the division of opinion was different. In 1945 members from The Pas, Flin Flon, and Sherridon argued for electoral co-operation with the Liberals and tempering "adventurist" socialist policy demands. Now they argued for more socialism. "[T]he cause of the setback suffered by the CCF in the recent [federal] election was that our party has failed to base its policies upon the socialist principles laid down in the Regina Manifesto," read their resolution.[87] Suspicion of such logic fed suspicion of collusion with the LPP. By a vote of fifty-six to eighteen the two anti-NATO MLAs were expelled from the party and the caucus. Although only the two MLAs were expelled, many rank and file delegates were still opposed to NATO, and an amendment to the expulsion resolution, disapproving of Richards's and Doneleyko's statement and actions, was defeated. The day after the expulsions, however, resolutions to rescind the party's 1948 resolution on the Marshall Plan and to endorse NATO for the first time were carried.

Not all anti-NATO elements in the CCF were treated as harshly as were Richards and Doneleyko. An interesting example was Fred Tipping. Nominated to contest Winnipeg South, Tipping spoke out often against NATO. When the national convention endorsed NATO he immediately offered to give up the nomination, since he differed on a major point of policy. His constituency association, however, voted to keep him on as their candidate and gave him complete liberty to speak his mind on this issue.[88] Similarly, when the provincial convention came along and Tipping stood shoulder to shoulder with Richards and Doneleyko in opposition to NATO, he was nominated for the chairmanship of the party. The vote, taken after the expulsion debate and Tipping's strong anti-NATO comments, was amazing: Tipping was elected! To Tipping such a situation was preposterous. How could the party elect him as chairman when he had so vigorously opposed NATO, an issue leading to the expulsion of two MLAs? He quickly tendered his resignation as chairman and despite the convention's plea to reconsider, refused to serve, although he remained a member in good standing.

The answer to Tipping's question was the real or assumed relationship of individuals, and particularly MLAs, to the Communist Party. Tipping, who had in principle not been opposed to co-operating with the Communists in the 1930s, had become very critical of the Communist "Labour-Liberal" unity line of the 1940s. It was on the basis that the Communists had given up on the anti-capitalist struggle that he had attacked the Richards–Johnson position of 1945. He also made it very clear at the 1949 convention that he was anti-communist. Richards, Johnson, and Doneleyko, on the other hand, were not as averse to co-operating with the

LPP. Richards had spoken on LPP platforms and refused to attack the LPP, as he did not consider it a foe of the CCF. "When I saw that anti-communism was apparently a basic tenet held by the CCF leadership," he recalled, "I decided it had to be defied, and fought. I never could see a socialist (if it were socialist) party getting anywhere as long as it thought of left-wingers and communists as being greater enemies than liberals and conservatives."[89] Johnson, as a Marxist in the CCF, had also been revolted by what he felt were unprincipled attacks on fellow Marxists. Doneleyko, although clearly not a Marxist, was very much influenced by Richards's thinking on international affairs[90] and did not fear closely co-operating with Communists. Around the time of his expulsion Doneleyko became a leading member of the Manitoba Peace Council, an organization closely identified with the LPP. Tipping, and other leftists like him, may have agreed with Communist positions at times and may even have supported joint actions. He never, however, suggested that the CCF negate its electoral role as Richards, Johnson, and the LPP did in 1945. For the CCF leaders and members, therefore, the criterion for expulsion was not necessarily the endorsing of a position held in common with the Communists. It was, rather, giving the *impression* that dissent from CCF policy was based on collusion with the Communist Party and its activities. It was into this trap that Richards, Johnson, and Doneleyko had fallen.

CCF leaders were concerned over any possible identification with the Communists. They were determined that Communist views, even those with which they sympathized, be ignored. An example of this syndrome arose when the *Manitoba Commonwealth* reprinted an article by a Communist. David Lewis, more angered by the authorship than the content, would have kept such an article from members' eyes: "Of course there is a great deal of truth in the Moscow article about working conditions in the United States and in Scott Nearing's analysis of the inner capitalist drive toward armaments, and the consequent danger of war," he wrote to Don Swailes, "but one thing is very clear. We are not likely to educate our members in the theory and practices, philosophy and objectives, of democratic socialism for which the CCF stands, by quoting sources like those mentioned."[91]

The leaders' concern over identification with the Communists was largely endorsed by the membership. Even though many in the CCF agreed with the LPP on the NATO question, many were afraid of having CCF criticism of NATO aired publicly, lest it be used by the press in smearing the CCF. There was great concern over the party's image. As Stanley Knowles commented: "We didn't have to worry too much about people who expressed divergent opinions on the right, but we did have to worry about... our image in the public eye if it looked as though we were playing footsie with the Communists."[92]

Reaction to the 1949 expulsions was predictable and consistent. Richards and Doneleyko claimed that the CCF had succumbed to red-baiting and that they would sit as Independents.[93] The *Free Press* was still unhappy with the CCF, despite the expulsions it had called for. How could Tipping have been elected party chairman, it wondered, if he was opposed to NATO?[94] The *Manitoba Commonwealth* took a slightly different approach: "Berry Richards and Wilbert Doneleyko were expelled from the CCF, not because they were opposed to the Atlantic Pact, but because of the opposition tactics they adopted. At no time were they curbed in stating their minority views on the Atlantic Pact at caucus meetings of the M.L.A.'s, at executive or provincial council meetings. They were likewise given space to state their views in the party organ, the *Manitoba Commonwealth*. However, they were not satisfied to confine themselves within these limits; they insisted in pressing their minority views as if they were the majority."[95] The editorial went on to level other charges: the use of the party's free radio time to deal with foreign rather than provincial affairs; the circulation of a letter attacking party policy; the ignoring of the constitution; and collusion with other parties (meaning, the LPP).

Rejected by their party, Richards and Doneleyko were soon to drift into political oblivion. In the summer of 1949 Richards declared himself a Northern Independent candidate for The Pas. The CCF association there, still firmly behind their MLA, refused, as they had in 1945, to nominate an official CCF candidate against him.[96] Encouraged by the provincial office, however, a rival CCF association, claiming to represent The Pas constituency, nominated their own "official" candidate. Richards was soundly beaten, but the CCF candidate ran a poor third.

Doneleyko fared better in dealing with the CCF, but his political fate was the same as Richards's. He declared himself an Independent CCF candidate and received the endorsement of a convention of over 150, which the *Winnipeg Tribune* described as being composed of CCF supporters and sympathizers.[97] A month later he wrote to the nomination convention of his former constituency, St. Clements, and urged those in attendance not to nominate an official CCF candidate in the interests of a "people's" victory.[98] To this they agreed. The Communists also declined to run a candidate in St. Clements, and instead, endorsed Doneleyko. Such political maneuvering went for naught, however, as Doneleyko lost the election.

After the 1949 election, CCF relations with the Communist Party reverted to what they had been before 1945. "As far as communism is concerned, we try to ignore them as far as possible; certainly we don't go out of our way to slam them," wrote Don Swailes. "If there is no communist candidate in the field, we will get their votes."[99] The CCF, therefore, recognized that many people identified it with the LPP. The LPP failed to improve on Kardash's lone seat in the legislature. Its influence on the CCF, which was itself declining in strength, became marginal.[100]

Being able to ignore the local Communists, however, did little to resolve the foreign policy dilemma facing the CCF. When isolated members in the party protested the federal party's anti-Sovietism and acquiessence to American foreign policy, the response was Cold War rhetoric. The provincial secretary wrote to one such protester: "On the other hand, much as they hate to do it, *ALL* the social democratic parties in the world, Norway, Sweden, Denmark, Germany and Great Britain, including Nye Bevan, have recognized the absolute necessity for maintaining defensive armament. I have an idea that if J.S. Woodsworth were alive today, knowing what is known about the slave labour camps, about the thought control and terrorism which the Soviet Union seeks to impose on all the people it controls, he would back to the hilt the program of the international socialist movement."[101]

In the final analysis the CCF's relations with the Communists were closely bound to the relations between the two major world camps. When Swailes wrote the CCF national secretary and questioned the wisdom and cost of the party's pro-US stand—a stand he felt had come about more by default than design—the reply was revealing:

We cannot afford to ignore the fact that at the present time the world is divided. I think socialists must realize that the predatory nature of American capitalism is as nothing compared with the imperialism of the U.S.S.R. . . . The aggression of communist Russia poses a much more serious threat [than Hitler's Nazis did] to the world in my opinion. Already the Russian Communists have succeeded in gaining control over a larger portion of the world, both in area and in population, than Hitler succeeded in doing. They may have done it to no small degree by relying on the treacherous and perverted 'idealism' of the non-Russian communists in the countries concerned. . . .

This poses a threat for the rest of us that simply cannot be ignored and in the division of the world into two camps which consequently follows from Russia's policies, socialists everywhere must not hesitate to state where they stand. So far there has been an overwhelming manifestation of support among socialists for the nations and forces which are determined to retain or to win democracy and freedom, even if this means, for the time being, alliances, pacts, etc. All I am saying here is that in the event of a showdown between the two major forces in the world today there is no question but that socialists would stand with the Western powers because only if the Western powers succeed in defeating communism in such a conflict would the ideals which we stand for have any chance of survival.[102]

The CCF prided itself on its British and Western European social democratic traditions and antecedents. The Communist Party, on the other hand, was viewed by the CCF as a puppet parroting and pushing Soviet foreign policy objectives. When the clash between East and West became the major post-war issue, the CCF came down firmly, as did other Western European social democrats, behind a "Western," if not a socialist, position. The decision was understandable and, some may argue, inevitable.

The forties and fifties:
the party's character and strategy

4

In 1943 the Co-operative Commonwealth Federation became a serious contender for political office both federally and provincially. At one point that year—and for the only time in the party's history—it led the national Gallup poll. One year later the CCF formed the government in Saskatchewan and was the largest opposition party in Manitoba, Ontario, British Columbia, and Alberta. A minor party in the 1930s, the CCF became a major party during the war years. But the Cold War brought setbacks, and by the late 1950s it was apparent to the CCF leadership that minor party status was a permanent feature of the CCF's existence. This analysis led the party's leaders to transform the CCF into the New Democratic Party in 1961. A survey of activities of the Manitoba CCF in the 1940s and 1950s shows how wartime optimism and strength gave way to post-war pessimism and weakness, which, in turn, gave way to renewed hope and moderate success.

THE PARTY'S ORGANIZATION

The Manitoba CCF was the provincial wing of a party which was also active on the national and municipal levels. At the municipal level, the Manitoba CCF was most active in the city of Winnipeg. Notable successes had been the mayoralty victories of ILP–CCFers S.J. Farmer and John Queen in the 1920s, 1930s and early 1940s. After Queen's departure, the CCF slowly lost its status as a serious mayoralty contender. When provincial party secretary Donovan Swailes ran for the job in 1952, he confided to others that he had no serious expectation of winning and spent a meagre $600 in a disappointing effort.[1] At the aldermanic level, the CCF continuously held between 30 and 40 per cent of the seats. In some suburban and rural areas CCFers often ran as independents but relied on CCF mailing lists. The CCF's municipal electoral performance was generally closely correlated to its provincial performance; the provincial and municipal CCFs did well together or poorly together in any given area.

The CCF's competitor at the municipal level was the Civic Election Committee. The formally "non-partisan" CEC was a loose coalition of Conservatives and Liberals. Ideologically and politically the CEC was the descendant of the 1919 Citizens' Committee which opposed the Winnipeg General Strike. Similarly, the CCF had ideological links with the Strike Committee. The CEC operated much as a conventional political party, nominating and endorsing candidates who usually had a business background. The CEC's program was simple and two-pronged: Winnipeg needs good business government; and there should be no party politics at the municipal level.[2] In response, the CCF spent much of its time merely trying to justify its municipal existence and argued that municipal issues were political issues.

The municipal CCF was an extension of the provincial CCF, which in turn saw itself as an extension of the national CCF. In theory the programs and policies of the provincial party were "subject to the approval of the National Council."[3] In practice, as the party's role in a provincial wartime coalition government had shown, the provincial party operated fairly autonomously. A monthly financial quota, assessed by the national party with provincial consent, permitted stronger CCF provincial sections to aid weaker ones. On the whole, the Manitoba party received more than it contributed. It was also assisted by the presence of a powerful neighbouring Saskatchewan CCF government. Saskatchewan cabinet ministers spoke on behalf of Manitoba CCF candidates in every election campaign between 1945 and 1959. Another example of the close link was provincial party leader Lloyd Stinson's soliciting of Premier T.C. Douglas's opinions before drafting a Manitoba CCF election platform.[4]

Some people continued to perceive the CCF as a movement and more than a party. The movement concept had been given substantial credibility by social gospel preachers, usually in the United Church, who were willing to associate themselves with CCF educational and organizational efforts. CCF organizers exploited this link to its full advantage. One such organizer, and future MP, Alistair Stewart, wrote to the national office about his "technique":

In the country I have started three [educational] groups recently. The technique I have evolved is this. I go to the United Church minister. I make my position clear. I don't want him in the CCF for he can usually do much better work outside the movement and in any event we have too many goddam ministers as it is. But I ask him to lead a study group on post war problems and tell him that the members will also be members of the CCF. I also ask him to instruct them in leadership and in the business of conducting a meeting, public speaking, etc. I begin with one group for it is no good being overly ambitious.[5]

As the war drew to an end the CCF became more a party than an educational crusade or movement. It attained "official opposition" status in the legislature when it left the Coalition government in 1942. Large membership gains, a paid circulation of over 5,000 for the provincial party newspaper,[6] and CCF electoral gains elsewhere fed unprecedented enthusiasm and optimism about the CCF's electoral possibilities in the mid-1940s. As an electoral party, the Manitoba CCF reached its apex in 1945 by amassing 35 per cent of the vote. The most it had ever received before was 17 per cent (in 1941) and it was never to gain more than 26 per cent after 1945. Of the fifty-seven legislative seats (fifty-five before 1949), the party never won fewer than three seats (in 1941) or more than eleven (in 1958).

The CCF's decline after 1945 was as dramatic as its earlier rise. By 1951 twenty-seven of the forty-five provincial constituencies had no viable CCF association,[7] and a year later the party organ, the *Manitoba Commonwealth*, folded. The party did not contest a majority of the seats in either the 1949 or 1953 provincial elections, and attendance at the annual provincial convention dropped so low that it was not held in 1953. The CCF was on the verge of internal collapse yet, somehow, it continued to maintain the voting support of a significant percentage of the population. After 1956 an upswing in rural memberships and party activity led to record slates being fielded in the 1958 and 1959 elections (see Table 4).

TABLE 4

Manitoba provincial elections, 1945–59

Party	1945		1949		1953		1958		1959	
	Seats	Popular vote (%)	Seats	Popular vote (%)	Seats	Popular vote (%)	Seats	Popular vote (%)	Seats	Popular vote (%)
Conservative	13	(16)	10	(13)	12	(21)	26	(41)	36	(47)
Liberal–Progressive	25	(33)	31	(40)	35	(41)	19	(35)	11	(30)
CCF	10	(35)	7	(26)	5	(17)	11	(20)	10	(22)
Other	7	(16)	9	(21)	5	(21)	1	(4)	—	(1)
Totals	55	(100)	57	(100)	57	(100)	57	(100)	57	(100)

Fear of being characterized by its opponents as little more than a Winnipeg labour party led to a concerted CCF rural effort. The leadership decided to run as many candidates as possible.[8] The St. George by-election of 1956 reflected the support the CCF could attain despite its internal organizational woes. St. George had not been contested by the CCF since 1945, and had only three party members; however, the CCF gained 21 per cent of the vote. "We just thought it incredible the number of votes we would get in spite of the poor organization," recalled a CCF organizer of the campaign. "Coming from Saskatchewan I just couldn't believe it."[9]

A look at the various provincial CCF parties places the Manitoba party in some perspective. National CCF membership never exceeded 40,000 after 1946 and at no time did the Manitoba CCF represent 10 per cent of the national membership total. The role of the Manitoba CCF in provincial politics was impressive, therefore, in light of its small membership size compared to the other provincial CCFs. In 1945, for example, one of every twelve eligible voters in Saskatchewan was a CCF member; in Ontario one of every sixty eligible voters was a CCF member.[10] In Manitoba, in contrast, one of every ninety-eight eligible voters was a party member. Manitoba membership figures were below those of Saskatchewan, Ontario, and British Columbia and were also lower than Alberta where CCF influence was minor in comparison to Manitoba. The unfavourable comparison of the Manitoba CCF to the other provincial parties operated at many levels (financial resources, number of labour affiliates, youth group size, etc.) except for representation in the legislature (see Table 5).

TABLE 5

CCF membership in the prairie provinces, 1947-1957

Year	Manitoba	Saskatchewan	Alberta
1947	1,932	10,821	3,739
1948	1,953	17,260	4,920
1949	1,589	14,858	3,329
1950	1,199	8,120	2,336
1951	1,064	12,800	1,826
1952	1,047	12,749	1,772
1953	1,034	12,271	1,452
1954	795	6,500	1,671
1955	717	9,000	1,889
1956	1,040	14,314	1,392
1957	1,361	16,125	1,029

SOURCES: Treasurer's Report, National Council minutes, November 1953; National Council minutes, January 15-16, 1955; and Auditor's Reports for 1956 and 1958, CCFR-PAC

The Manitoba CCF tried to finance its activities through membership fees, contributions, and fees from affiliated groups. Appeals to the membership for contributions proudly stressed the CCF's grass-roots financing and implied that the other parties were agents of major financial interests.[11] Such appeals failed. Fees from affiliated trade unions were insignificant and individual membership fees amounted to very little because the party was so small. A fund-raising device known as the "500 Club" was instituted in the early 1950s in an attempt to get a small number of affluent party members to make large contributions. This program was more successful than any other CCF fund-raising scheme: contributions from twenty members of the "500 Club" produced 50 per cent more income than all membership fees.[12]

Financial difficulties at times rendered the CCF inactive outside its role in the legislature. An operating budget of $42,200 in 1945 shrunk to $3,500 in the mid-1950s.[13] In contrast, the Saskatchewan CCF had annual operating budgets of about $30,000 and election budgets of $150,000 during the same period. For a large part of 1954, provincial secretary Don Swailes had a staff of one: himself. His services, moreover, were often provided free.[14] The post of provincial leader was part-time and without remuneration. After 1956 an upturn in membership took place, partially related to the demise of the D.L. Campbell Liberal–Progressive regime and the financial assistance of the national CCF.

Expenditures by the CCF showed little relationship to the number of seats won. In the 1949 election in multi-member Winnipeg South, for example, both Liberal Resources Minister J.S. McDiarmid and CCFer Lloyd Stinson were elected with about the same number of votes. McDiarmid, however, spent $4,736 while Stinson spent only $876.[15] This pattern operated in federal elections as well. Although the party consistently attracted a fair percentage of the popular vote, CCF–NDP per-candidate expenditures in the province in the 1949–65 period were even lower than those of Social Credit,[16] a party that has never come close to returning a Member of Parliament from Manitoba.

Greater Winnipeg constituencies consistently returned a majority of the CCF MLAs, although the city contained a minority of the CCF's total membership. In 1958, for example, nine of the CCF's eleven seats were urban. In those nine seats, however, total CCF membership was only 131 before the election. Winnipeg CCF strongholds such as St. John's had eleven members, Elmwood eleven, Seven Oaks nine, Inkster eight, and Burrows three.[17] In the constituency with the most CCF members, Flin Flon, the party lost its deposit. CCF organizers knew they could win north

Winnipeg constituencies with little membership recruitment. The organizational paradox for the CCF in the late 1950s was that it increased the number of urban seats it held and the number of rural party members but its number of urban party members and rural seats remained low.

In the 1940s and 1950s there were a number of formal leadership changes in the CCF: from S.J. Farmer to E.A. Hansford to William (Scottie) Bryce to Lloyd Stinson to A.R. (Russ) Paulley. Other figures playing important leadership roles were party secretary Donovan Swailes and Winnipeg's two CCF MPs, Stanley Knowles and Alistair Stewart.

The mere length of Swailes's service to the party as secretary and MLA placed him in a position of significant importance. Swailes became active in Winnipeg labour circles soon after his arrival from Britain in 1920. A member of the musicians' union, he became the chairman of the Winnipeg Trades and Labour Council and the first president of the Manitoba Federation of Labour. In 1944 Swailes took on the job of provincial treasurer and director of organization for the CCF. Soon after he became the provincial secretary. From 1945 to 1959 he also sat as an MLA. Although he was neither an ideologue nor a brilliant tactician, Swailes was indispensable to the party. At times he was its only full-time functionary. In 1949, when he had an opportunity to become an organizer for the American Federation of Labor, Stanley Knowles and David Lewis pleaded that he stay on as CCF secretary on the grounds that his loss would be insurmountable.[18] Swailes was important for internal administrative reasons, but he never attained the stature nor influence in the provincial party of his national counterpart, David Lewis.

Formal party leadership first changed in 1948. J. Farmer resigned in 1947 after having been leader since the party's formation. At the 1948 convention, St. Boniface MLA and mayor E.A. Hansford was elected to replace him. Hansford led the party through only one campaign and was less effective than others in his caucus, notably Swailes and Stinson. Hansford resigned the leadership in 1951, stayed on as house leader in 1952, and then returned to municipal politics. His replacement as party leader was MP Scottie Bryce. He was chosen because of the possibility that his federal seat would disappear through redistribution, thus permitting him to enter the provincial field.[19] Bryce, however, did not enter provincial politics and a new leader was soon thereafter elected.

Lloyd Stinson, a United Church minister and an insurance agent, was elected acting leader by the provincial council in 1953. His selection was subsequently confirmed in convention. A capable and articulate parliamentarian, Stinson was the CCF's most effective leader. His effectiveness, however, was greater in the house than outside it. Despite his rural Manitoba origins, Stinson had little impact in rural Manitoba. After his defeat in 1959 the house leadership was taken over by Russ Paulley. Paulley became the last CCF leader in 1960 and the first NDP leader in 1961. All the CCF leaders were elected by acclamation and all had previously served as house leaders, elected either by the provincial council or the caucus. Formal leadership was never a contentious issue in the CCF.

THE PARTY IN THE LEGISLATURE

Between the 1941 and 1945 provincial elections, the Liberal–Progressive, Conservative, and Social Credit parties became, more or less, organically linked. Rumps within each party existed, but the three effectively merged, often nominating candidates at joint or "coalition" conventions. Although such a formidable alliance was convenient for CCF propaganda purposes, the party could not entirely avoid the stigma of its past association in a coalition government with the very forces it now fought.

Ironically a contributing factor to the coalition's demise was the CCF's own loss of strength. In 1945, the CCF had been a potent and real threat. By 1949, in contrast, the CCF was declining. The Cold War and post-war prosperity led to a general drop in membership. The expulsion of three of the party's MLAs between 1945 and 1949, for opposing the party's pro-Western foreign policy, reflected the day's Cold War hysteria, something the CCF was not immune to.

Part of the political logic of coalition government was "non-partisanship." But an equally important part was keeping the CCF out of power. CCF losses undermined the logic behind the latter argument. The results of the 1949 election showed why. The CCF's loss in strength and Social Credit's departure from the scene left the province's two major parties coalesced for no apparent reason. More Liberal–Progressives and fewer Conservatives, however, had been elected in 1949 than in 1945. This led to squabbling over the number of Cabinet portfolios each would hold, and the Conservatives left the coalition and reclaimed from the CCF the status of official opposition.[20]

Duff Roblin more than any other individual was responsible for the Conservative resurgence of the 1950s. After gaining the Conservative leadership in 1954 he moved the Conservatives to the left, undercutting the CCF's position. In 1955, for example, he supported virtually every CCF resolution introduced in the legislature. On some issues, such as nationalizing Winnipeg's natural gas distribution utility and increasing social development expenditures, the Conservative caucus split its votes. Rather than hurting the party, this helped it. It permitted Conservative urban candidates to appear as reformers while Conservative rural candidates could still be seen as fiscal conservatives.

As the D.L. Campbell Liberal-Progressive government fell from public favour in the late 1950s, the Conservatives, rather than the CCF, were the major beneficiaries of the anti-government feeling. The meteoric rise of John Diefenbaker in the federal arena and Duff Roblin's ability to attract many well-known candidates also helped the Conservatives. The CCF response to the Conservative resurgence was unrealistic. CCF spokesmen kept insisting that there was no difference between the Liberals and Conservatives. Such an argument was dubious to a large part of the electorate that saw Roblin as a "new" and "progressive" force.

When the Liberal-Progressives were rejected at the polls in June 1958, however, the CCF was put into a position it had not attained even as the official opposition. Since no party had a majority of seats, the balance of power held by the CCF could make or break either a Liberal or Conservative minority administration. This led to a period of post-election negotiations between Stinson and Campbell which held open the possibility of yet another Manitoba coalition government.

The CCF's position in the negotiations reflected its willingness to exchange legislative votes for immediate reforms. Campbell's initial inclination was to resign, but his cabinet disagreed. Campbell then met with Stinson and they "agreed the Tories should be kept out if it was possible."[21] Campbell offered the CCF two portfolios (Stinson in Welfare, Swailes in Labour), and the speakership (Russ Paulley). Stinson suggested, instead, CCF parliamentary support for a Liberal government in return for five specific pieces of legislation, including improvements in the provincial hospital service scheme, farm security legislation, some labour legislation, increased mining royalties, and public ownership of Winnipeg's natural gas distribution utility.

There was opposition to any formal agreement in both camps. Developments, moreover, were complicated by editorials and inaccurate stories in the *Winnipeg Free Press* that kept misrepresenting what was taking place. For a week Roblin was left waiting to find out if he would be called upon to form a government. The Liberal-Progressives wanted to stay in power but rejected Campbell's offer of portfolios and refused to promise specific legislation to the CCF. Stinson, meanwhile, solicited the advice of senior CCFers in and out of the province. A few urged coalition or a working arrangement with the Liberals; others, however, including Saskatchewan's

Premier Douglas, national leader M.J. Coldwell, Stanley Knowles, and national secretary Carl Hamilton, all strongly opposed any formal arrangement. The CCF caucus and executive decided by a vote of thirty-one to three to refuse any formal agreement with the Liberals.[22] Campbell resigned and Duff Roblin was sworn in as premier.

Faced with a new minority administration whose legislative direction was not yet altogether clear, the CCF had a number of alternatives. The importance of the party's leverage status was not lost on its leadership. Soon after the Conservatives took office the party executive discussed the options open to it: "Some thought the CCF should take an active role as opposition from the outset. Others thought it would be advantageous to gain time. The view was expressed that the CCF members in parliament made a mistake in harassing the Diefenbaker government too much, thus precipitating the election by creating an 'intolerable' position. It was firmly agreed that the CCF should continue to take the initiative by repeatedly publishing its legislative objectives...."[23] In effect, the CCF pursued the course of action which Stinson had proposed earlier with respect to the Liberals. In return for the introduction of certain pieces of legislation, the CCF would support the Conservatives. Although no formal or even verbal arrangement was made, Roblin gladly obliged. Many of his programs, some dealing with labour, social welfare, and economic development, were similar to the CCF platform. The Conservatives, for example, introduced a hospital insurance scheme, reorganized and centralized the public school system, and restructured the Winnipeg area municipal governments into a metropolitan system. These were all policies the CCF favoured. The Conservatives also adopted a CCF resolution on old age pensions that had been voted down for seventeen consecutive years.

The CCF strategy of voting with the government on bills it supported, however, did not advance the party's fortunes. When the 1959 election came, the CCF was in a defensive position. No longer could it charge that the Conservatives and Liberals were the same. Much of the CCF campaign was simply devoted to keeping the seats it held arguing that the voters should not give one party too many seats.[24]

With Roblin's Conservatives in power, the role of the CCF was again questioned. "As the Conservative party edges over to the left, and widens the gap between it and the Liberal party," noted one newspaper analyst, "it starts to trespass on CCF territory."[25] Stinson insisted that the important distinguishing feature between the Conservatives and the CCF was the latter's commitment to more public ownership. Aside from the fledgling natural gas distribution utility, however, the CCF platform named no industries the C C F wanted nationalized. The C C F seemed satisfied with Roblin's welfare and labour legislation and when that was implemented the C C F had little room within which to manoeuvre.

Roblin's success in the 1958 legislative session led to frustration among C C F officials and caucus members. One prominent C C Fer summed up the quandary:

> Look at our position. The Roblin government is putting into effect good legislation. The people want it: they need it, and they should have it. Are we going to defeat them and face the charge that we obstructed the very things we have been calling for over the years?
>
> The only thing we can say is that they are not doing enough... On the other hand, we're supposed to be socialists. We believe in an entirely different system. We're supposed to want to change the whole order of things, not just vote for this improvement here and that one there.[26]

Before the 1959 session, C C F provincial councillors voiced opinions ranging from continued support for the Conservatives to defeating the Conservatives at the first opportunity. "In the end it was generally agreed that the C C F should go into the next session as a fighting organization for the implementation of C C F policy."[27] A rash of C C F nominating meetings in early 1959 indicated that the party anticipated an election, and a few M L A s openly predicted one. The assumption in C C F circles, however, was that the Roblin government would be defeated at a time and on an issue of the C C F's choosing.

Roblin, astutely, again undercut the C C F. He introduced a sunshine budget and engineered his own government's defeat, on a procedural motion, before the budget could be debated. In the ensuing election the Conservatives swept to majority power despite a slight gain in the C C F popular vote and an overall loss of only one seat for the party. The Conservatives capitalized on the continuing Liberal demise. In the new majority government (Conservatives, thirty-six seats; Liberals, eleven; C C F, ten), the C C F reverted to its traditional third party role and no longer held the balance of power.

One factor that had limited the success of the C C F in the legislature was the electoral system. There was no redistribution of seats between 1920 and 1949, although the urban population had increased much more than the rural population. This worked against the C C F which relied heavily on greater Winnipeg support. Thus, without redistribution, the C C F could not easily gain more seats as the province became more urbanized. In approximate terms, over one-half the province had only one-quarter of the seats. Before the redistribution legislation of 1949 the ten CCF MLAS represented about 216,000 people while ten cabinet ministers represented only 119,000 people. After redistribution the CCF was still disadvantaged, having been gerrymandered by the coalition. One particular urban riding (represented by the CCF) had, after redistribution, six times the population of the smallest rural riding (represented by the government). Redistribution itself, therefore, became an issue championed by the CCF. In the early 1950s it commanded more attention from the CCF caucus than any other issue. Prodded by Stinson in particular, the Liberal-Progressives agreed to changes before the 1958 election. The new legislation established Canada's first independent boundaries commission and instituted an urban-rural vote ratio (in which seven urban votes equalled four rural votes). It also did away with the large multi-member Winnipeg ridings and dropped the transferable ballot in favour of the plurality system. Although this was far from what it wanted, the CCF supported the legislation on grounds of self-interest.[28] In part, this Liberal-Progressive bill led to the Liberal-Progressive government's demise.

THE PARTY'S PHILOSOPHY AND PROGRAM

Two conflicting, although not inconsistent, interpretations of CCF ideology have been developed. One view maintains that an other-worldly and doctrinaire political movement became a worldly and conventional reform political party as it evolved and had to face the exigencies of electoral politics.[29] Another view, fostered by CCF-NDP spokesmen, maintains that party ideology was "refined"[30] with the passage of time and that the original principles of the 1933 Regina Manifesto were never repudiated. The former school of thought cites the anti-capitalist rhetoric of party publications in the 1930s and 1940s and contrasts it with the mild political pronouncements of the 1950s. The latter school of thought relates the CCF welfarist demands of the 1950s to the pioneering welfarist demands of J.S. Woodsworth in the 1920s and 1930s.

Both the anti-capitalist rhetoric of the early years and the liberal reform demands of the latter years reflected responses to social and economic changes. There was no conscious or unconscious "break" or dividing line in CCF thinking. Always an aggregation of both socialist and liberal elements, the CCF responded to changing conditions by falling back on that part of its philosophy which seemed most appropriate, at any given time, for political advancement. The tensions between socialism and liberalism, radicalism and reformism, movement and party, education and electioneering, were permanent features of the CCF's character. Just as the CCF was never a centralized Marxist sect, it was never simply another small-l liberal party. CCF leaders, like their social democratic counterparts elsewhere, called for the replacement of capitalism when the capitalist system seemed to be tottering and for the reformation of capitalism when its strength seemed unassailable.

Although they rarely posited a class analysis of society, both national and provincial CCF leaders in the 1940s claimed that private corporations were competitors with Parliament for economic and political supremacy. The issue, as the CCF defined it, was public versus private power. S.J. Farmer, the provincial party leader in the 1940s, argued that "There must be a complete change, not only of government, but a change in the economic system. Mr. Bracken...talked of a 'reformed capitalism'...rather than give the people control of the means by which they live."[31] When it came to specifics, however, CCF leaders defined socialism as little more than the acceptance of the principle of public planning.[32]

Post-war prosperity compounded the CCF's difficulties. Keynesian innovations on the part of the federal government contradicted a major CCF claim and a major CCF assumption. The disproven claim was that the older parties would refuse to undertake broad economic planning. The discredited assumption was that a post-war depression was inevitable. The CCF also found itself saddled with a growing mood of anti-communism and, indirectly, anti-socialism in Canada. Before the war the CCF characterized itself as the socialist alternative to the capitalist parties, and after the war the CCF pleaded that it represented a middle road between the false gods of Capitalism and Communism. But that imaginary middle road had been staked out and occupied by the Liberals, who, with the help of others like the *Free Press,* depicted the agents of the false gods to be the Conservatives and CCF respectively.

The dilemma facing the CCF led to a so-called rethinking initiated by national chairman Frank Scott at the 1950 national convention. Scott insisted that socialism must remain the objective and disagreed "with those who say that the issue today is not between capitalism and socialism, but between freedom and totalitarianism.... Capitalist forces," he maintained, "...are still bitter enemies of social progress; still potent sources of reaction." His prescription was a reformed type of capitalism; the CCF should preach more state planning and less nationalization. Capitalism was to be managed, to be humanized, to be made to work for all. Thus, he insisted, "We do not oppose the making of profit, in all its forms; on the contrary, the profit motive, under proper control, is now and will be for a long time a most valuable stimulus to production."[33] Scott's views were not really a departure from the thinking, if not always the language, of the drafters of the Regina Manifesto. Manitoba's S.J. Farmer, neither a radical nor an ideologue, had also pointed out as party leader in 1945 that "we are not opposed to genuine 'private enterprise,' but we are opposed to what usually parades under this disguise... 'monopoly Capitalism.'" "In fact," proclaimed one party pamphlet that year, "the CCF aims *to increase the private property* of the bulk of the Canadian people."[34] The formal restatement, as opposed to revision, of the CCF's position was completed by 1956 with the adoption of the Winnipeg Declaration. To be sure, the CCF "watered down" its language, but it had never been committed, despite isolated phrases in the Regina Manifesto, to the scale of socialization often attributed to it by others.

For a large part of its life the CCF was identified as a depression-preaching party. Part of this image was fostered by the fact that it had been born in the midst of depression and sustained by many who had memories of depression. Changes in social conditions, however, required changes in a doom-and-gloom theory. Throughout the 1940s "security" was the watchword of every CCF campaign. Although a post-war boom was taking place, the CCF's director of education was telling a Manitoba CCF convention that "time is short. This spell of industrial activity will not last much longer, and then will come the day of depression.... The purpose of the CCF in Manitoba is to convince the people of the province that they [may] have a new and better way of life that will remove the injustice and insecurity which is the common lot of our people."[35] The director of organization assured the 1946 convention that capitalist governments will have exhibited their failures by 1949 and the CCF could come to power in Manitoba. In 1949, however, the CCF convention drafted an election program which assumed that the depression that had not occurred was still imminent: "Will the prosperity last?" asked its platform preamble. "Judged by the past history of Manitoba the answer is *NO*."[36] CCF advertisements reflected this depression psychology. One pamphlet featured a cartoon depicting a coffin and a bereaved family with the widow commenting on the lack of security in society. Stanley Knowles's pamphlets in both the 1945 and 1949 elections displayed photographs of a relief soup kitchen and hundreds of unemployed men milling around trains that were taking workers, from coast to coast, looking for non-existent jobs. The caption under the photographs in the 1945 pamphlet was "This must not happen again," and in the 1949 pamphlet, "Beat the Depression Now."[37]

The "depression ahead" philosophy was the result of the party sincerely believing that hard times were inevitable under old party rule. When membership figures inched slightly upwards in 1948, party secretary Swailes traced this directly to "the reappearance of all the worst features of capitalism, which were partially concealed during the war years."[38] As late as 1954 Swailes was still predicting depression "unless socialistic measures are used pretty freely."[39] A similar sentiment was expressed that year by the Brandon CCF Association which foresaw a "challenge presented by the inevitable deflation of wartime prosperity under the old system of capitalism, and the unnecessary distress it will entail."[40] The CCF finally forsook its depression-preaching position by the late 1950s.

Differing conceptions of socialism led to differing reactions to the national CCF's Winnipeg Declaration of 1956. Senior party officials, at both the provincial and national levels, variably referred to it as "nothing new," "something new," "in the tradition of the Regina Manifesto," "changing policies for changing times," etc. In reality, the document was not a departure from the CCF's past, for the party had always supported a mixed economy. The major difference was that the CCF had never gone to the same lengths in defining the private sphere. The moderate tone of the Winnipeg Declaration was largely designed to attract more electoral support. For many in the CCF, however, a restatement of principles was welcome, not only on those grounds, but also because they simply did not believe in large-scale public ownership.[41] There were, of course, those few who opposed any new statement of principles. The tiny opposition to the Winnipeg Declaration was led by Winnipeg's Fred Tipping and it included more CCFers from Manitoba than from any other provincial section. By 1956, however, there was no significant or viable left caucus within the CCF at either the national or Manitoba level.

An examination of the Manitoba CCF's specific policy proposals reflects its reformist nature. Despite explicit anti-capitalist slogans employed in the 1945, 1949, and 1953 campaigns, the policies offered to the electorate were, almost exclusively, welfare reforms. The 1945 platform called for better labour legislation, farm security, higher wages for teachers, and free medical care for the aged. It also called for government encouragement to co-operatives and the development of more secondary industries under public control, but none were named. The 1949 and 1953 platforms were even less explicit in the field of economic development: policies included dividing the Health and Welfare department, reorganization of municipalities, establishment of agricultural marketing boards, free treat-

ment for cancer patients, electoral reforms, and public automobile insurance. In the 1958 and 1959 campaigns the CCF also called for the nationalization of Winnipeg's natural gas distribution utility and an industrial
development fund to aid and lend capital to private entrepreneurs. The
notion that a CCF government would nationalize sectors of the natural
resource industry was eliminated. The CCF explicitly accepted private
development in the resources field and asked merely for higher royalties.
Resolutions debated and passed at party conventions reflected the thinking of the CCF membership. At the 1959 convention, for example, policies
passed dealt with increases in workmen's compensation benefits, a medical
care scheme, the banning of commercial trading stamps, a reduction in
beer prices, legalized lotteries, and restrictions in advertising.[42]

CCF leaders in the late 1950s were sometimes in a difficult position
when it came to convincing voters that they should vote CCF rather than
Conservative. One argument employed was that voters should elect
CCFers to ensure that Conservative promises were kept. M.J. Coldwell,
campaigning in Portage la Prairie in the 1959 election, urged voters to
reject the candidates of the other parties and elect CCFers who "will fight
every inch of the way to force the fulfillment of the promises which the
other parties are making."[43] The CCF house leader in the 1959 session,
Russ Paulley, claimed that the CCF had to remain vigilant because "in a
couple of years, the reactionary forces within the government will become
dominant and future legislation will become typically Conservative."[44]
The self-defined role of the CCF, therefore, had become one of prodding the
Conservatives. CCFers felt their role contributed to pushing the Roblin
government to the left.

The CCF took pride in presenting itself as part of a national and international social democratic movement. The Saskatchewan, British,
Australian, and New Zealand governments were frequently cited as models
which the Manitoba CCF intended to follow. In its early years the CCF looked
to the British Labour Party as an ideological mentor. Party leaders hoped,
and expected, an evolution toward the British experience where one of the
older parties would disappear and a polarized two party system would
emerge, with one party on the right and the CCF on the left. Lloyd Stinson,
for example, expected the provincial and national political system to
"inevitably follow the same course" as Britain. After Roblin appeared on the
political scene in 1949, Stinson dismissed the possibility of a Conservative
resurgence: "even his eloquence will never revive this party. You can't stem
the tide of history."[45] Ironically it was to be Roblin's very success a
decade later which toppled Stinson as an MLA and party leader.

An image that the CCF cultivated was that it was the party of the common man, worker or farmer. As a counterpoint it presented the older parties as the agents of financiers and industrialists. Party literature stressed the democratic nature of the CCF with its delegate conventions and open policy debates. Some election pamphlets printed the net profits of major corporations, showed how they had multiplied over the years, and contrasted these figures to the much slower rise in wages and farm income. "Farmers, industrial and middle workers make up 99.4 per cent of the population," declared one pamphlet. "Only 0.6 per cent are in the capitalist class. But the 0.6 per cent rule and control the lives of 99.4 per cent."

The corporate sector was depicted by the CCF as ogre-like. "In the last few years," read a 1953 letter to the CCF membership, "the forces of big business have been greatly strengthening their position; they are striving to bind the people of Canada hand and foot."[46] The letter featured a cartoon, common in CCF literature, showing a worker being tied down by a number of Lilliputian-size men in tuxedos and top hats. The Lilliputians, by label, represented the steel industry, the *Winnipeg Free Press,* the packing industry, the machine industry, and middlemen. Clearly, the CCF and the corporations did not care for each other and in 1956 three large Manitoba breweries revealed that they contributed regularly to the Liberal, Conservative, and Social Credit provincial parties.[47] The CCF, making much of this revelation, argued that it neither sought nor accepted financial support from large corporations.

The most vociferous and consistent critic of the Manitoba CCF was the *Winnipeg Free Press;* a paper which, Mackenzie King noted, "rendered yeomen service"[48] for the Liberal Party. If CCFers were Liberals in a hurry to Louis St. Laurent, they were Bolsheviks in disguise to the *Free Press.* The *Free Press*'s attack on the CCF had many facets. In 1945 it assailed the Manitoba party for bringing Saskatchewan CCF cabinet ministers into the province during the provincial election campaign. "The issue in Manitoba," noted the *Free Press Weekly Farmer,* "has nothing to do with the record of Mr. Douglas in Saskatchewan."[49] This attitude, however, did not keep the *Free Press* from publishing daily columns on its editorial page in October 1947, and during the 1949 provincial campaign, that attacked the CCF record in Saskatchewan and insisted that the same alleged problems of that province would befall Manitoba under CCF rule. While attacking the appearance of T.C. Douglas in Manitoba as an unwarranted intrusion into Manitoba affairs, the *Free Press* was publishing anti-CCF articles authored by the Saskatchewan Liberal leader.[50] Despite the Manitoba CCF's strong anti-communist bias, the *Free Press* continued to insist "that the C.C.F. is shot full of Communists, should-be Communists and pro-Communists."[51]

In Manitoba, the older parties and their supporters, such as the daily newspapers, presented the CCF as alien and radical. Liberal and Conservative politicians accurately viewed the population as, on the whole, suspicious of dramatic changes. The CCF, on the other hand, hoped the public was less tradition-bound. It considered the economic condition of individuals and groups to be a variable that affected support for the party. When relative economic prosperity existed the CCF accepted a lower level of public support as similarly inevitable. "Times are good," reported the provincial organizer in 1954, "people are not worrying very much. They are too lazy to think."[52] When four rural vacancies occurred in the legislature in 1959 members in those constituencies recommended against contesting them. Times, it appeared, were still too good. "If the people in general were to have hard times come in a big way on account of nature being unkind, then they might vote CCF," wrote one rural member. "That would not make much sense but that seems to be the set up."[53]

THE PARTY AND ORGANIZED LABOUR

Organized labour in Manitoba had three distinct and competing elements in the 1940s. The smallest was the One Big Union (OBU) which had continued beyond the General Strike period. In 1942 it included twenty-eight units representing diverse groups such as civic employees, bakers, projectionists, carpenters, and mental hospital attendants. In Winnipeg the OBU units were represented on the Winnipeg Central Labour Council. On occasion the OBU contributed financially and otherwise to CCF campaigns.[54] A second union element was the Canadian Congress of Labour (CCL) and its local, the Winnipeg Labour Council. This group was the most receptive to the CCF and endorsed it in 1943 as the political arm of the labour movement. The third and oldest element in the union movement was the Trades and Labour Congress (TLC) and its local, the Winnipeg and District Trades and Labour Council. The CCL was based on industrial unionism, that is, organized by industries, while the TLC was based on craft unionism, organized by occupations. Although many prominent CCFers were also prominent local TLCers, the TLC, on a formal level, was less receptive to the CCF than was the CCL. The provincial TLC and CCL merged in 1956 to form a new Manitoba Federation of Labour (MFL). This paralleled the national TLC-CCL merger which produced the Canadian Labour Congress (CLC). At the local level the three Winnipeg labour councils also merged to form the Winnipeg and District Labour Council (WDLC).

CCF success in attracting trade union affiliates, as its constitution permitted, was not great. In 1952 there were less than 15,000 affiliated unionists in Canada and 10,000 of these were from the miners' union in Nova Scotia.[55] There were no union affiliates at all, at that date, from Manitoba. The two cent per month per member affiliate fee, whenever and wherever collected, provided only marginal income for the CCF; the Manitoba party collected $80 from this source in 1945 and $50 in 1950.[56] Rather, the major financial union contributions to the CCF came in lump sums at election time. The Manitoba and national CCF organizations were usually dependent on three unions for substantial financial support: the United Steelworkers of America, the United Packinghouse Workers, and the United Auto Workers.

The CCF, characterizing itself as labour's spokesman, made special and specific appeals to union members. One typical letter sent to all Manitoba locals, carried photographs of CCF unionists Swailes and Knowles with pro-labour slogans: "Human Labour Produces All Wealth," "Humanity Before Profit," and "Canada's Wealth for Canadian Workers."[57] CCF literature distributed in Winnipeg for both provincial and municipal campaigns emphasized to workers that organized labour endorsed the CCF. In return for organized labour's support, the CCF endorsed labour's demands. This was easily done in the 1950s when the reforms sought by the union movement were similar to the reforms promised in the CCF platform. Leaders of both groups had accepted, although some continued to dislike, a capitalist economic order. The conservatism of the labour movement was reflected in successive issues of Winnipeg's *Labour Annual:* regular articles appeared discussing the social responsibility exhibited by the labour movement and its contribution to "Labour-management co-operation." The CCF gave voice in the legislature to labour's objectives. CCF proposals in the field of labour were two-pronged: first, they called on the government to enact and improve labour welfare legislation, e.g., a higher minimum wage, vacations with pay, improved employment standards, etc.; second, they called for the establishment of a Bureau of Industrial Relations which would promote and harmonize the common interests of labour and management in the interests of economic "efficiency."[58]

The main links between the CCF and the labour movement were individuals holding senior posts in both groups. Party secretary Don Swailes, for example, had been president of Winnipeg's TLC council in

1942 (the year that council endorsed Knowles's CCF candidature in Winnipeg North Centre) and a Canadian Labour Congress (CLC) vice-president in the late 1950s. Len Aylen, chairman of the Winnipeg CCL political action committee, was also an active CCFer. He was a party candidate in 1953 and made annual reports to CCF conventions on party-union relations. Other links between the CCF and the union movement were Jimmy James, the MFL president, and Art Coulter, the executive secretary of the WDLC. James had urged the Winnipeg Labour Council's voluntary two cent per month per capita contribution to the Manitoba CCF.[59] Stanley Knowles was yet another individual whose influence and status was significant in both CCF and union circles.

Labour leaders in Manitoba, perhaps more so than in Canada as a whole, identified their interests with the CCF. A sample survey of Canadian union leaders in the 1950s indicated that 93 per cent of the CCLers supported the CCF and that among TLCers 45 per cent supported the CCF.[60] There is good reason to believe that, in class-conscious Winnipeg, TLC support for the CCF was higher than the national average. For a time, the majority of Winnipeg CCF public office holders, at all three levels of government, were TLCers.[61] Specific election contributions by the unions were more important to the CCF than formal affiliates contributing negligible fees. With few exceptions, in the 1940s and 1950s the Winnipeg Labour Council (CCL) endorsed CCF candidates while the local Trades and Labour Council (TLC) rejected such a move. CCFers on the TLC council, including Swailes, opposed affiliation or endorsation of CCF candidates (including Swailes) for various national and tactical considerations.

Significant assistance to the CCF was rendered by the CCL beginning with the 1949 provincial election. In that campaign the CCL provided the services of a full-time organizer as well as financial assistance. Local political action committees of the steelworkers and packinghouse workers also made contributions. They sent letters to their members encouraging them to work for CCF candidates and, on occasion, placed advertisements in the Winnipeg dailies endorsing the CCF as labour's voice. The CCF made financial appeals to all Manitoba union locals and large numbers of them, TLC as well as CCL, contributed small (usually $10 to $100) but significant amounts. Union contributions represented between one-third and one-sixth of the cost of the CCF provincial election campaigns in the 1950s. Large union contributions came from national sources: the Ontario-based United Auto Workers, for example, contributed $4,000 to hire a Manitoba CCF organizer in 1952, and the national CCL political action committee made possible the payment of other salaries at the provincial level.[62] After 1956, national CLC leaders gave active encouragement to Manitoba unionists in all pro-CCF efforts. Labour assistance was stepped up. The groundwork was being laid for the creation of the NDP, a formal merger of the CCF and the political side of the CLC.

THE PARTY AND THE FARMERS

A striking feature of the Manitoba CCF was its overall failure to win seats in the rural areas. Many have erroneously depicted the CCF as little more than a Western agrarian protest party. In reality the Manitoba CCF, like its sister parties in Ontario and British Columbia, was always urban-based and urban-led. In the 1949 election, for example, all seven successful CCF candidates were from greater Winnipeg.

The party's weakness in rural areas is partly explained by the diversity of rural Manitoba, both in the differing quality and uses of the land and in the ethnic settlement patterns. In general, the fertile southwestern part of the province was occupied first by Anglo-Saxon, primarily Ontarian, settlers. The northwestern, interlake, and eastern regions were less fertile; they required more clearing, included fishing and dairy farming, and were invariably less profitable for the occupants than the southwest. Into these areas flocked European immigrant settlers—Ukrainians, Germans, Icelanders, and others. Northern Manitoba, above the fifty-third parallel, grew slowly and mainly around developing mining sites in a non-agricultural setting.

Whatever rural successes were scored by the CCF were in the poorer farming areas. On occasion the constituencies of The Pas, Brokenhead, Fisher, Gimli, and Ethelbert were won. In the southwest wheat belt seats were never won except for the city of Brandon which was captured in a by-election in 1943 and held for a brief two-year period. It was a major task for the CCF to find candidates in the southwestern constituencies. When, in 1959, there were four by-elections in that part of the province and a single CCF victory in any riding would have tied the CCF with the Liberals in the legislature, the CCF let all four ridings go uncontested. Any effort in these areas, CCF leaders concluded, was futile.

Most of rural Manitoba was rooted in Ontario's Liberal and Conservative traditions. The Manitoba Farmers' Section, which affiliated with the CCF in the 1930s as a protest against the non-partisanship of the United Farmers of Manitoba, had been a small group. In the 1940s not even a tiny radical farmers group existed. To be sure, there were isolated farmers in the agrarian radical tradition. Some of them occasionally complained to the provincial office that the CCF had become a city-centred party with no radical agricultural policies.[63] The overwhelming majority of Manitoba farmers, however, supported the older parties. An argument which rural CCF organizers often "ran into, was, that in the minds of many farmers, they felt it was better to have a representative who was on the government side, rather than one who was in the opposition."[64]

In its attempt to capture more farm votes, the CCF offered an agricultural program that included crop insurance, flood assistance, farm security legislation, and producer marketing boards. As in other policy areas the CCF stressed the accomplishments of social democratic parties elsewhere. One election pamphlet claimed that farmers and industrial workers were brothers exploited by the same monopolies. Farmers, it argued, needed political as well as economic organizations to fight for them. The pamphlet went on to cite the success of the "labour-farmer" coalition in New Zealand.[65] The CCF's failure to capture more rural seats was the major impediment to its coming to power. This state of affairs troubled CCF leaders, and one of them, former ILP-CCF MLA Bill Ivens, told the 1949 convention "that the best interests of the CCF would be served if the farmers' organizations break away from the old political parties and form their own political organization. Then perhaps," he continued, "they will come to realize that their best interests are with the CCF."[66] The speech was somewhat prophetic as it came just when a rival to the Liberal-dominated Manitoba Federation of Agriculture and Co-operation (MFAC) was being formed. The new Manitoba Farmers Union (MFU) became the CCF's new rural hope in the 1950s.

There should have been a natural affinity between the CCF and the MFU. Whatever rural strength the CCF had was precisely in those areas where the MFU was strongest. The MFU's membership was, generally, from poorer areas and was ethnically heterogeneous in composition. The MFAC's strength, on the other hand, was mainly in the Anglo-Saxon southwest, where the CCF had always been rejected. Whereas the MFU tried to build a united farmers movement through individual memberships, the MFAC was organized around affiliated commodity producers' co-operatives. It relied heavily on the Manitoba Pool Elevators, the United Grain Growers, and other co-operatives. A CCFer who belonged to both the MFU and the MFAC recalls that CCF support in the MFAC was "very small. They [MFAC members] were almost Liberal to the core."[67] If it was natural for Manitoba's political outsiders to gravitate to the CCF, it was just as natural for the outsiders in the agricultural community to gravitate to the MFU.

The MFU was founded in the late 1940s by future CCF MP Jake Schulz. It was a new response to the established MFAC and the party with which it was identified—the Liberals. This was an ideal focal point, from the CCF's point of view, for CCF-MFU co-operation. Both groups stood for the same agricultural policies. The MFU's priority, however, was to expand its own membership. Its CCF-inclined leaders, therefore, took a "no politics" position in the hope of attracting as many farmers as possible to their cause. This meant no open identification with the CCF for fear of alienating anti-CCF farmers who would refuse to join any organization, such as the MFU, if it were overtly sympathetic to the CCF. CCF leaders accepted this position and saw it as advantageous in the long run. Any weakening of the MFAC, they reasoned, meant a weakening of the Liberals. Conversely, any gains for the MFU meant an eventual gain for the CCF. When farm incomes began to decline sharply in 1953, and MFU membership reached a peak of 30,000,[68] CCFers hoped for a rural breakthrough.

In effect, the CCF rural strategy was to count on the MFU to "ripen" farmers, to develop them politically, to break down their resistance, slowly but surely, to the CCF. "The whole of the Farmers' Union platform is CCF," wrote Swailes with considerable enthusiasm after attending the 1952 MFU convention. "It could easily have been a CCF convention, only the farmers didn't know it. The union is slanting farmers' minds towards CCF policy without mentioning CCF, and I have an idea that it will affect the voting in the next election."[69] A long-time CCFer, who along with his wife became senior MFU functionaries, was similarly enthusiastic about rural developments:

We feel that we can get the CCF ideas across to the people better through the union than any other way. It is true that both movements are very similar. That is because a large number of CCFers were the first in the union. If anyone asks why there are so many CCF in the union the answer is "because they are the type of people who think their problems through. They thought their way into the CCF as they had no previous heritage of political attachment to that party, so they were able to think their way into the union in the same manner." At present we are able to talk to people and get them out to meetings which you wouldn't be able to do if politics were mentioned.[70]

The CCF rural strategy was ingenious, but it failed. Paradoxically, the attitude of separateness in CCF and MFU affairs weakened whatever rural base the CCF did have. Many farmers who had been CCFers became so committed to the MFU that they dropped their party memberships and devoted most of their energies to the new union.[71] Other CCFers in the MFU continued to be party members but silent ones, fearful of scaring away potential MFU recruits by identifying themselves politically. "The policy of the Farmers' Union, in leaning over backward to be non-political, particularly non-CCF-political, is helping to kill us in the country," wrote Swailes to the CCF's national secretary. "Quite a lot of our members are holding official positions in the Union, and some of them are so scared that they don't want to be seen in the company of known CCFers."[72] The CCF was in a trap: the few spokesmen it did have on agricultural policies had embraced the MFU which, in turn, usually meant fewer CCF rural spokesmen. This, of course, made it increasingly difficult for the CCF to attract more farmers to its banner.

The MFU did fulfil one of the functions foreseen for it by CCFers: it weaned many farmers away from the federal and provincial Liberals. It did not necessarily "ripen" these same farmers, however, for the CCF. As the 1950s wore on, Manitoba farmers were more willing to leave their Liberal past but, when they did, most of them opted for the Diefenbaker and Roblin Conservatives rather than for the CCF.

THE PARTY AND THE ETHNIC MINORITIES

Since 1941, a majority of Manitobans have been of non-Anglo-Saxon origin, but the non-Anglo-Saxon group has been diverse: no specific ethnic group has ever represented more than 12 per cent (Germans and Ukrainians) of the total population. This striking feature of Manitoba has had its political expression.

Before the Winnipeg General Strike, the Social Democratic Party was organized on the principle of language locals with five such locals operating in Winnipeg.[73] Some ethnic locals also operated as CCF Clubs in the party's formative years. Ethnicity was definitely a calculation in certain party decisions. One long-time CCF-NDPer recalls that part of the logic behind the CCF nomination of Alistair Stewart in ethnically heterogeneous Winnipeg North in 1945 was his British background. An Anglo-Saxon, it was reasoned, would be the most acceptable in an area with ethnic animosities and diversity.[74] In the rural areas CCFers also perceived that ethnicity was a factor in CCF support: in the Anglo-Saxon southwest the party was not a force; while in the non-Anglo-Saxon areas it received a more positive response. One rural CCF-NDPer explained that an "out" party not dependent on the votes of the "ins" of the rural community could gain a certain type of protest vote: "One of the reasons the ethnics supported the CCF was because it was different. It was going to rival the status quo that had discriminated against them over the years. The status quo was the

Anglo-Saxon domination of everything that happened — the trustees, the Councils — everything."[75] In general, CCF organizers found that the Anglo-Saxon rural settlers who had come from Ontario in the latter part of the nineteenth century reflected ideological traditions that were unsympathetic to the CCF. The non–Anglo-Saxon farmers, in contrast, "brought a different attitude with them from Europe than the conservative element from Ontario," claimed one CCF rural organizer. "And I refer to the conservative element from Ontario as being both Liberal and Conservative."[76]

In certain years, particularly during the 1940s, the CCF made special efforts to attract non–Anglo-Saxon voters. An unsuccessful attempt was made in 1944 by the provincial party to launch a Western Canadian Ukrainian CCF newspaper based in Winnipeg. For the 1945 provincial election two Ukrainian- and one French-speaking organizers were hired. Occasional foreign language election pamphlets (a regular feature of north Winnipeg politics) were supplemented in 1945 with a CCF French newspaper, *Le Nouveau Canada,* and in 1948 a Flemish pamphlet appeared.[77] In most ridings ethnic background was an important consideration in the process of candidate selection. In 1959, as one example, the CCF consciously searched out an Indian candidate, Manitoba's first, to contest Rupertsland, a riding with a large number of Indians and Metis. But ethnic prejudices persisted too as Swailes's evaluation of the Ukrainian vote in the rural areas revealed. He suggested that it reflected sheer ethnocentric opportunism. "I have sensed that Ukrainians in particular are very interested in political positions," he wrote to one rural member. "Not that they want to advance any particular social principles, but just to enjoy the prestige of being in office. They are very proud of anyone who holds a public position, whether he be Liberal, Tory, Social Credit, CCF, or Communist."[78] That assessment of the Ukrainian vote was clearly untenable in Winnipeg.

In an area as heterogeneous as north Winnipeg deep political divisions precluded an electoral victory based strictly on an ethnic appeal. All parties could, and often did, recruit candidates of different ethnic backgrounds but the CCF-NDP's success with Anglo-Saxon and Jewish as well as Ukrainian candidates in Ukrainian areas indicated that more than ethnic consciousness was at work. In north Winnipeg the Ukrainian community was sharply divided between anti-communist and pro-communist elements; the former tending toward the Conservatives and Liberals, the latter toward the Communist Party. In this polarization, the CCF had very few Slavic members and no Slavic elected representatives before 1945 in Winnipeg. As late as 1958, the CCF victory in Winnipeg's Burrows constituency could be traced to the support received by the CCF candidate from two pro-Liberal

Ukrainian newspapers which were determined to have the incumbent Ukrainian Communist defeated.[79] After 1945 the CCF gained many Ukrainian members from the previously pro- and anti-communist sides. Each side saw the CCF as an opponent of the other side's ideology. Increased assimilation, less immigration, intermarriage, and the passing of time broke down earlier ethnic political divisions. The NDP MP for Winnipeg North, an elected representative at all levels of government from that area since 1945, summed up the Winnipeg Ukrainian vote: "Both the communists and the anti-communists...had their politics determined by the Russian Revolution. You were pro-Bolshevik or anti. As time has gone along that generation of people is disappearing. Their children, on both sides, don't care...I would say, in a general way, that Ukrainian people forty-five and under take their politics from work and not from the church or from the fraternal organizations. A very large percentage of them work in the packing houses and in steel plants and in the railways. And those unions are sympathetic to the NDP, so they, the workers, are sympathetic to the NDP."[80] In brief, class as well as ethnic factors were determinants of voting behaviour.[81]

The Manitoba CCF in the 1940s and 1950s commanded a fair share of public support despite its organizational difficulties and lack of consistent rural support. It was a Winnipeg-based party with potential strength in the poorer rural districts and among ethnic minorities. When the Manitoba NDP followed and scored an electoral victory in 1969 it capitalized on the foundations built by the CCF in earlier years.

Although the CCF had become an established national and provincial party by the 1940s, its hopes of gaining power in Ottawa and Winnipeg were dashed. By the 1950s it seemed to be going nowhere, relegated to permanent status as a third party. Party leaders were eager to broaden the party's base and to make victories at the polls more likely. The emergence of a unified Canadian trade union movement (the CLC) in 1956, along with strong support in that movement for the CCF, led to the forging of a new political party. Between 1958 and 1960 joint CCF–CLC and CCF–MFL committees met in Ottawa and Winnipeg to negotiate the terms and the complexion of a merger of political efforts. An attempt was made to rekindle the movement spirit of the 1930s with a broad appeal made to workers, farmers, small businessmen, and professionals. In its ideology and in its program the early NDP reflected the ideas of the CCF of the late 1950s and the Canadian labour movement. It promised to manage the economy better than the other parties, to bring more equity in society, and to generate higher levels of social welfare.

The new party

5

In the late 1950s a debate took place within the CCF respecting the formation of the New Democratic Party. A similar debate had taken place in the 1930s in Manitoba regarding the establishment of the CCF and the inevitable disintegration of the ILP. Both times the advocates of a broader social democratic party won out. In the 1930s the Depression helped the national CCF become more than merely a loose federation of small urban parties. The CCF's brand of socialism expanded beyond the British immigrant urban pockets that had proven receptive to such parties as the ILP. In the late 1950s the support of Canada's newly consolidated organized labour movement, the Canadian Labour Congress, helped the NDP become more than merely a party of individual members. By the early 1970s, the NDP had formed three provincial governments and gained a permanent place in Parliament.

The advocates of a broader social democratic party won in both the 1930s and the late 1950s partly because the outlook of social democracy, with its emphasis on national economic planning and universal welfare schemes, has always been more relevant to the federal than to the provincial level of government. Successful provincial and municipal social democratic parties such as the Saskatchewan CCF in the 1960s and the Winnipeg ILP in the 1930s accepted, however hesitantly, their roles as components in a broader, national, movement and party. Unlike their Conservative and Liberal counterparts, the national and provincial CCF–NDP sections have always seen and organized themselves as organically linked fraternal parties. As in the 1930s, a determined effort was made by some Manitoba social democrats in the late 1950s to thwart a movement to broaden the party's base. And, as in the 1930s, they failed.

The genesis of the strategy leading to the NDP's formation has been traced to a speech by Saskatchewn Premier T.C. Douglas at a CCF national council meeting in 1956.[1] Douglas envisaged a federation of forces, including labour, co-operative, and farm organizations, that would be led by a core of convinced democratic socialists. Douglas felt that such a coalition could win elections as the CCF had in Saskatchewan. An expression of Douglas's thinking was Stanley Knowles's book, *The New Party*. Knowles became a CLC vice-president and then chairman of the National Committee for a New Party (NCNP) after his defeat as an MP in the Diefenbaker landslide of 1958. He wrote his book in intentionally broad terms, hoping to attract a broad cross-section of sympathizers. The aim of the New Party proponents, according to Knowles, was a "political realignment through the creation of a broadly based people's political movement embracing the CCF, the labour movement, farm organizations, professional people, and liberally minded persons interested in basic social reform and reconstruction through our parliamentary system of government."[2]

Although the New Party idea did not crystallize until 1958, Manitoba's CCF leader, Lloyd Stinson, was receptive to such an idea not long after Douglas's national council comments. "I find," wrote Stinson after a tour of the province, "This sentiment [for a new political alignment] common among those who are on the fringe of the CCF."[3] For Stinson the aftermath of the federal Conservative victory of 1958 was an opportunity for Canada's socialists to achieve major party status. A social democratic party,in this view, would gain at the expense of one of the older parties, as had occurred earlier in the century in Britain. "If there is any logic in Canadian affairs," Stinson told a foreign observer of Canadian politics, "now is the time when there should be a good chance for a third party to slip in and take the place formerly occupied by the Liberals against the older Conservatives."[4] In Manitoba the idea was certainly plausible: after the 1959 election the Liberals were the official opposition by virtue of a single seat advantage over the CCF. Provincial secretary Donovan Swailes was, like Stinson, also enthusiastic about a formal political realignment. Although substantial trade union support already existed in the province for the CCF, he reported "a feeling that there should be a political movement more directly associated with the trade unions, and more closely identified with them." He wanted a stronger link with labour. As early as 1957 he favoured the title Labour Party of Canada for a new party.[5]

The CLC's 1958 decision to initiate discussions with the CCF on the creation of a new political party was in part a result of the Douglas strategy. The CLC was an amalgamation of the craft unions in the

Trades and Labour Congress and the industrial unions in the Canadian Congress of Labour. Under the Manitoba CCF's constitution, union locals could affiliate with the party, but none did in the 1950s. In the 1940s the party had had only four union local affiliates and their affiliations lapsed. In Winnipeg organized labour's formal public endorsement of the CCF, and then the NDP, meant little because strong labour support in terms of votes had always been present. "In Winnipeg," noted David Orlikow, "we had that tradition which goes back to even before the 1919 strike, and which was reinforced by the 1919 strike. The party, whether it was called the Independent Labor Party, or the CCF, or the New Democratic Party, is looked on by a very substantial number of workers — I'm not talking about their unions or their leadership or the constitution of the union — they [the workers] have looked on this party as *their* party. . . . The important factor is that this is [to them] a worker's party, period."[6] The CLC's formal strength in Manitoba (35,000 in 635 locals[7]) during the New Party's formation, however, was not enough to boost the New Party to power even if all unionists supported it. The labour initiative was important because it helped contribute to the impression that the New Party was a "new" movement based on a "new" coalition of forces that could, unlike the CCF, succeed at the polls. It was necessary for tactical reasons, moreover, that Manitoba developments parallel national CCF–CLC developments. CCFers favouring a direct link with the union movement did not fear union dominance at conventions because they felt that labour's interests could be easily accommodated. "I don't think that the labour boys at that point made any strong representations about platform and I don't think our platform altered at all because of labour participation," recalled Lloyd Stinson.[8]

Although the majority of CCFers were enthusiastic about the CCF–CLC merger proposals, some older members and younger CCF executive officials were not. Some veteran members opposed the provisions for direct union representation and recalled that even in the labour-oriented ILP membership was by individual application only. These members did not always see the union movement as a progressive force. Charles Biesick, a party secretary in the 1940s, had reservations "because our trade union movement here is too much oriented along the lines of the American trade union movement, and that is certainly not a radical orientation."[9] For Beatrice Brigden, party secretary in the late 1930s, the New Party represented a betrayal of the CCF idea: "A New Democratic Party — what under the sun does it mean? It means nothing to me; but the Co-operative Commonwealth did, that has meaning to it, but what's a 'New Democrat'?"

She "was very disappointed with the stand that Stanley [Knowles] took... Mr. Woodsworth... wouldn't have given into any one group [labour] becoming sort of dominant as they did."[10] Another veteran CCFer felt that the Winnipeg Declaration of 1956, which he had fought, had no purpose but to facilitate the future alliance with organized labour.[11]

There were also reservations about the New Party voiced by some younger CCF officials. They did not so much object to a new party as to a new structure. Al Mackling, provincial party chairman in 1959-60, opposed what he called a "class" party. He argued that the unions could not help attract voters, but would only hinder. "I don't think the New Party's future will be very rosy if it is just devoted to one class," he told the *Winnipeg Free Press*. "We must win the support of all citizens, whether they be labourers, doctors, lawyers or farmers.... We'll have to achieve this recognition to win in Manitoba."[12] Mackling feared the disintegration of the constituency associations, something he foresaw if reliance for funds and organization fell on the unions.

Howard Pawley, Mackling's predecessor as provincial chairman, was another leading executive member opposed to the merger proposals. Although the two fought union affiliation together, their reasoning was somewhat different. Pawley's major concern was socialist content. He was one of a small handful who had voted against the Winnipeg Declaration and feared that the New Party would become a pale image of its competitors. "I was concerned about this tendency to want to become similar, wanting to become respectable, wanting to become no different from the two old-line parties," he recollected. "I didn't think it [the New Party] would work. Philosophically, I thought it was wrong."[13] He saw the union movement as pushing the New Party towards the centre of the political spectrum.

There were other opponents of the New Party proposals. One was Magnus Eliason, the party's provincial organizer responsible for the rural areas, who feared that close labour identification would hurt the CCF in Manitoba. Others feared that radical and communist influences might enter the New Party via the unions. One CCF executive member, Allan Denton, a unionist and former vice-president of the Winnipeg and District Labour Council, was led by this fear to quit the party and join the Conservatives. Concern about communist infiltration was dubious since the CLC and the MFL kept Communist-led unions out of the Congress and the Federation. Minor opposition to a CCF–labour merger also existed in some union circles. Most of these opponents were former TLCers of the "non-partisan" school who were considered by pro-CCF unionists as sympathetic to the Liberals or Conservatives.[14] The overwhelming majority of union leaders, however, former CCLers and TLCers alike, supported or accepted the New Party idea.

In addition to organized labour, the architects of the New Party hoped to attract organized farmers. The farm movement in Manitoba however, unlike the labour movement, was divided into two competing groups: the Manitoba Federation of Agriculture and the Manitoba Farmers' Union. By the late 1950s the MFU was more vibrant than the MFA. The MFA drew only 57 delegates to its June 1959 convention whereas the MFU drew 775 delegates to its district conventions that same month. After temporarily reorganizing on a direct membership basis, the MFA attracted 2,640 members. MFU membership, in contrast, hovered between 17,000 and 20,000 in the late 1950s.[15] Active rural CCFers in the MFU included its founder Jake Schulz, Peter Burtniak, Herb and Mary McIntosh, Fred Tufford, Ed Schreyer, and Sam Uskiw. Mary McIntosh was the MFU's women's president, and Burtniak and Uskiw were to become cabinet ministers in 1969 in the government led by Ed Schreyer. Tufford, a CCF member of both the MFU and MFA estimated that in the late 1950s 60 per cent of all MFUers were sympathetic to the CCF.[16] A determined effort was mounted, therefore, to attract the ethnically heterogeneous MFU, but New Party overtures were not made to the MFA because of its largely Liberal and established, Anglo-Saxon, identity.

Some in the CCF hoped and expected that the MFU would move towards the New Party at the 1958 MFU convention.[17] This optimism, however, was deflated when a resolution calling on the MFU to enter negotiations with the CCF and the MFL was soundly defeated. Most CCFers in the MFU voted against it. Both James Patterson and Rudy Usick, successive MFU presidents at the time, opposed any negotiations on affiliation with a political party. Ironically, opponents of the pro-New Party resolution quoted from a book Schulz had written that supported a "no politics" position for organized farmers.[18] The MFU's decision did not surprise CCF leaders, but it was, nonetheless, a blow to their strategy.

CCF and MFU leaders were both opposed to the Campbell Liberal–Progressives in the 1950s, but they had different interests and different strategies. The CCF was committed to building a new party that could replace the government through the electoral process. The MFU, on the other hand, opted for the farmers' traditional route of economic organization. Its priority was organizing a maximum number of farmers. Among other things this meant attempting to amalgamate with the MFA.[19] Organized farmers saw themselves as a pressure group lobbying for favourable legislation. Like the MFA, and the UFM before it, the MFU was constitutionally non-partisan. Despite substantial sympathy for the CCF, the MFU rejected entry into the New Party for a number of related reasons: a fear of jeopardizing its chances for amalgamation with the MFA; the traditional agrarian suspicion of political parties as "evil" and "corrupting;" the belief in organizing on economic rather than political grounds; a suspicion in some minds of organized labour; the continuing popularity of the Diefenbaker Conservatives among many farmers; and the dislike in some MFU circles of the CCF and its New Party offspring. These fears were disguised diplomatically in public by MFU leaders who pointed out the non-partisan provisions of their constitution.[20] Privately, they complained at one point to the CCF for mentioning the MFU in campaign literature.[21]

The links between the MFU, the CCF, and the MFL in the 1950s were largely informal. In 1954 a liaison committee was established by the MFU, the TLC, and the CCL,[22] but little came out of it. MFU executives and CCF MLAs met occasionally, but the New Party was kept off the agenda.[23]

Some CCFers were disappointed with the CCF–MFU relationship. Although the CCF supported many of the MFU's demands in the legislature, the support was not reciprocated. In both the 1958 and 1959 provincial elections the MFU's newspaper went to great lengths to project impartiality.[24] After the 1959 election, the MFU's *The Voice of the Farmer* pointed proudly to the fact that MFUers had been elected to all three party caucuses. This approach reflected the MFU's central objective—expanding its own base. Some CCFers hoped that affiliation of the MFU would be easier to accomplish after the NDP's creation in 1961, but they were to be disappointed. NDPers in the MFU were given a further blow when MFU president Usick emerged later as a Liberal candidate. In brief, "there was enough of the other parties in the Farmers' Union to prevent it ... from going political."[25]

The third element which was expected to complete the New Party according to its architects was "liberally-minded individuals." In effect this meant small-l liberals, small businessmen, and professionals. They were ineligible to join the New Party via labour or farmers' unions and were considered understandably hesitant about joining via the CCF, a party many of them had rejected before. A mechanism for their entry was needed. Created by the CCF and labour leaders on the NCNP, the New Party clubs were expected to capitalize on the demise of the federal and provincial Liberal governments. New Party clubs were formed in Winnipeg, Brandon, Killarney, Minnedosa, Hamiota, Flin Flon, Thompson, and Transcona.[26] Lloyd Stinson played a major role in their formation.

MLA Morris Gray also formed a Paole Zion (Labour–Zionist) New Party club in north Winnipeg. The two Winnipeg New Party clubs, the largest ones in the province, contained more students and academics than small businessmen and professionals. In large part the clubs were regroupings of CCFers not active in constituency associations. The clubs, although not particularly successful in recruiting new "liberals" to the social democratic banner, contributed to the desired impression that they were.

A partial test of the appeal of the CCF–New Party to small-l liberals came in the 1959 provincial election. In the 1958 election the CCF had argued that there was no difference between the Conservatives and Liberals. The focus in the 1959 election shifted slightly with Stinson appealing to "progressive Liberal-thinking" people to vote CCF.[27] The CCF hoped to replace the Liberals as the opposition by capitalizing on an anticipated further decline in the Liberal vote. A political reporter for the *Winnipeg Tribune* noted that: "Mr Stinson is driving to replace the Liberals as the 'liberal' element in the legislature. With the new CCF–CLC party looming in the future, this election will indicate success or failure, in the CCF attempt to bring 'liberal-minded' voters into their ranks."[28] The Liberal vote did decline, but the CCF picked up only three percentage points in the popular vote. New voters and disaffected Liberals, of both the small- and large-l variety, tended to turn to the Conservatives. If the election represented a test of popularity for the CCF–New Party among "liberal-minded individuals," the results were negative.

One group rejected for affiliation with the New Party was the communist Labour Progressive Party. Soon after the CLC's 1958 call for a new political movement, W.A. Kardash, on behalf of the provincial LPP, made a bid to discuss the basis of possible LPP affiliation. The overture was quickly rebuffed by both CCF and union officials. When national LPP leader Tim Buck later suggested that communist trade unionists were joining the New Party via the labour route, Winnipeg union officers dismissed his views as either wishful thinking or intentional adverse publicity.[29] Despite the apprehensions of some CCFers, there was no communist infiltration of the New Party.

Press reaction in Manitoba to the New Party was not any more sympathetic than it had been to the CCF. The *Free Press* and *Tribune* argued that farm organizations should not affiliate because the interests of farmers and workers were in opposition, and both newspapers applauded the MFU's decision to reject consideration of New Party affiliation. The only difference in the views of the two newspapers was that the *Free Press* contended that the New Party was nothing but a Labour party, while the

Tribune argued that if the New Party was not labour-dominated, as its leaders claimed, labour could not trust it to implement its desires.[30]

The press's contention that an irreconcilable antagonism existed between urban unionists and farmers was shared by many outside the CCF. Although the CCF rejected such a contention, some party members believed it too. Provincial organizer Magnus Eliason feared that rural supporters would desert the CCF–NDP once the unions were formally incorporated, but the CCF had never attracted the dominant, charter group of the province's farmers. Whatever rural support the CCF did have came from the poorer, immigrant-origin, ethnically heterogeneous areas. When these farmers voted for the labour-oriented CCF in the 1940s and 1950s they indicated that they did not subscribe to the urban-rural, worker-farmer, conflict theory. "Of course, Magnus was right if you're talking about the old Anglo-Saxon MFAC pool elevator's farmer" commented farmer Fred Tufford, "but on the other hand some of the ethnic groups ... Ukrainian people in Swan River and Dauphin for example, saw right past this [argument]. They understood that there is need for co-operation between labour and farmer because one is the customer of the other. They didn't swallow [the press's logic] at all."[31] Tufford's views were confirmed by membership records in party files. Swan River, although never represented by a CCF or NDP MLA, had the largest constituency association in the province in 1957.

Party secretary Don Swailes played a similar role in the formation of the Manitoba NDP to Knowles's role nationally. Before becoming a CLC vice-president and its first political education committee chairman in 1956, TLCer Swailes had been the first president of the MFL. He gave up that position to CCLer Jimmy James to facilitate the CCL–TLC merger in Manitoba.[32] Throughout the late 1950s Swailes sat on the MFL's executive committee. Swailes represented, therefore, a natural link between the MFL and the CCF. Other senior labour officials in the CCF–MFL talks included Sam Goodman, an MFL vice-president and an outspoken labour advocate for the New Party although not a CCFer; Jimmy James, MFL president and a CCFer; Art Coulter, secretary-treasurer of the Winnipeg and District Labour Council and a 1958 CCF candidate; and Grant McLeod, president of the WDLC and a CCFer. R.B. Russell, executive-secretary of the WDLC and a 1919 strike leader who had never joined the CCF took no active role in the deliberations, although he appeared briefly on one New Party committee. Opposing MFL sponsorship of a new party were Peter McSheffrey, the MFL secretary-treasurer from Flin Flon, Lawrence Taylor, an MFL vice-president from Pine Falls, and Frank Armstrong, a former president of the

Winnipeg TLC council. But pro-CCFers were clearly in the ascendancy, particularly in Winnipeg.

Early in 1959 the WDLC's political education committee sponsored a major conference to discuss the CLC proposals. With Swailes as chairman, a meeting of 250 Winnipeg unionists overwhelmingly endorsed the principle of establishing a new political party.[33] They voted in favour of a system of per-capita affiliation dues rather than ad hoc financial support, labour's major contribution to the CCF in the past. This was followed by a CCF-sponsored conference in March with ninety-seven members in attendance. Stanley Knowles, as guest speaker, compared the New Party proposals to the formation of the Manitoba CCF in the 1930s. Majority opinion among the CCFers at the meeting, in contrast to the unionists, favoured individual memberships only, no membership of organizations, in the New Party.[34] A month earlier a labour delegation including MFL president James and WDLC officials had met with the CCF executive and agreed to establish a joint exploratory committee with equal representation from each side.[35] The role of the committee was defined as promoting a wider understanding of the envisaged new party. The labour leaders, although not eager to see the Roblin government defeated,[36] also committed themselves to aiding the CCF in any forthcoming election.

By June 1959 there was organized opposition to the New Party proposals in the CCF. An unnamed party official announced that a "rebel group" had been formed to fight the CCF-CLC proposals. He listed four major objections: fear that the New Party was not an expression of rank and file opinion but was "being superimposed by top CCF and Canadian Labor Congress officials"; concern by some CCFers about joining with large American-based international unions; fear that in appealing to labour there would be a move to the right, away from socialism, to "become almost a second Liberal party"; and a belief that opportunities for a strong CCF showing in a future federal election were being jeopardized by the New Party diversion and "wrangling with labor."[37] Concern about the New Party being imposed from above was aired openly by junior members at the June provincial council meeting. "[M]any people," they reported, "were of the opinion that the whole thing was already planned by the 'top brass' of the CCF and CLC, and that the New Party was in effect, already in being." Similar sentiments were expressed by a few members of the WDLC, but they were neither influential nor united.[38]

Two New Party conferences for CCF members, held at Onanole in 1959, resulted in partial victories for the rebel group. The first conference, on Mackling's motion, opposed corporate or bloc membership, and favoured individual voluntary membership only.[39] But this was overridden at a national CCF–CLC seminar in Winnipeg a few weeks later. The second Onanole conference recommended that Manitoba New Party clubs be organized as vehicles to attract non-CCFers and proposed "Social Democratic Party" as a name for the New Party. The Mackling group, however, succeeded in having the conference recommend that affiliated organizations, no matter what their size, be permitted only one delegate each to conventions. Unions could have obtained better representation in the CCF.

The Conference also featured a discussion of a New Party program. Some talked of the need to be "pragmatic" and "modern." This led others to urge that any new program not mean a departure from socialism to sheer reformism. Some argued that public ownership had little to do with socialism:

Outlining the subject, Mr. Schreyer [as chairman], pointed out that nationalization was not a complete answer, it was guidance, and direction of the general economy that was most important. . . .

E. Shellborn. Surely we are not going to abandon public ownership. Mr. McWilliams. Competition is wasteful and expensive. If a product is under a monopoly, it should be publicly owned. [Fred] Zaplitny. It is up to the public to determine what should be publicly owned. Demand should come from the public. A socialist party should be an expression of public opinion. H. Pawley. A socialist party should lead public thought, even though an idea might be unpopular at a certain time.[40]

Many CCFers felt that explicit rejection of large scale public ownership meant little "[I]t wasn't an idea held in the CCF anyway," commented one long-time CCF–NDPer. "It was a matter of some people conceding the point who hadn't already conceded it."[41]

Formal negotiations on the New Party were spurred on by the 1959 MFL and CCF conventions. The former authorized its executive "to take whatever action may be necessary to assist in the formation of the New Political Party in Manitoba, including meetings with the Manitoba Section of the CCF, the Manitoba Farmers' Union, and any other organization which may be interested in a similar program."[42] The MFL, like the CLC, would not affiliate with the New Party but would encourage its locals to do so. As the federation representing unions in the province, it would negotiate the terms of labour participation. The proposal had substantial support; only 12 of the 228 delegates representing a total of 150 locals voted against it.[43]

An immediate result of the CCF and MFL conventions of 1959 was the creation of the New Party committee. Since no other groups came forward, it was basically a CCF–MFL body. Each side provided three members: Stinson, Mackling, and Pawley for the CCF; Swailes, Goodman, and a third MFL vice-president for the unions. Swailes, like Knowles nationally, represented labour while wearing hats in both organizations. For a chairman the group agreed upon Fred Tufford, a CCFer from Portage and a member of both the MFU and MFA. Tufford's rural background was seen as an asset since it gave the group an image of representing a broader spectrum of Manitoba society. Tufford thought that he was made chairman "because I took a fairly neutral stance between the people who were so afraid of this new venture and those who wanted it very badly. I was very anxious to see the New Party concept come into being, but I wasn't prepared to take it at any cost. . . . We didn't want to lose the socialist philosophy of our party."[44] The official role of Tufford's committee was to publicize the New Party through conferences and seminars, laying the groundwork for its creation at the provincial level. Throughout 1960 the New Party committee was a focal point for political infighting between supporters and opponents of trade union affiliation.

Mackling, Pawley, and Eliason, who were opposed to the membership provisions adopted by the NCNP, fought the proposals on the provincial council, on the executive, and on the New Party committee. At one council meeting they successfully carried a resolution indicating concern about the proposed federal constitution and arguing that all affiliated members be required to be members of constituency associations.[45] Their key argument was that affiliate memberships would only weaken the constituencies since both union members and their contributions would by-pass them.[46] The NCNP rejected these protests and hired Stinson and another organizer to stir up enthusiasm for the New Party in a provincial section that now appeared quite recalcitrant.

An example of the differences between Manitoba's New Party supporters and opponents was the Fisher debate. Mackling proposed that CCF MP Doug Fisher be the guest speaker at the 1960 convention. Fisher had wondered publicly about the wisdom of the New Party strategy. Stinson, aware that Fisher's appearance could be detrimental to his own efforts on behalf of the New Party, fought the proposed invitation. In the Fisher debate, Mackling's forces won the support of executive members such as Ed Schreyer, who was somewhere in the middle between the two factions. Schreyer's reason for supporting Mackling on this point reflected the views of many in the middle of the debate. "Clearly I felt that he [Fisher] was an asset to the party and that it was important to hear his views and so on. But at the time," recalled Schreyer, "he was not particularly in favour of transforming the party. Nevertheless, while I disagreed with him on that, I still thought that it was important to keep his counsel."[47]

Such a position, Schreyer thought, endeared him to neither side. But the Stinson forces decided to support Schreyer against Mackling for chairman of the party. Schreyer, although not an enthusiastic supporter of the New Party, had been discouraged by the infighting that surrounded the discussions. The Stinson forces knew that in the end Schreyer would go along with the New Party proposals. By choosing as a candidate an apparent neutral like Schreyer, rather than an identifiable New Party partisan, they hoped they could defeat Mackling for the chairmanship. For Stinson, Mackling's defeat seemed essential. A month before the convention he was in doubt abut the outcome and feared that Mackling would be successful in keeping the provincial CCF from accepting union affiliates. "At the moment I'm not sure we can win, and we must win," he wrote Knowles. "We can't allow these malcontents to take over *our* party."[48]

The reaction of many constituency associations was also a cause of anxiety to the New Party partisans. Many constituencies favoured a representation formula that would ensure constituency paramountcy.[49] Stinson travelled through the province encouraging constituency associations to support the NCNP proposals, which gave no such assurance. The NCNP convention representation formula provided for one delegate per fifty members for the first 200 members in constituency associations and then for one delegate per every 100 members or major portion thereof thereafter. Each constituency was guaranteed one delegate. For the unions each affiliated local was allowed one delegate per 1,000 members or major fraction thereof with a guaranteed minimum of one delegate. Such a formula made union domination possible.

The 1960 CCF convention went more smoothly for Stinson than he expected. Mackling and Eliason argued that the convention should support the New Party idea nationally but should hold up provincial endorsement for a while, perhaps a year. The idea was rejected and the decision to create the New Party within one year carried by a two-to-one margin. The representation problem was dealt with behind closed doors at an executive meeting during the convention. Both sides agreed on a compromise resolution that called on the NCNP to explore "the possibility of a constitutional formula which would encourage affiliate members to become constituency members."[50] Mackling took this concession as a victory. For Stinson it was an insignificant concession that tied neither the NCNP nor the provincial CCF to anything. Stinson's efforts had prevailed over Mackling's and for his victory David Lewis sent Stinson a congratulatory telegram.[51]

The note of harmony that the compromise resolution seemed to represent was superficial. Both the Stinson and Mackling groups fielded slates for the election of officers on the convention's last day. One group was fighting for a smooth transition to the New Party; the other, for continued agitation on the representation formula. The results of the voting were much closer than the vote on the New Party itself. Schreyer defeated Mackling for the party chairmanship by less than a handful of votes. Pawley then defeated Tufford (who was now identified with the Stinson group) for the vice-chairmanship by a similar count. Both sides claimed a victory. Mackling pointed to his supporters taking six of ten executive posts and to the resolution urging the NCNP to consider changes. Stinson pointed to the comfortable majority attained by the New Party resolution and to the defeat of the attempt to extend the CCF's life.[52] Stinson was closer to the mark. No matter how many of Mackling's group had been elected, the important decision had been made: the CCF committed itself to a political alliance with the union movement. Mackling realized the inevitable and declined renomination to the New Party committee.

The CCF's last convention also elected a new provincial leader. After Stinson's defeat at the polls in 1959 the party operated in the legislature with A.R. (Russ) Paulley, a unionist and the mayor of Transcona, as house leader. Stinson had initially intended to resign as leader in 1959 but decided to stay on and work from his position for the New Party. Since his position as leader added to his stature as a New Party organizer, Mackling and Pawley wanted him replaced. They supported Paulley, who declined to run against Stinson in 1959, but did run in 1960 when Stinson announced he would vacate the leadership. Their support for Paulley seemed logical. Paulley had voted with Mackling and Pawley for Hazen Argue at the 1960 national convention at which Lewis and Knowles had tried unsuccessfully, with informal CLC backing, to keep Argue from being elected national leader. Paulley had been only on the fringes of the New Party debate and had not worked as Stinson and Swailes had for the CCF–CLC alliance.

But Paulley's few public statements about the New Party could not have cheered Mackling and Pawley. Paulley told the Winnipeg and District Labour Council not to worry about elements in the CCF who were charging that labour would dominate the New Party and encouraged the New Party idea. The same day that Mackling and Pawley publicly endorsed him for the leadership, Paulley told the press that he was not concerned if labour dominated the New Party as long as the basic philosophy of the New Party was that of the CCF. Immediately after his election as leader, and coming from a convention that recommended constituency paramountcy in the New Party, he encouraged farmers at a meeting in Arborg to try to get the Manitoba Farmers Union and the Manitoba Federation of Agriculture affiliated with the New Party. Paulley was committed all along to the New Party idea and its provisions for affiliated representation,[53] a position Mackling and Pawley had strongly opposed.

A month before the CCF convention, the MFL voted to proceed with the New Party. The approximate vote, according to a press account, was 188 to 12 in favour.[54] Opposing views were booed. There were some elements in the MFL so committed to direct political action that they claimed they were prepared to go it alone, if need be, without the CCF.[55]

In contrast, organized farm support continued to elude the New Party. MFU executive members continued to insist that their organization was constitutionally non-partisan. The farmers at their 1960 convention were so determined to avoid politics that they shelved a proposal to establish a political education committee.[56] Their position was consistent with that of the Interprovincial Farm Union Council of which the MFU was a member. The 1960 MFU convention was only different from the preceding ones in that Jake Schulz finally made a direct appeal for supporting the New Party. Speaking as its honorary president and founder, Schulz was listened to and applauded. His comments on the New Party, however, were not endorsed. His argument was that organized farmers should be "getting in on the ground floor of the New Party or they might be left out in the cold."[57] Schulz's efforts did not budge the convention.

Throughout the New Party's formation no formal overtures were made to the co-operative movement. CCFers were certain they would be rejected. Public appeals and the subsequent public rejections would be bad publicity. One large Winnipeg consumers' co-operative, Red River Co-op, voted to maintain the politically non-partisan position it had adopted when formed.[58] As for rural producers' co-operatives, such as those in the MFA, their reaction was certain to be negative. Tufford, a director of one of the MFA's co-operatives, felt that a New Party appeal at any co-op convention or meeting he had ever attended would have been rejected out of hand. He thought that, apart from a few exceptions, the co-operative movement in Manitoba, unlike Saskatchewan's, was a politically reactionary force.[59]

Outside the CCF, therefore, most new funds and new members were expected to come from organized labour. To overcome constitutional restrictions that could keep locals of international unions from contributing funds for political activity, Goodman encouraged the creation of New Party clubs within the locals. A small number of such clubs was formed but the club status was largely symbolic. The largest portion of union contributions in 1961, when a target of $4,000 had been set, came from the WDLC. Less than a quarter of this sum, however, reached the provincial CCF office; most of it went to the NCNP.[60] The same unions that had supported the CCF in Manitoba in the past, notably the Steel and Packinghouse Workers, were the ones that supported the New Party idea.[61]

Despite the continuing differences within the CCF, membership rose dramatically. Eliason's rural organizational efforts brought membership to a point not attained since 1945. Ironically, it had been Eliason who had argued that an alliance with labour would hurt the CCF in the rural areas. At the end of 1957, before the New Party debate began, membership stood at 1,361.[62] Between then and the 1960 provincial convention it remained fairly constant despite the activity generated by general elections, three of which took place in 1958 and 1959. After the 1960 convention, the CCF's last, membership expanded rapidly. The New Party debate had obviously not hurt the CCF. New members were told that their memberships would automatically be converted to New Party memberships after the founding convention. In the first two months of 1961 Eliason reported signing over 1,000 members. He told the provincial council that interest in the New Party was a major factor in these gains.[63]

By the time of the NDP's provincial founding convention in 1961 membership was 3,554. Only about one-quarter of the members were from Winnipeg. A year later, when the NDP was firmly established, the total stood at 3,259 of which 2,000 were in rural areas. The tripling of members that had taken place in the first eight months of 1961 reflected support for the CCF in the marginal farming communities of the northwest, the interlake, and the east. Despite this rural support, only two of the CCF's ten seats were from these areas; the rest were in metropolitan Winnipeg. No relationship existed between the number of members and electoral success. CCF electoral victories in north and central Winnipeg, where membership figures were fairly low, were testimony that Winnipeg's working class identified with the CCF, whether or not they joined the party.

At the national founding convention of the NDP in July 1961 the overwhelming number of delegates from Manitoba were veteran and active CCFers. Most of the union delegates were active in the CCF and had attended former CCF conventions.[64] It is doubtful that more than five of the Manitoba delegation would have been ineligible to attend had it been simply another CCF convention. In effect, the CCF was joining with unionists who had all along supported the CCF and some of whom had been elected to public office as CCFers. The largest number of Manitoba union delegates at the national convention represented Steel, Packinghouse, the Retail, Wholesale and Department Store Workers, and the Brewery Workers—all of whose locals had contributed to CCF campaigns in the past.

Manitoba's role at the national convention was minor. Paulley, Schreyer, Swailes, James, and Coulter were elected to the national council. Four of the five were both trade unionists and CCFers. Mackling's supporters played no significant role and, upon returning to Winnipeg, Mackling announced he was fed up and was going to just "sit and watch."[65] He had no intention of leaving the NDP, however, and one year later contested the provincial election for the NDP.

MFU president Rudy Usick returned to Manitoba from the national NDP convention and depicted the party as "ready to win." He looked favourably on the NDP's structure, constitution, cross-section of delegates, and its agricultural policies.[66] Usick's sympathetic comments led to renewed hope on the part of CCF officials that the MFU would reverse its stand on affiliation. But, again, the MFU disappointed the CCFers. Usick made it clear that his comments were not to be taken as endorsing the NDP and that he would oppose any change in MFU policy.[67] As a guest speaker at the NDP's founding provincial convention he reported a favourable response in the MFU to the NDP. But if the party hoped to gain MFU support, he continued, it would have to seek out farmers on an individual basis and not expect MFU locals to affiliate.[68]

The representation formula at the provincial convention was, surprisingly, weighted a bit more in favour of union representation than it had been nationally. Allowance was made for one CCF delegate per five CCF members from constituency associations. For affiliated union locals the ratio was one delegate per twenty-five affiliates. Neither group filled its quota. The New Party clubs and the CCF–New Party youth groups were also given one delegate per five members. Others entitled to attend as delegates were members of the CCF provincial council, the New Party committee, the MFL executive committee, and three delegates from each labour council. This formula yielded 355 convention delegates with 191 from the CCF, 132 from unions, and 32 from New Party clubs.[69]

The change in composition of delegates from CCF conventions was more apparent than real. The new affiliation provisions permitted many CCFers to appear as labour delegates, adding to the broadening image desired by the New Party architects. The lack of substantive change in membership and leadership was reflected in the NDP's first executive committee. Every one of them had been a CCF member and the majority had been active CCFers. Paulley was elected leader and Alistair Stewart president. Both of Paulley's opponents for the leadership were non-unionist CCFers and neither had opposed the New Party affiliation proposals.

The content of the NDP's program was also little different from that of the CCF. The article of the constitution dealing with objectives simply asserted that the role of the provincial NDP was to unite all progressive people and organizations into a democratic party and to further the objectives of the national NDP.[70] As for policies, the resolutions adopted reiterated the CCF's election platforms of 1958 and 1959: a provincial health plan, an extensive housing program, public auto insurance, incentives for industrial growth in the private, co-operative, and public sectors, assistance to private industries interested in locating in Manitoba, more aid to education, reallocation of municipal responsibilities and revenues, assistance to small farmers, and lowering the voting age to eighteen. To pay for this program the convention proposed higher corporate taxes, higher mineral royalties, the diversion of more beer profits to the public purse without increasing the price to consumers, and a higher tax for commercial highway users.

The one important new figure in the NDP executive who was not a CCFer was Sam Goodman. He was appointed provincial secretary by the provincial council. His selection reflected a number of factors: personal determination, external NDP influence, financial circumstances, and a desire to make the CCF transformation into the NDP appear as a genuine combination of CCF–Labour efforts. Goodman had been the major driving force in both the MFL and WDLC for the New Party. Less than a month before the convention he lost in a bid for the MFL presidency. Both Eliason and Mackling had expressed false fears that Goodman was a Communist.[71] To Pawley, Goodman's selection was merely a symbol of where the NDP was going, i.e., to becoming a "labour" party.[72] Ironically, to his fellow labour leaders, Goodman was a rightist and an opportunist.[73] The decision of the provincial council to appoint Goodman surprised Coulter. Neither Coulter nor James considered Goodman a "labour" candidate for the secretary's post. Goodman's candidacy, according to Lloyd Stinson, was "a brainwave of Stephen Lewis." The younger Lewis, perhaps with encouragement of national NDP officials, sold Goodman to Stinson and "between us we sold Sam to the party."[74] Goodman's candidacy was aided by the international union he represented in Manitoba. It agreed to continue to pay his salary if he took the full-time position of party secretary.[75] Thus there was no expense to the NDP for his services. Swailes, who had been both CCF secretary and treasurer, moved over voluntarily to retain only the treasurer's post. Even if Goodman was neither favoured nor particularly liked in the labour movement, his selection, some CCFers felt, would aid NDP interests.

The creation of the NDP was seen by CCF leaders as a necessary development if Canada's social democrats were ever to come to power. Nationally and provincially the CCF could not escape its third party status. The CCL–TLC merger of 1956 provided the CCF an opportunity to gain the endorsement and support of a united labour movement. Electoral triumphs by John Diefenbaker and Duff Roblin, however, proved that reform and protest votes could go as easily to the Conservatives as to the CCF. To capitalize on their labour gains and de-emphasize the CCF's image of perennial loser, CCF leaders looked for a new political formula. In the transformation from CCF to NDP the leadership secured, at every crucial juncture, majority support from the rank and file. After almost three decades of electoral reversals the CCF dissolved and the New Party was launched as a new and tenable hope.

The sixties: the party's rise to power

6

The NDP's rise to power in the late 1960s was meteoric. In less than seven years and three elections, between 1962 and 1969, the party boosted its popular vote from 15 per cent to 39 per cent. Few in or out of the party expected such a dramatic rise in light of the CCF's performance between the 1930s and 1950s and the NDP's initial poor showing in the 1962 election. In a sense the NDP's rise to power represented the victory of Manitoba's traditional political outsiders over its traditional political establishment. A number of factors, including a redistribution of seats and a change in leadership, favoured the NDP. In addition, Manitoba society by the 1960s had once again been remade; this time not suddenly through the force of new waves of immigrants but gradually through the long-term effects of ethnic and immigrant assimilation. The NDP's rise to power was partly a reflection of this remaking of Manitoba politics and partly a reflection of the continuing traditional rivalries in Manitoba politics.

In the 1969 election, a party identified with the tradition of the Winnipeg General Strike of exactly a half century earlier was elected to office. It defeated the other two major parties who were identified with opposition to the Strike and its subsequent political tradition. The NDP's victory has been presented as both an "ethnic revolt"[1] and as a victory of class politics over ethnic politics.[2] Because ethnic cleavages often complement class cleavages and party division[3] these descriptions of the 1969 election are complementary (i.e., only apparently contradictory) ways of expressing the same phenomenon. Manitoba's non–Anglo-Saxon communities have generally been located in the poorer urban and rural areas. Any party winning office in Manitoba has had to secure a significant measure of non–Anglo-Saxon support. A strictly British (Anglo-Saxon) versus non–British (non–Anglo-Saxon) approach, which is implicit in the perspective of "ethnic revolt," belies the CCF–NDP's history. British Anglo-Saxons, who form the core of Winnipeg's working class in areas such as Weston, Brooklands, Transcona, and Elmwood, always gave strong support to the CCF–NDP. This group provided the leadership and most stable base of support for the party through most of its history.

THE 1962 AND 1966 ELECTIONS

The Roblin government of the late 1950s and 1960s was a formidable foe for a reform party of the left. In the early 1960s, during the years the NDP was being established, the Conservative government introduced and received credit for its major achievements: new schools, highways, parks, a Red River floodway to protect Winnipeg, and an improved welfare system. The early 1960s represented a peak in the government's expansiveness and popularity.

The government's strength lay more in its political dexterity than in its progressiveness. It tried to convey an image of being pragmatic, competent, efficient, and "non-ideological" in character. Composed of both reform and conservative elements, the Roblin government moved back and forth, from right to left and back again, as necessary, to outmanoeuvre its parliamentary opponents. The government's strength, moreover, was reinforced by the opposition's weakness. The Liberals were never a serious threat to Roblin's paramountcy. Saddled with an image of extreme frugality in government, they were unable to attract enough voters to give them more than two of greater Winnipeg's twenty seats during most of the 1960s. Liberal difficulties by themselves, however, did not result in any upsurge of support for the NDP. Reform-minded voters were not willing to desert what appeared to be a reform party in power (the Conservatives) for a reform party in opposition (the NDP).

The NDP's early platforms were virtually identical to the CCF platforms of the late 1950s. The 1962 and 1963 NDP conventions called for a reformed tax policy, public automobile insurance, medicare, more federal and provincial monies for health, education and welfare, the establishment of agricultural marketing boards, a tax on advertising, and more progressive labour legislation. In the field of economic development, a number of party conventions called for the establishment of a Manitoba Development Corporation to provide public loans to private, co-operative, and Crown corporations.[4] (The Conservatives' Manitoba Development

Fund had these powers already, although they were in practice only exercised selectively within the private sector.) The NDP program did not attract a flock of new supporters. There was no rush of small-l liberals to the party as had been hoped for, and the progressive farm organization, the MFU, did not come any closer to the party either. Like the CCF, the party was attacked by the *Winnipeg Free Press*. Its editorial refrains were that the NDP was a tool of large American trade unions and that its platform was far too costly to entertain.

In its first provincial election the new party lost ground. In 1959 the CCF had gained ten seats with 22 per cent of the popular vote; in 1962 the NDP dropped to seven seats with 15 per cent of the vote. NDPers, in comparison to 1959 CCF showings, lost votes in every constituency except one and in that one the candidate still lost his deposit. Dauphin, Selkirk, and Churchill, all constituencies with a strong CCF-NDP base, were not contested in 1962 for lack of candidates. For the first time in decades Manitoba's major party of the left trailed both the old parties in popular vote in the Winnipeg area (see Table 6).

TABLE 6

Manitoba provincial election, 1962

Party	Seats	Percentage of popular vote
Conservative	36	45
Liberal	13	36
NDP	7	15
Other	1	4
Total	57	100

The 1962 results were not altogether surprising. The NDP had not anticipated a December election and had fielded only thirty-nine candidates. This contributed to an impression that the party was not a serious contender for power. Earlier that year the NDP's popular vote in the federal election in Manitoba was no better than the CCF's 1958 performance in the Diefenbaker landslide. In the 1963 federal election this downward trend continued with the NDP being the only party in Manitoba to lose votes.

These reversals led some NDP leaders to stock-taking. Two senior party members wrote Stanley Knowles, a New Party architect, commenting on the irony of the new broader-based party doing more poorly than its unsuccessful predecessor.[5] "The 'image' our Brass is attempting to create is a liberal one, and many voters cannot distinguish 'liberal' from 'Liberal,'" wrote one veteran rural member after the 1963 federal election campaign. "We disappoint our friends by this attempt to mollify our enemies, and the latter are implacable."[6] Magnus Eliason thought that "there is skepticism over the NDP in rural areas. Under the CCF we had trust. I doubt if we have it now."[7] Leader Russ Paulley's reaction to the 1962 provincial setback was "that the NDP had been too honest in the presentation of its program to the people, laying it on the line from the commencement of the campaign. Perhaps more thought should have been given on the basis of giving the people what they want."[8] But this was a surprising reaction. The party had presented a program no more radical, and if anything less so, than in the past. At the federal level the NDP depicted the Liberals and Conservatives as Tweedledum and Tweedledee. The party's billboards and leaflets in the 1965 federal election, for example, offered cartoons of Lester Pearson and John Diefenbaker wrestling with each other next to the slogans "Fed up with politicians and old-line political parties?" "Fed up with ineffectual leadership?", "If you're fed up—speak up!" Vote NDP.[9] One campaign leaflet spelled out the acronym NDP as "Neither Diefenbaker nor Pearson."

An image that the NDP tried to project provincially was that of competent technician: "Elect us because the Liberals and Conservatives are mismanaging affairs. We will manage them more efficiently." This appeal was more "We can do things better" than "We will do different things." It was this theme which provincial leader Russ Paulley stressed in the 1966 election. In an address to his candidates he listed specific proposals, of a technical nature, that the NDP wanted implemented in various government departments.[10] In the field of education, for example, the NDP stood for more schools, improved facilities, more bursaries and scholarships, more teachers, more technical training, etc. Nowhere, however, was there an NDP position on the role of the education system or a statement on how the NDP's position was different, in non-quantitative terms, from that of the other parties. One issue of the *Manitoba New Democrat* offered a series of quotations emphasizing the need for more social and economic reforms. Rhetorically the publication asked if Paulley had said these things. Did NDP deputy leader Saul Cherniack say them? Did other NDP MLAS say them? "No," proclaimed the party publication–members of the Roblin government had said all these progressive things.[11] The message conveyed was that an NDP government should be elected to ensure the implementation of Roblin's progressive platform.

After 1963 a resurgence in NDP support occurred nationally and in the provinces. In the 1965 federal election NDP support in Manitoba went up by about 50 per cent over 1963. In Winnipeg constituencies NDP candidates garnered 31 per cent of the vote, roughly the same percentage as each of the older parties. At one point in 1967 the NDP pulled ahead of the Conservatives in the national Gallup poll. And despite the Liberal party's Trudeaumania in 1968, the NDP further increased its percentage of votes received in Manitoba over 1965.

This general rise in NDP support was reflected in the 1966 provincial election. The popularity of the Roblin regime was beginning to falter, and the NDP, rather than the Liberals, began to make gains (see Table 7). The NDP was the only party to gain both seats and votes and fielded a record fifty-two candidates. These candidates represented every major ethnic group (including native Indian) and religious group in the province. The slate was also occupationally diverse, containing lawyers, unionists, businessmen, teachers, clergymen, and two senior MFU officials, one a past president. Both the party and the press depicted the NDP's 1966 showing as a major victory, although the party barely exceeded the CCF's 1959 popular vote.

TABLE 7

Manitoba provincial election, 1966

Party	Seats	Percentage of popular vote
Conservative	31	40
Liberal	14	33
NDP	11	23
Other	1	4
Total	57	100

After the election, the NDP's position was further strengthened. Roblin's progressive image began to fade. One sign of this was an unpopular and regressive sales tax introduced in 1967. The Liberals, meanwhile, were unable to shake free from their image as a rural-based, tight-fisted, party. When Roblin vacated the premiership in 1967, the rural conservative rather than the urban reform wing of his party came to the fore. Walter Weir, the new Conservative premier, broke with the "non-ideological" nature of the previous regime and steered the goverment onto a conscious right-wing course. Now both the government party and the major opposition party appeared on the right side of the political spectrum, a situation wholly unlike that prevailing in the early 1960s. The late 1960s, therefore, were conducive for NDP electoral gains.

THE PARTY'S MEMBERSHIP AND ORGANIZATION

The NDP membership was consistently larger than the CCF's, particularly after 1966. Through most of the 1950s, CCF membership was below 1500, but it tripled in 1961 from its 1960 level through concentrated rural canvassing by New Party organizers. During the 1960s the NDP's size tended to reflect its general electoral performance; the low point coming after the 1962 election setback and the high point coming on the eve of the 1969 election victory (see Table 8). A large majority of the party's seats always came from the Winnipeg area, but only occasionally did a slight majority of the membership live there. In Winnipeg constituencies membership numbers were usually fairly uniform, while in the rural areas there were great differences. Often there were a few southwestern constituencies with no members at all, while others, in the northwest and east, contained the largest numbers of NDP members in the province. As had been the case with the CCF, there was little relationship between numbers of NDP members and electoral success in specific constituencies. In 1969, for example, Rupertsland and The Pas with nine and thirty-seven members respectively both returned NDP MLAs, while Swan River and Roblin with 216 and 175 members respectively failed to do so.

TABLE 8

Manitoba NDP membership, 1961-70

Year	Total	Metropolitan Winnipeg	Non-Winnipeg
1961	3554	888*	2666*
1962	3259	1204	2055
1963	1590	793	797
1964	2011	872	1139
1965	2934	1500	1434
1966	2693	1342	1351
1967	3662	1778	1884
1968	3958	1964	1994
1969	5205	2689	2516
1970	5341	2625	2716

SOURCE: NDP Papers, Winnipeg
* approximations

Although the NDP was larger than the old CCF, its composition was not all that different. Less than a handful of provincial executive and council members in 1961-62 had been brought in by the New Party drive. "New Party types are not coming forward to take positions of leadership in the New Party but rather, are standing in the wings waiting to see whether the New Democratic Party is really the old C.C.F. with some artificial respiration," wrote the provincial secretary to the national leader.[12] The NDP's membership, like the CCF's, was less rural- and business-oriented, especially at the senior levels, than that of the older parties. A typical NDP executive committee was the one of 1965: it contained seven trade unionists, five teachers and professors, two lawyers, two housewives, and a small businessman. It was also common to have a farmer on the executive. An analysis of over 4000 open-ended questionnaires completed by NDP members showed that in the late 1960s and early 1970s roughly 30 per cent were blue collar workers, 12 per cent were retired, 10 per cent were white collar workers, and 5 per cent were students.[13]

Constituency associations often lay dormant and their executive committees sometimes disappeared. In 1962, despite a membership of over 3000, twenty-seven of the province's fifty-seven constituencies had no executive committees.[14] When letters went out to the NDP membership in 1962 asking for membership renewals by mail the appeal received less than 1 per cent response.[15] This meant that the few organizers the party did have spent much of their time simply renewing annual memberships rather than actively expanding the party's base of support. As late as December 1968, six months before the NDP's election, three constituencies had no members and seventeen constituencies, including a few that were to be won, had no executive committees.[16] Thus, in the more difficult early 1960s, a major party problem was finding candidates who would accept nominations. Membership participation reached a low point in 1964 when atypical affair, a party membership of around 3000 yielded only 78 constituency delegates, whereas the party's constitution provided for a possible 300.[17]

Like its national and provincial counterparts, the Manitoba NDP became a more polished electoral machine than its CCF predecessor. Comprehensive and refined organization manuals, some thirty and forty pages in length, were used. A preoccupation with technique led one provincial party research director to recommend renting computer services to facilitate opinion poll analysis and "game theory for optimal exploitation of 'possible' class names on voters' lists."[18] But nothing so elaborate was undertaken. In an attempt to revitalize the policy formulation function, which poorly prepared constituency delegates almost let lapse at conventions, the party executive established a number of ongoing policy committees in 1965-66. About a hundred people, many not party members but interested professionals, served on health, education, natural resources, and other committees devising policies to be presented to the annual convention.

The most important organizational position was that of party secretary, elected by the council rather than the convention. During the 1960s the NDP had four provincial secretaries. The first, Sam Goodman, was a union official whose union continued to pay his salary during his service to the NDP. Goodman's union, however, terminated its salary support in 1963 and he resigned and moved to Montreal. Don Swailes, party treasurer and long-time CCF secretary, took over as secretary-treasurer and held the post until 1966. Ben Hanuschak, a teacher and a newly elected north Winnipeg MLA, then held it for two years. The provincial secretary who led the party through the 1969 election was Betty Klein, a former union and party organizer from Saskatchewan.

The appointment of MLA Hanuschak as a senior party official was an indirect comment on the weakness of the Manitoba NDP. In Saskatchewan there was a tradition of excluding members of the caucus from official party posts.[19] In part, this reflected concern about internal party democracy. But it also revealed party strength in that many competent members, outside the legislature, were available to serve the Saskatchewan party. The weaker Manitoba party, in contrast, relied in the mid-1960s on one MLA to serve as secretary and another MLA, Sidney Green, to serve as president. At a number of conventions there was substantial difficulty in attracting candidates for executive party posts. In 1962 the outgoing executive presented the convention with a slate of suggested executive members. Although nominations were permitted from the floor, few members of the slate were challenged and none was defeated.[20] The Manitoba NDP rank and file was not only weaker than Saskatchewan's but also deferred more consistently to its leaders.

After the NDP's creation a modest attempt was made by some members to revive the role which the LSR had fulfilled in the 1930s. A group of about twenty members, calling itself New Society, met monthly in Winnipeg. New Society defined itself as "liberal-minded, left-of-centre ... committed to study, discussion and publication on specific problems of political concern."[21] It was intended primarily for academics who were either NDP members or, failing that, not members of any other political party. This group did not survive long beyond 1962 and its impact was not great. A more typical form of party education were the schools for candidates. They were generally held immediately before an election and dealt with election organizing, public relations, finance, recruiting, etc. Policy issues were generally discussed in an incidental fashion, in terms of how to present them effectively, rather than in terms of content. In the mid-1960s a permanent political education committee was created by the party. Most of its energy was devoted to propaganda work: public relations, preparing free time television broadcasts, and organizing a billboard campaign. The content of these activities was attacks on the government, aimed at attracting disenchanted voters to the NDP.

As for the party's finances, many parallels abounded in CCF and NDP funding. Financial and membership quotas were assigned to each constituency, party members holding public office were expected to contribute percentages of their legislative indemnities, and there were appeals to and from sister provincial parties and the national party. The party faced a steady succession of financial crises. Party expenditures in the 1960s were larger than those of the CCF in the 1950s,[22] but it was reasonable to assume that they were still significantly lower than those of the two older parties. This was reflected in the amounts spent in campaigns. In the 1965 federal election, for example, the provincial office and NDP candidates spent much less than a third of Liberal expenditures yet elected three Manitoba MPs to the Liberals' one.[23] There seemed to be no link between the size of campaign expenditures and electoral success, although the NDP harboured such a suspicion. A series of deficits led the party to favour legislated ceilings on campaign expenditures.[24] The largest percentage of NDP funds for most campaigns came neither from membership fees, union affiliate fees, or union contributions but from general contributions by members and supporters.

THE PARTY AND THE LABOUR MOVEMENT

One way of determining the location of a party on the political spectrum is to examine its ideology and program. Another way is to look for the bases of the party's electoral support. From both these perspectives the NDP qualified as a party of the left. The ideology of the NDP was the social democracy of the Socialist International, a federation of parties that describe themselves as commited to transforming capitalist societies into socialist commonwealths. In the late 1960s the Socialist International included over fifty parties representing 15,000,000 members and a voting strength of 78,000,000. The NDP program, essentially, was no more and no less radical than the programs of sister Labour and social democratic parties such as those in Britain, Sweden, West Germany, Israel, and Australia. As for the party's voters, many NDP supporters considered themselves to be members or sympathizers of the working class. An affinity between working class consciousness and voting for the NDP was more pronounced in parts of Winnipeg than anywhere else in Canada.[25]

In the 1960s, as before, there were close bonds between Manitoba's organized labour movement and the province's social democratic party. The majority of provincial labour leaders were members and supporters of the CCF-NDP. In metropolitan Winnipeg the CCF-NDP fared exceptionally well in those areas containing large numbers of unionized workers. The changeover from the CCF to the NDP represented a formal consolidation of the links between the union movement and social democratic politics. The logic behind trade union leadership support for the CCF-NDP was summed up elsewhere:

Support of the CCF-NDP becomes an established policy. It becomes one of the leadership traits which would-be leaders must adopt in order to be co-opted into leadership positions. The party world and the labour world begin to merge, or at least to interlock, so that the prestige, power, and success of a unionist in one of these worlds becomes a base from which power, prestige, and success can be sought in the other.

Union interests become vested in the party. Effort, loyalty, and enthusiasm are invested in the party over a period of years to such a degree that harm to the party is perceived as harm to the union. The union has an investment in the party which it will not lightly withdraw. The question "why does labour support the CCF-NDP?" becomes misleading because the interlocking, the vesting of interest has reached the point where labour, in a sense, *is* the CCF-NDP.[26]

This relationship was reflected in the 1961 Winnipeg municipal elections when ten of the thirteen CCF-NDP candidates were active trade union members.

Although the overwhelming number of Manitoba union locals did not affiliate with the NDP in the 1960s this did not particularly concern party or union leaders. Affiliation fees were a small fraction of union contributions. For the provincial party, affiliation was primarily a symbolic act. "I never looked on it as a financial thing," commented David Orlikow. "It was more a sort of status thing. By the unions coming in you put the onus on them to go out and convince their membership that this is their party."[27] Informal and indirect contributions were attracted with little or no publicity. For example: a number of union locals contributed per capita sums to their labour councils and to the MFL for the broad purposes of "political education" and "political action." Many of these locals were not affiliated with the NDP, but their officers knew that the MFL used the money directly to aid the NDP. This arrangement was convenient for pro-NDP union officials and eliminated potential adverse publicity and controversy in union locals. "Why rock the boat by maybe the odd dissident having something to harp on" at a large open meeting, asked the MFL executive secretary.[28] This is not to imply that the MFL did not go through the formal motions of soliciting affiliations and direct check-offs for the NDP. It did.[29] But formal affiliations were not very important in union-party relations.

The large majority of unionized workers in the province resided in greater Winnipeg. In 1966, for example, Winnipeg had 53,000 of Manitoba's 63,000 unionists.[30] Throughout the 1960s the number of NDP union affiliates in Manitoba fluctuated between 5000 and 7500. In 1966 there were 6274 such affiliates in thirty-two locals while there were almost one-quarter million national affiliates in 679 locals.[31] There were more affiliates in British Columbia, Alberta, Ontario, Quebec, and Nova Scotia than in Manitoba. Every affiliated Manitoba local, however, was in the Winnipeg area. Outside the Winnipeg area formal NDP links with the union movement were virtually non-existent. Winnipeg, the historical heart of the Manitoba CCF-NDP, was also the core of the Manitoba labour movement. The largest union in Manitoba, the Steelworkers, had most of its members outside Winnipeg, and none of these affiliated with the NDP. In Winnipeg, in contrast, most of the Steelworkers affiliated. The overwhelming majority of the party's affiliates belonged to the Packinghouse Workers (later the Food and Allied Workers), Retail, Wholesale and Department Store Workers, Railway Workers, and Steelworkers.

The conditions of union affiliation varied from province to province. Affiliation fees were five cents per month with three cents going to the national NDP office and two cents to the provincial office. There were no guaranteed union positions on either the provincial council or executive, although such guarantees did exist in the constitutions of the national, Ontario, and British Columbia parties. In all cases neither urban labour councils nor provincial labour federations directly affiliated. They were, however, entitled to a small number of delegates at conventions. Affiliation was only open to locals and not to parent bodies. Union affiliation had a much greater impact on the national than on the Manitoba party. In the 1960s union affiliation fees represented about 45 per cent of national office receipts, a figure never approached in the CCF.[32] This income far exceeded income from individual membership fees. The pattern of financing beyond fees was that the NDP national office had access to the national offices of unions, and the NDP provincial office had access to locals, urban labour councils, and provincial labour federations. In 1965 this pattern of operation yielded the national office 72 per cent of its expenses for that year's election campaign. The major union contributors, at both the national and Manitoba levels, were the Packinghouse and Steelworkers unions.[33]

In contrast to the national party's financial reliance on union fees the provincial party's income from affiliates was small. The two cent per month per affiliate levy never gave the party more than $1689 in any one year in the 1960s.[34] Voluntary check-offs by certain locals over and above the affiliation fee produced even less income: $671, for example, in 1969. Individual membership fees were generally three to four times the total of affiliate fees. General contributions by individuals, in turn, were usually three to four times the total of all fees combined. With the possible exception of the 1969 election campaign it appears that general and election contributions from unions never exceeded one-third of the party's income and were usually substantially less. Most union funds came to the NDP through the MFL and the Winnipeg and District Labour Council. In 1969, the Ontario Autoworkers sent the party $2,000.[35] The Manitoba NDP may have been beholden to the union movement in the 1960s, but it was for other than financial reasons. The union movement provided the NDP with a solid base for membership recruits and electoral support as well as finances. The Manitoba NDP, however, was always more than just a labour party.

Another measure of union participation in party affairs was labour's role at the annual provincial conventions. That role, both in numbers and influence, was significant but never dominant. At some conventions no resolutions came from any of the affiliated unions. At others the resolutions presented were almost always restricted to the specific legislative concerns of organized labour, e.g., the Minimum Wage Act, Vacations with Pay Act, Labour Relations Act, Workman's Compensation Act, etc. Generally, union delegates made up one-quarter to one-third of the provincial convention. In 1962 they numbered 59 of 202 delegates; in 1965, 56 of 149.

THE PARTY'S LEADERSHIP

Leadership and personality considerations are important features of politics. This is reinforced in political systems where the policies of the competing parties are not too dissimilar. Mandates given to parties at elections are often mandates to particular leaders. Many voters vote for "the best man" because there is little differentiation of the parties. Some of the Conservative provincial strength in Manitoba was based on the popularity of Duff Roblin just as much Conservative national strength was based on the popularity of John Diefenbaker. But when Roblin left provincial politics, his party selected more than a successor. It also signalled an ideological shift in direction in its leadership choice—Walter Weir.

The image of the party leader was not stressed in the Manitoba CCF-NDP through most of its history, and the first serious challenge for the leader's post did not come until 1968. This striking consensus in the leadership selection process was, perhaps, reasonable in a party which touted principle above personality. Until 1969 every leader of the party came from greater Winnipeg and was of British extraction. In many ways John Queen, S.J. Farmer, E.A. Hansford, Lloyd Stinson, and Russ Paulley were reflections of the party's origins and electoral base: generally British, Protestant, working class, urban, and with only marginal appeal in the rural areas. The rural and conservative inclinations of the Conservative and Liberal parties, in contrast, were expressed in the late 1960s in the leadership selections of Walter Weir and R.B. Bend. Both of them defeated urban, "reform" image, candidates.

The NDP leadership conventions of 1968 and 1969 reflected ideological differences, as had the Conservative and Liberal leadership contests. In both conventions, MLA Sidney Green appeared to the public and to members of his party as the left-wing candidate. Paulley and Ed Schreyer appeared as the right-wing or centrist candidates. Prior to the 1968 convention Green asked Schreyer to quit his federal seat and to run for the party leadership. Green's motive was to provide the recently defeated national NDP leader, T.C. Douglas, with a parliamentary seat—Schreyer's Selkirk constituency.[36] When this plan did not materialize Green ran for the leadership. "I indicated at all times that there was no disagreement between Mr. Paulley and myself on policy" recalled Green. Although most party members, including Schreyer, took the challenge as a leftist one,[37] "There was absolutely no suggestion by myself that the policies of the party would be any different under myself or Mr. Paulley" insisted Green. "It was not a policy debate." It was in his view, rather, a contest that would be healthy for the party's image. Russ Paulley, party leader since 1960, took Green's challenge quite personally and replied by insisting that he would step down for one person only—Schreyer, a former MLA and a man

Paulley considered his natural successor "from the first time I had met him in [his home town] Beausejour."[38]

The 1968 convention retained Paulley by a vote of 213 to 168. Despite his urban background and experience as a labour lawyer, Green fared well among rural, northern, and university delegates. Paulley won the support of the majority of the trade union and the urban delegates, many of whom were influenced by their pro-Paulley MLAs. A large part of Paulley's support was provisional; it was predicated on Paulley's promise to vacate the leadership in a year's time and to open the way for a Schreyer candidacy,[39] despite Schreyer's refusal to commit himself to being a candidate in the future. A crucial factor in Green's defeat was his inability to secure the support of more than one MLA—Ben Hanuschak. The eight pro-Paulley MLAs endorsed a Draft Schreyer campaign for 1969 and argued against a "precipitous" change in leadership.[40] A cartoon in the *Winnipeg Tribune* summed up the situation: Green and Paulley were seated at a table playing poker while Schreyer was under the table playing with all the chips.[41]

The 1969 convention, unlike most NDP affairs, dealt only with the leadership question. In this respect it resembled the leadership conventions of the other parties. Ed Schreyer, a popular MP who had first been elected an MLA at twenty-two and had never been defeated at the polls returned to provincial politics with a touch of fanfare. It was a development he himself had predicted: "I wouldn't rule out the possibility [of returning to lead the NDP]—say in three years from now," he had told the press in 1966.[42] Schreyer's decision to run, however, did not come until May 1969; he felt uncertain about how his federal constituents would regard his leaving them less than one year after they had elected him.[43] For most of the provincial caucus, senior party members, and rank and file members, Schreyer represented the type of personality and ideological orientation they felt would produce unprecedented NDP gains. Paulley thought so too and personally endorsed Schreyer upon his own resignation.

The calling of a snap election by Weir for late June forced the party to reschedule its convention to early June. In their race for the leadership Green and Schreyer apppreared together at joint meetings throughout the province, supported the same policies, and spoke highly of each other. Green, recalled Schreyer, had been erroneously labelled as a classical and doctrinaire socialist by many, including himself.[44] Schreyer's own political philosophy was a mixture of American New Deal liberalism and Swedish-style social democracy.[45] Schreyer overwhelmed Green by a vote of 506 to 177. Many rural delegates, who one year earlier voted for Green against

Paulley, now had a genuine rural choice in Schreyer. Schreyer, noted a former rural organizer for the party, had "the rural touch," a quality shared by Roblin but never held by any former provincial CCF–NDP leader.[46] Most delegates believed that Schreyer's leadership in an election would reap the party many more seats than they could hope for under Green.

One important feature of the convention was the extent of free television coverage it was given. This was the first time in the party's history that a convention was televised. Since the convention took place during an election campaign, both Schreyer and the party were given more exposure than the NDP could ever hope to buy. The NDP was thus able to accomplish two important tasks simultaneously. First, there was a changeover in leadership to a personality whose background and appeal offered the party reasonable expectations for advancement. Second, the media generated an unprecedented level of public awareness of the provincial NDP.

THE 1969 ELECTION

The late 1960s presented an exceptional opportunity for a surge in support for the NDP. A number of coincidental developments, the foremost being the election of Ed Schreyer to the NDP leadership, facilitated the party's jump from third party to government party. Four by-elections were held in February 1969. The Conservatives won three and the NDP one. The results consolidated the position of the government, but they also elevated the NDP to twelve seats, just one less than the Liberals. Liberal leader Gildas Molgat resigned immediately.

R.B. Bend's subsequent election as the new Liberal leader had a profound effect on the fortunes of the NDP. Bend, a former government minister under Campbell, represented the more rural and status-quo elements in his party. In effect the Liberals chose a fiscal conservative to fight another fiscal conservative (Weir). The shift of both the older parties to the right permitted the NDP to make an effective appeal to Liberal and Conservative supporters who considered themselves progressives and reformers. Between Bend's election in May and the NDP leadership convention in June three thousand members, according to the NDP, joined the party.[47] These gains for the NDP reflected interest in the Schreyer–Green leadership contest, the unpopularity of the federal Liberals in the rural areas, and a reaction to Bend's election as Liberal leader. A former president of the Manitoba Young Liberals summed up the feelings of many disenchanted Liberals by joining the NDP on the grounds that the NDP best represented small-l liberalism.[48] After the 1969 election a survey of one hundred Liberals showed that thirty deserted their party, "and of these, twenty-six voted NDP—the consensus being 'that party was doing what the Liberal party ought to be doing'."[49]

The NDP's platform contained planks that were attractive to the more progressive wings of the opposition parties. They included lower medicare premiums, public auto insurance, an ombudsman, lowering of the voting age, raising of the minimum wage, and a review of a controversial Conservative decision respecting northern hydro-electric development. This policy orientation, in combination with Schreyer's leadership, the caucus's performance in the legislature, and perceptible ideological shifts in the other parties, made the NDP a formidable force. "You have the NDP with a program. Call it what you want—social democratic, democratic socialist, or small 'l' liberal," commented David Orlikow. "But it has that kind of program [and] it has a pretty competent group of members from the legislature...and you have this leader who personifies in himself, sort of, Manitoba."[50]

One of the major assumptions underlying the shift of both the Liberals and Conservatives to the right in the late 1960s was that the NDP was a permanent minor party in Manitoba politics. One reason that the CCF–NDP had been a minority force in the past, however, was that one of the older parties usually covered enough of the centre of the ideological spectrum to successfully compete with the CCF–NDP for a centre, swing, bloc of voters. In the late 1960s both older parties vacated the centre of the ideological spectrum almost simultaneously. The NDP, in contrast, moved closer to the centre of the spectrum by electing a popular leader who was on the right wing of the party. Ed Schreyer predicted and wanted a more "pragmatic party" and one with more "moderate centrists." In a 1965 survey of seventy journalists, intellectuals, and politicians, he was the only respondent who viewed the possibility of a national Liberal-NDP rapprochement with equanimity.[51]

A host of factors contributed to the NDP's success. A redistribution of seats, based more closely on the principle of one man one vote, rather than on the old seven-to-four urban–rural ratio, gave the NDP an advantage in many of the new urban ridings. Winnipeg's representation in the legislature expanded from twenty to twenty-seven seats with a corresponding shrinkage in rural seats. In addition to the extensive exposure of the leadership convention, the NDP received more press coverage than it ever had in the past. The party also had more money than ever before for campaigning. In calling the election when it did the Weir government killed many bills, including one that lowered transit fares for pensioners.

This provoked charges of insensitivity. The NDP's focus on high medicare premiums was inadvertently highlighted by the arrival of the government's medicare bills at voters' homes within days of the vote. The Conservatives, furthermore, ran a low-key campaign, misjudging the mood of a volatile electorate.

Leadership was the most easily distinguishable factor in the NDP's favour. This was partly because of the media's preference for reporting on personalities. Walter Weir conducted a campaign of relative aloofness. Press photographs of him conveyed an image of an obese and distant politician, always smoking a big cigar. The *Free Press* carried such a front page photograph two days before the vote. R.B. Bend appeared as a figure from the past—the discredited, stingy, Campbell years. Bend and his party were endorsed in a successive number of *Free Press* editorials and only his photograph appeared on that paper's front page the day before the election. In brief, both Weir and Bend appeared as sons of liberal–conservative, dominant, Anglo-Saxon, rural southwestern Manitoba.

Ed Schreyer, in contrast, was presented by the NDP as a dynamic young leader with an appeal to people of diverse backgrounds. His photograph appeared in almost every piece of party literature. Although he was born in rural Manitoba, unlike most rural politicians he also conveyed an urban image, having been a university teacher in Winnipeg. He could also communicate in four languages, three more than his opponents. He attracted personal support among large numbers in the French and Indian communities, historically unsympathetic to the NDP. He was the only party leader to endorse the federal government's bilingualism and biculturalism policies. Schreyer's style and language were both simple and sophisticated, employed in varying doses, as required, for any particular setting or audience. His Catholicism was not a handicap but an advantage. It strengthened the NDP's position in traditionally unsympathetic Catholic areas yet did not weaken existing or potential support for the party in Protestant areas. Early in 1969, before Schreyer's return, a senior NDP organizer considered that only twenty-three of the province's fifty-seven seats were "winnable."[52] With Schreyer as leader the NDP had a reasonable chance in almost every constituency outside the southwest.

The funding of the campaign revealed differences between the NDP and the other parties. The two older parties appeared to rely on a small number of large contributions. Under the Manitoba Election Act the central campaign committee of each party filed a declaration listing its income and expenditures within a legal ceiling of $25,000. None of the parties stayed within that ceiling, but they filed, nevertheless, declarations covering sums up to that amount. The NDP attracted a relatively large number of small contributions. Its declaration claimed $21,400 in expenditures and $18,900 in contributions. This included $1600 in personal contributions, $2900 in membership and affiliate contributions, $6400 from trade unions, $4000 from constituency associations, and $4000 from members who remembered the party in their wills.[53] In fact, the NDP provincial office appeared to have spent $45,321 and raised $30,761. The NDP's statutory declaration underrepresented the full extent of trade union contributions.[54] These union contributions came from a large number of union locals rather than from one or two sources. Most of the party's expenditures were on advertising, travel, and the posting of deposits for weaker riding associations.

The Liberals and Conservatives, in contrast, raised and spent their money differently. The Liberal party claimed revenues and expenditures of $24,600.[55] It listed over 125 separate contributors to make up that amount. One contributor, however, the Winnipeg law firm of Walsh, Micay accounted for $21,600 of the total from an unspecified "trust" fund. The Conservatives declared receipts and expenditures of $20,100.[56] This figure represented donations by three Winnipeg professionals: lawyers Duncan Jessiman, Q.C. ($10,000), W.L. Palk ($5700), and chartered acountant Donald Gordon ($4400). For $2000 the Conservatives hired an advertising firm for one month to provide public relations advice, arrange news conferences, write press releases, attend strategy meetings, act as Weir's press secretary, and provide "general consulting services to the Party on matters pertaining to election."[57] The Conservatives also hired F. Clifton White and Associates of New York, a firm claiming to specialize in "political counseling." White was retained for $500 per meeting plus expenses and provided his services from early May, before the election was called, throughout the campaign on a weekly basis. The professional assistance the Conservatives purchased, as well as the editorial support given them by the *Winnipeg Tribune,* were of little avail. It was clear that there was no relationship between money spent (the Conservatives undoubtedly ranked highest with the Liberals second), or press support, and the election results.

The election brought the NDP to the verge of a majority position, winning twenty-eight seats (see Table 9). NDP gains in the popular vote came from all other parties but particularly from the Liberals. This led to a toppling of many Conservatives. The NDP picked up ten seats from the Conservatives, two from the Liberals, and six of the new ridings produced by redistribution. Parts of every constituency won by the NDP had been in the CCF–NDP column at either the federal or provincial level sometime in the past. The only part of the province where the NDP was denied a seat was the traditional, rural, Ontario-origin southwest. Virtually every one of those seats returned a Conservative MLA. One analysis of the election showed that although the NDP received an impressive 43 per cent of the vote in the fourteen northern and eastern ridings, it could only garner 19 per cent of the the vote in the southwestern constituencies.[58] One week after the election the Liberal party's demise continued: its St. Boniface MLA, Larry Desjardins, defected and, proclaiming himself a Liberal Democrat, announced that he would join the NDP caucus and give it a bare majority. Schreyer, Desjardins told the public, represented the kind of liberalism he had always supported.

TABLE 9

Manitoba provincial election, 1969

Party	Seats	Percentage of popular vote
Conservative	22	35
Liberal	5	24
NDP	28	39
Other	2	2
Total	57	100

In the 1969 election, a small plurality of votes gave the NDP a near majority of the seats. The Conservatives received only 4 per cent less in the popular vote and the Liberals,despite their drop in terms of seats, still held 24 per cent of the vote. The level of NDP support in 1969 was only 4 per cent higher than the CCF's 1945 showing, but in that election a rural-oriented electoral map yielded the party only ten seats or roughly one-third of its 1969 total.

An NDP victory was increasingly possible with the passing of time. Long-term trends towards ethnic assimilation and integration, urbanization, and policy convergence among the parties worked to the advantage of the NDP. The party's early British working-class character was transformed over time. By 1969 the CCF-NDP had become a party whose leadership and membership, like Manitoba's population, was increasingly indigenous and of non-British extraction. In its early years the party was seen by many, incorrectly, as a foreign and revolutionary force. It did not disappear or wither, as other left-wing parties had, and it successfully moved toward the centre of the political spectrum. The NDP program and leadership had become a moderate and respectable alternative to the older parties.

The seventies: the party in power

7

It is possible to view the Manitoba NDP in the 1970s from two perspectives. One is to examine the party's bases of support: who elected it and what that meant. From this perspective, the NDP's election in 1969 and re-election in 1973 represented a victory of the traditional outsiders over the traditional insiders in Manitoba politics. It was the victory of the poorer parts of the province—the marginal farming areas and the working class areas of Winnipeg—over the well-to-do farming areas of the southwest and the wealthier suburban areas of Winnipeg. It was also a victory produced by a successful voting coalition of the ethnic minorities, the traditional outsiders in Manitoba society and politics: Ukrainians and Poles, Indians and Metis, and large numbers of French, Germans, and Scandinavians. It was a victory, too, for the party supported by organized labour over the parties supported by the business community. When the NDP won two by-elections in 1971 in areas never before represented by the party, it gained a majority in the legislature and proved that its election in 1969 had not been a fluke.

The NDP's success also stood for the ascendancy of one political philosophy or outlook over another. Thus, another way of looking at the NDP's role in Manitoba in the 1970s is from an ideological perspective. Did the election of a social democratic party lead to a more equal distribution of wealth and power in society? Did the NDP government deliver on the promise held out by its philosophy? The NDP's legislative achievements during its two terms—from 1969 to 1977—were remarkable for their similarity to programs in other provinces. Little was done that had not been done elsewhere in Canada, and little at all of a controversial nature was done after the first few years in office. Over the years, the NDP had mellowed ideologically, and this process continued once it gained office. Its vision of social democracy represented little more than some minor social, economic, and tax reforms. Although they were consistent with many specific legislative proposals made by the CCF–NDP between the 1940s and 1960s, they were far from the radicalism and socialism ascribed to the NDP by its opponents and sometimes proclaimed by NDPers at party meetings.

From a national perspective, the Manitoba NDP's success seemed related to NDP success in two other Western provinces. It was tempting for observers in other parts of Canada to see the NDP in the early 1970s as a strong Western, regional, party forming three of the four provincial governments west of Ontario. But although the electoral efforts of the national and provincial NDP sections were closely coordinated in terms of organizational resources, the success and failure of various party sections in and outside of the West had little to do with each other. Within Manitoba the national NDP's fortunes were similarly unaffected by the provincial NDP's success. In the three federal elections between 1968 and 1974 the national NDP's vote in Manitoba barely fluctuated (from 25 per cent to 26.5 and back to 25), and it lost one of the three seats it held before the Manitoba NDP came to power. Conversely, after the provincial NDP's defeat in 1977, the national party gained a record five seats and 32 per cent of the provincial vote in the 1979 federal election.

Surveys of the electorate in the early 1970s identified the social bases of party support. They showed that the NDP did better among blue-collar and white-collar workers than either the Conservatives or Liberals.[1] In contrast, more than ten times as many farmers supported the Conservatives as the NDP. As for those who described themselves as "working class," almost equal numbers supported the Conservatives and the NDP. Similarly, the two leading parties had almost equal support among those calling themselves "middle class." But while the Conservatives were favoured by a majority of Protestants, the NDP was favoured by a majority of Catholics. And while a majority of those of Anglo-Saxon or British ethnicity supported the Conservatives, a near majority of non-British voters supported the NDP. The NDP was also preferred by a majority of those under thirty-five years of age while a majority of those between thirty-six and fifty-five preferred the Conservatives. Although the NDP government was strongly identified with working-class support, its composition, in occupational terms, did not fully reflect this. A majority of its MLAs were professionals, less than a fifth were manual workers, and a tenth were farmers.[2]

The make-up of Manitoba's first NDP administration revealed something of the NDP's transformation and the province's political evolution. For the first time Anglo-Saxons were in a minority in the cabinet; and, for a period in the 1970s, none of the five provincial party leaders was from the historically dominant ethnic group. When the NDP went down to defeat in 1977, its cabinet contained six Anglo-Saxons, four Ukrainians, two Franco-Manitobans, two Jews, one Dutchman, one German, and one Metis. At one point there were four Unitarians, and, throughout the NDP's tenure, there were a large number of Catholics in the cabinet. The increasing acceptance of minority ethnic and religious representation in politics was partly a result of continuing assimilation in a province where the major migrations had taken place more than a half-century earlier. To be sure, candidates' ethnic backgrounds sometimes affected electoral success, but political deference on the part of the minorities as exhibited in earlier years was no longer necessary or expected. Anglo-Saxon Protestants were a continuing minority of Manitoba's population.

A primary source of the NDP's strength — a source that was not present before 1969 — was the popular image of its leader. Ed Schreyer in a 1973 survey was preferred as premier by Conservative and Liberal supporters to their own respective leaders.[3] Schreyer was so magnetic that over a fifth of those surveyed who did dislike him gave as their reason that he was "in the wrong party,"[4] essentially a comment on the NDP rather than its leader. Without Schreyer it was doubtful that the NDP would have been elected in 1969 or re-elected in 1973.

THE 1973 AND 1977 ELECTIONS

The NDP's rise and fall in the 1970s could also be related to the ideological shifts within the Liberal Party and the impact of these shifts on the traditional bases of party support in Manitoba. In the 1969 and 1973 elections the Liberal Party moved to the right and lost many of its urban voters, left-wing supporters, and Catholics to the NDP. The Liberals replaced a Franco-Manitoban Catholic leader with a Protestant who did not support the federal Liberal bilingualism and biculturalism policies. The NDP, in contrast, replaced a Protestant leader with a Catholic who was sympathetic to state aid to private schools. In the 1977 election, the Liberals shifted again, moving to the left, and lost many of their remaining rural voters and right-wingers to the Conservatives. One result of the Liberal decline (they sank from 36 to 12 per cent of the vote between 1962 and 1977) was that Manitoba moved closer to a two-party system, with one party on the left (the NDP) and one party on the right (the Conservatives). It was a development that many in the CCF-NDP had predicted, and hoped for, for years (see Table 10).

There were also changes within the Conservative Party in the 1970s but they had a lesser effect on the outcome of the elections. Walter Weir, opposition leader between 1969 and 1971, wildly and erroneously portrayed the government as being subject to "Marxist-Communist infiltration."[5] He was out of touch with the thinking of the government and the electorate. His successor, Sidney Spivak—a progressive-minded Jewish lawyer— was ethnically and ideologically out of tune with his caucus. Although the Conservatives gained seats and votes under Spivak in the 1973 election, he was replaced in 1975 by Sterling Lyon, a former minister in the Roblin government. The Conservatives moved enthusiastically to the right and were determined, as Lyon put it, to "throw out the socialists who follow alien doctrines laid down in Europe in the 19th century."[6] Although the Conservatives were decidedly anti-socialist in image, their 1977 platform was described in the *Winnipeg Free Press* as "a watered-down version of the government platform."[7] There seemed to be little that the NDP had done in its eight years in office that the Conservatives could not live with.

TABLE 10

Manitoba provincial elections, 1973 and 1977

| | | 1973 | | 1977 |
Party	Seats	Percentage of popular vote (%)	Seats	Percentage of popular vote (%)
Conservative	21	37	33	49
Liberal	5	19	1	12
NDP	31	42	23	39
Other	–	2	–	–
Total	57	100	57	100

The character and interests of the NDP government were displayed in both the 1973 and 1977 campaigns. The NDP slates included MFU members, clergymen, unionists, lawyers, teachers, and people involved in providing social services. In 1977, six women ran for the party, and for the first time a woman became party president. The candidates reflected Manitoba's ethnic mix, and, collectively, they had more university degrees than former party slates.

In both elections the government ran mainly on its record. Some of its planks in 1973 included government entry into the fire and general insurance fields, a dental care program for children, an increase in mining royalties, subsidization of prescription drug costs, and increased support for urban transit. Party literature and candidates also referred repeatedly to Churchill Forest Industries, an economic debacle of the Conservatives in the 1960s into which $137 million in public funds had been sunk by 1973. Some of the 1973 promises, such as forming a provincial bank and providing an assisted home ownership program for those with incomes below $10,000, were not kept, but few noticed or complained. In the 1977 campaign there were fewer promises and those that were made represented little more than administrative adjustments to programs in place. In Schreyer's mind the NDP had gone, perhaps, too quickly. Addressing the 1977 party convention, "he said his government will run basically on its eight year record which he said showed that, rather than doing too little, the NDP administration ran the risk of having attempted too much too fast."[8]

The government's campaign style was reminiscent of the style employed by the older parties when they were in power. The premier and his cabinet, like so many Manitoba premiers and cabinets before, paraded through rural constituencies in 1973 promising bridges, roads, and sewer construction.[9] Opposition parties' promises were financially evaluated by the NDP's finance minister who reported that the proposals were "pie in the sky" and far too expensive.[10] The CCF-NDP had faced identical charges respecting its program proposals by former Liberal and Conservative finance ministers in every election campaign in the 1950s and 1960s. In 1977, as in the 1950s with the Campbell Liberal-Progressives and in the late 1960s with the Weir Conservatives, the government's sentiment for restraint overshadowed any sentiment for change.

The essence of both the NDP campaigns was Schreyer. In 1973 a slick half-hour film featuring him and his family was broadcast on all provincial television stations. In 1977 Schreyer's image was stressed in the party's campaign slogan, "Leadership you can trust." "There were times on the campaign trail" noted a journalist, "when the premier was greeted almost as a figure of royalty."[11] But a difference between 1973 and 1977 was that Schreyer was falling somewhat out of touch with the electorate. "If the Tories think that they will do even as well in this election as they did in 1973," he brashly asserted, "then they have absolutely no sense of the public mood."[12]

An area of the province where the NDP developed a strong electoral base was the north. During the NDP government's tenure northern

Manitoba entered a new stage of economic, social, and political maturity. These two developments were related: the NDP devoted more energy and attention to the area than any government or party in the past. The north responded by electing NDPers in all five northern ridings in 1973. Northern Manitoba's growing mining centres and its established Indian and Metis settlements became an important, identifiable, arena for electoral competition, and both the NDP and the Conservatives looked to the north as the major potential swing area in voting. Politically it represented a new, albeit still minor, component in the traditional struggle between the forces represented by rural Manitoba (dominated by the Conservative southwest) and the city (dominated by the NDP's hold on the north, east, and centre of Winnipeg). Unlike these regions, with their more fixed voting patterns, the north historically supported the winning party. It shifted from the Liberal-Progressives to the Conservatives to the NDP between the 1930s and the 1970s just as power shifted in the legislature from and to those parties. In a break with this tradition, and as a sign of the NDP's successful courtship of the north, four of the five northern seats remained in the NDP column in the 1977 election.

Support for the NDP among northern unionists was not surprising. It was similar to NDP support in northern British Columbia and northern Ontario. Certainly as significant as the union vote, however, was the northern Indian and Metis vote. In three northern ridings (Rupertsland, The Pas, and Churchill) the Indian and Metis vote was essential for victory, and in four north central ridings (Swan River, St. George, Roblin, and Ste. Rose), it could swing close contests. All three parties appreciated the importance of attracting Indian and Metis candidates. In the 1970s the NDP instituted many northern programs and once the Indians and Metis identified the NDP as the party most sympathetic to them they tended to vote for it en masse.

The NDP's major opponent outside the electoral arena was, as in the past, the *Winnipeg Free Press*. It provided active, continuous criticism and became an agent in the promotion of a coalition of Conservative and Liberal voters to oust the NDP. The *Free Press* argued its case ideologically (free enterprise versus socialism), mathematically (the NDP was in power by virtue of a plurality, not a majority of voters), and politically (by selective news reporting). The government, in particular the premier, in turn attacked the *Free Press* at public and party meetings. The feud between the *Free Press* and the parties of the left, the ILP, CCF, NDP, was a continuous one, begun over fifty years earlier.

PARTY POLITICS

The election success of 1969 transformed the NDP. A major feature of the party's transformation was its sheer growth in size and operations. In 1962, the NDP had been a dormant force in about half the provincial constituencies; a decade later it was a relatively booming operation with organized party structures in all ridings. In 1964 it had dispensed with its annual convention due to membership and organizational weakness; by 1976 it staged a convention of 721 delegates, or more delegates than there were CCF members in 1955. Growth was meteoric in areas where the party had been traditionally weakest. In the southwest, where deposits had always been lost, the party became sufficiently strong to form a regional council with its own newsletter, to hire a full-time organizer for the area, and to search out and appoint zone captains in places where the party had never been able to stock an executive committee.[13] The party also recruited a broader range of candidates including the brother of a former Conservative minister of agriculture. Similarly, in the vast and far-flung Churchill riding, where prohibitive campaign costs had been an impediment to nominating a candidate in the past, the party was sufficiently resourceful by 1973 to conduct a four-stage travelling nomination convention, counting and carrying ballots from place to place.

Party operations in terms of resources, budget, and activities took on the air of a medium-sized business. Staff and physical facilities, as well as membership, expanded. In 1971 the party began using computers to compile membership remittance reports that provided financial data on members' contributions and fees. In 1974 the party retained the services of a management consulting firm as well as a company specializing in data processing. It undertook a systems analysis of its office procedures and began computer programming its accounts. In 1975, a midterm off election year, when party activities are usually at an ebb, it employed a full-time staff of about a dozen, including six organizers. The party's annual budget reached approximately $100,000 in 1970 and grew to over $400,000 by 1976.[14] All this was in striking contrast to the days when the provincial secretary (sometimes without remuneration) ran the party's day-to-day operations on a part-time basis.

As premier and leader, Ed Schreyer's influence in party affairs was supreme. In 1972 a reporter at the annual convention observed that the party had "delivered itself into the hands of one man."[15] An example of Schreyer's influence in ongoing party activities was his directive in 1971 (for unspecified reasons) to the party secretary that constituency associations be discouraged "from holding a nominating convention until late 1972, particularly in those ridings that are presently represented by a New Democratic party M.L.A."[16] On one occasion the Saskatchewan NDP asked for (and was denied) Schreyer's permission to allow the Manitoba party secretary to work in that province for a short by-election period.[17] Schreyer's political astuteness led him to exert his weight sparingly but effectively, attaining broad-based support and confidence within the party and among the voting public. "In his four years as head of the party," noted a journalist in 1973, "he threw his full political weight behind only one issue: the volatile one of state aid to private and parochial schools."[18] Schreyer lost that fight. But what was significant in the intraparty debate was not that his views were repudiated but that his side had come very close to winning its point in a party that for decades had refused even to consider the state aid proposal. Schreyer was sufficiently powerful that his threatened resignation convinced a largely antipathetic convention, cabinet and caucus to permit a free vote on the issue in the legislature. Similarly, Schreyer's power was again exhibited in 1976 when the party in convention backed him in his support for the federal Liberals' price and wage controls policy—a policy strongly attacked by the federal NDP.

The government took note of party policies passed in convention, but it was clear to all that the cabinet and caucus, not the party, took responsibility for making government policy. Schreyer's attitude to his role of party leader was one of stewardship rather than party agent. Party policies were merely "guidelines."[19] His paramount responsibility, he felt, was that of premier rather than party leader. Most convention resolutions prudently "urged" or "recommended." The realization that party policies now had their greatest likelihood of becoming government policies elicited better researched and more precise proposals than in the past. Some of them were formulated by party members working in the government bureaucracy. The primary role of cabinet ministers in convention, however, was to dampen and dilute resolutions critical of their own department's activities.

Although deference to the government was the major feature of party–government relations, occasional criticism of the government was heard. In 1970, for example, the party's southwest regional council bluntly told the minister of agriculture that "this government's policies in dealing with the farm crisis have not diverged significantly from those of Walter Weir's government."[20] A former party vice-president protested in 1974 that many party policies, particularly in the area of natural resource development, were being ignored by the government.[21] A year later a number of provincial council members complained that the government's image was defensive and apologetic and that it was communicating poorly with the public. The party's MLAs were also mildly reprimanded for not attending the council's meetings.[22] Despite these criticisms, the party enthusiastically supported its government. The party's official organ, the *Manitoba New Democrat*, was for a while edited by a ministerial assistant using a pseudonym. It published a regular column of government press releases.

Party membership grew rapidly although not uniformly in the 1970s. Between 1970 and 1973 it tripled to a record high of 17,205 with a slight majority of members resident in non-Winnipeg ridings.[23] Membership grew in all parts of the province but most profoundly in the traditionally antagonistic southwest. Between the 1969 and 1973 elections, while membership grew in the north Winnipeg NDP ridings by 108 per cent (from 654 to 1360) it grew a phenomenal 687 per cent (from 252 to 1958) in the southwest where the NDP held only Brandon's working-class seat. Rising and falling membership levels, however, were dependent on nomination contests, periods of intensive electioneering, and professionally organized drives. They are therefore poor guides to genuine popular support. Examples of the questionable relevance of membership numbers are not hard to find. In Rupertsland riding, where the party had only nine members yet elected an MLA in 1969, membership by 1973 rose to an extraordinary 48 per cent of the NDP's popular vote. In Winnipeg's NDP Point Douglas riding, in contrast, memberships represented only 4 per cent of the party's vote. After the 1973 pre-election membership drive (in a single two-week period membership rose by 2,200)[24] the party's size declined dramatically, although not to pre-1970s levels. In 1975-76 it hovered between 8,000 and 10,000 and reached 16,000 during the 1977 election campaign.

More significant than the membership's size was its transformation. A study of the membership showed that less than 5 per cent of the NDP's 1973 members had been CCF members. A remarkable 70 per cent of the 1973 members had not been in the party as recently as 1970 and over half of them had joined since 1972. Although the NDP executive preferred that party organizers devote most of their efforts to increasing membership,[25] such activity did not necessarily bring financial benefits: "With 10,000 members we can raise more money than we did with 17,000," noted the party secretary.[26] There was some reason to believe that the larger NDP also meant a slightly different party. The ephemeral character of the membership in the 1970s led one party organizer to the following analysis: "These figures suggest that the NDP is not broadening its base, but shifting in character, conceivably from the left to the right. The party base has been wholly transformed not only from what it was in 1969 but also from what it was in 1971. No definite evidence of the ideological bias of those leaving the party is available yet it is the feeling of some observers within the party that as senior members exit quietly via the left door, the NDP is welcoming large numbers of novice members through the right door."[27] Despite the party's size, it was not particularly vibrant. "The Party is in the doldrums," wrote the provincial secretary to the premier. "The membership is largely inactive and unenthusiastic."[28]

The party was particularly listless and depressed at the municipal level where, in the 1930s as the ILP-CCF, it had had more success than at the provincial level. For decades the CCF-NDP municipal wing had called for the amalgamation of greater Winnipeg and for campaigns based on party platforms rather than personality. Paradoxically, the provincial NDP government's amalgamation bill (creating what became known as "unicity") undercut the electoral prospects of its Winnipeg municipal wing. Although the legislation had been designed to foster party politics by the creation of a parliamentary size fifty-member council, with a mayor elected by that council, the Schreyer government brought in a late amendment providing for the mayor's election at large. This served the interests of Winnipeg's perennial mayor, Stephen Juba, a member of no party and a friend of Schreyer's who was now assured re-election. It also aided the Independent Citizens Election Committee (ICEC), the 1970s version of a half-century-long string of informal Liberal–Conservative municipal coalitions. The ICEC's political line—"put public interest ahead of political party loyalties"[29]—was a contrast to the municipal NDP's line—"There is no way in which council can be made to work for the people *without* the *unity* and organization of a *party*,"[30] a line that rang hollow in light of the government's reversal on the legislation providing for a mayor selected by the council.

Opposition to amalgamation came from Winnipeg's suburbs and from a former suburban mayor in the cabinet (who, ironically, later became responsible for the legislation as urban affairs minister). When the government's "unicity" bill was attacked at a few suburban town hall meetings the party quickly responded in aid of its government by urging its Winnipeg members to attend future public meetings "to act as a countervailing force to opponents of the proposal and of our government" because "it is now apparent that the opposition parties are using this public forum as a springboard to attack and discredit our New Democratic Government."[31] But this support was not reciprocated by the government. It remained aloof, doing virtually nothing to aid the municipal wing's slate of candidates. Schreyer was opposed to a strong municipal NDP presence and preferred a loose coalition of reform-minded municipal groups of which the NDP would only be one component. "The party should not insist in over-codifying the party's involvement in municipal politics but should allow for a strengthening of municipal involvement through working alliances with other municipal groups,"[32] he told the provincial executive two months before the municipal wing codified its platform and ignored political alliances at a policy convention. That platform's main plank was an assault on private real estate, property development, and construction interests, something the government was not interested in pursuing.

Controversy surrounding the new legislation brought a record voter turnout in unicity's first elections in 1971. The NDP was trounced, returning only seven inner city members to the ICEC's suburban-anchored majority of thirty-seven seats. The rout was not surprising and it had its Brandon parallel, where NDP candidates polled a meagre 21 per cent of the votes in their wards. Schreyer and his cabinet's detachment from the campaign effort logically led him to dismiss the abysmal results "as no reflection of the status of the party on a provincial level."[33] The Winnipeg municipal wing in 1974, labouring under the same disadvantages, was deflated and fielded only twenty-two candidates. By 1977 the government gave up any pretence of fostering parliamentary-style politics at the municipal level and shrank the council by almost half.

More reciprocal than the links between the provincial government and the municipal NDP were the links with other provincial NDPs. Although political developments in different provinces seemed to go forward independently of each other, the various NDP provincial sections saw themselves as component parts of a broader national movement and operated accordingly; so much so that no one thought it peculiar that of the Manitoba party's five provincial secretaries between the 1969 and 1977 elections two were from Saskatchewan, and one each from Ontario, Alberta, and British Columbia. Membership and financial arrangements between provincial sections and the federal party were organic and constitutional. Often, one level of the party owed money to another level. In 1974, for example, the politically successful Manitoba party owed the relatively unsuccessful federal party $45,000.[34] The most important feature of interprovincial assistance came at election time. In the 1973 Manitoba election campaign, for example, the Saskatchewan party contributed fourteen organizers, Ontario twelve, British Columbia eleven, and Alberta two.[35] Manitoba, in turn, sent some of its organizers to campaigns in those and other provinces.

Not as significant as the NDP's interprovincial links, but notable nonetheless, was the party's identification with the international social democratic movement and the Democratic Party in the United States. Through the national party the NDP was a continuing affiliate of the Socialist International, a loose voluntary association re-established after the Second World War under the auspices of the British Labour Party. On one occasion the Swedish prime minister was invited to address a party rally in Winnipeg[36] and on two other occasions, in 1970 and 1974, Schreyer invited West Germany's Willy Brandt for the same purpose.[37] More successful was the invitation extended south of the border, to a North Dakota member of the US Democratic National Committee, in 1972. He was sufficiently sympathetic to the Manitoba NDP's activities that he offered to provide advice on fund-raising procedures.[38] Schreyer repeatedly identified himself with Franklin Roosevelt's New Deal philosophy of forty years earlier. In budget speeches and elsewhere Schreyer quoted Roosevelt more often than anyone else. The only American political organization that saw merit in sending an invitation for a Manitoba NDP spokesman was the tiny Socialist Party of Wisconsin.[39]

As in the past the union movement was an important, although not dominant, part of the party. The number of affiliates grew from 7,700 in 1969, to 9,300 in 1972, to 11,800 in 1978.[40] Affiliated locals grew in this period from 36 to 50 with three of them, for the first time, coming from outside Winnipeg. The overwhelming majority of affiliates came from the Steelworkers, the Retail, Wholesale and Department Store Workers Union, the Canadian Food and Allied Workers, the International Association of Machinists, the Canadian Brotherhood of Railway, Transport and General Workers, and the Railway, Airline and Steamship Clerks unions. Although the unions were entitled to approximately 300 delegates at the 1977 party convention, they sent only 98, while constituencies sponsored over 500 delegates.[41] A figure at the junction of party and labour affairs in Manitoba was Steelworkers official H.L. Stevens who, in the 1970s, was MFL president, a leading party fund raiser, a member of the NDP national council, and the chairman of the Manitoba party's trade union liaison committee. Another leading figure who symbolized interlocked NDP–CLC interests was Art Coulter, the NDP's leader in the 1971 unicity elections, the MFL's executive secretary, and chairman of the party's legislative liaison committee in 1974. In both the 1973 and 1977 elections the larger union organizations such as the CLC, MFL, Steelworkers, CFAW, and CUPE contributed organizers, support staff, and money. Small contributions came from many locals but the lion's share of union support, as in the 1960s, came from the Steelworkers.[42] The party, in turn, cultivated its support among unions by hiring a labour liaison organizer, but even his salary was paid by the union movement.[43]

Income to fund the party's operations came from a number of sources, many of them non-traditional. As in the past the party solicited and received large numbers of small donations, but grassroots fund raising among rank and file members did not add up to much. The party could certainly have operated in the 1970s without grassroots funds. Nor did membership and union affiliate fees count for much: the party's 1974 finance committee estimated that these two sources of funds represented only $13,000 in a revenue budget of $248,500.[44] A more significant traditional source of funds came from party MLAs who paid a 10 per cent levy on their legislative indemnities and were required to raise other contributions.[45] Another traditional fund-raising technique, but one that was discarded in 1975, was setting financial quotas to be met by each constituency association.

Most party funds came from non-member sources: from well-to-do sympathizers, from small and big businesses, and from lotteries. Contributions in the $25-$100 range from small businesses and professionals grew increasingly common, especially during election campaigns. (Even Walsh Micay, an established Winnipeg Liberal law firm and trustee of that party's election fund, contributed $200 to Schreyer's re-election in 1973.)[46] Another form of income was the sale of advertisements in the *Manitoba New Democrat*. Alongside the large number of small advertisements appeared more expensive ones from the province's wineries, breweries, distilleries, construction corporations, major hotels, and other large concerns such as the Xerox Corporation and Winnipeg-based Investors Syndicate. These were not the kinds of businesses that advertised in the party's newspaper when it was in opposition. Under Schreyer's urging the party adopted a policy in 1970 of refusing donations of more than $500 from any single corporate contributor, and the party's table officers reaffirmed that policy in 1973.[47] In practice, however, larger corporate contributions were solicited and secured. Information filed by the party with the province's Chief Electoral Officer showed that donations over $500 were received from construction firms, Winnipeg's largest taxi business, large trucking companies, a number of professional firms, one of the province's largest mining companies (Sherritt Gordon), and the liquor-oriented hotel industry.[48] Less than twenty years earlier the CCF had tried to make political capital of the fact that it was the only Manitoba political party (excluding the Communists) that received no funds from liquor and

corporate concerns. The attitude of the NDP to corporations and their attitude to the party obviously changed once the NDP formed the government.
These developments were consistent with the party's shifts in character over time. Winnipeg, the location of Canada's most important general
strike, was the home of a governing social democratic party and a labour
movement with direct ties to that strike. But in the 1970s it was a party
and a labour movement with a different image. (One NDP affiliated union
local, for example, only narrowly defeated a bid to disaffiliate in protest of
the federal NDP's anti-War Measures Act stance.)[49] The NDP in the 1970s
styled itself as pragmatic, non-ideological, and politically respectable. It
also sported something of the conservative cautiousness that imbued all
of Manitoba's governing parties. The Manitoba party and its leader were
less radical in their philosophy and rhetoric than other NDP provincial
parties and leaders, although all the NDP provincial parties and leaders
stood for much the same things. One minimal principle that all the parties
adhered to, and one that led to the forced defection of Rupertsland NDP
MLA Jean Allard, was that membership in the NDP was politically
exclusive. When Allard, a former Liberal candidate who like so many
other Liberals had been brought into the party by Schreyer, continued to
attend Liberal meetings and indicated his possible candidature as a federal
Liberal, he was driven out of the NDP.

More helpful in explaining something of the party's ideological colour-
ation is tracing the role of its left wing (which Allard foolishly and erroneously attacked as having taken over the NDP when he resigned from the
caucus). The leading leftist in the legislature was Cy Gonick, a university
professor who had signed the 1969 nationalist, socialist, Waffle manifesto.
In contrast, all of Manitoba's cabinet ministers attending the 1969 national
NDP convention in Winnipeg voted against the manifesto. The two left
groupings in the Manitoba party, both composed mainly of academics and
students—the Waffle and the New Democratic Youth (NDY)—disappeared after their challenge to the government's direction was rebuffed
in convention. When the NDY dissolved itself in 1972 it put its opposition
to Schreyer's NDP this way:

The NDP's election platforms and legislative records in Manitoba and Saskatchewan
differ only in emphasis from those of the capitalist parties. The latter stress private
investment incentives, while the NDP preaches "social security" programs. These
two planks do not contradict each other. In fact, they are mutually supportive. Vari-
ations of both are found among the policies and practice of the NDP as well as the
capitalist parties. Premier Schreyer's appeals for harmony with private business, his
reluctance to confront even the drug industry profiteers, his inclusion of "ex"-Liberal

Larry Desjardins in his cabinet, his opposition to removal of abortion from the criminal code, his desire to aid private schools with public funds, and his support for Trudeau's use of the War Measures Act, are among examples of non-socialist NDP leadership in Manitoba.[50]

When Gonick declined renomination in 1973 he cited the government's refusal to promote greater worker control in crown corporations and private industries, its failure to bring about a major redistribution in incomes, and its failure to move toward public ownership of natural resource industries and urban land.[51] Gonick, the Waffle, and the NDY unrealistically expected the NDP to do more than social democratic governments are willing to do in Western industrialized states. When the NDY was resurrected in 1974 and once again in 1976, it featured all new faces with no sign of its past as a thorn in the party's side. It reverted to the role it played in the early 1960s and as the CCYM before that, as a faithful support group for the senior party.

GOVERNMENT POLITICS

Little in the NDP government's performance diverged from what non-NDP provincial governments did. The NDP operated in office much like its political opponents when they were in office. The NDP government, although it permanently etched its mark on the province through various legislative acts, certainly did not transform or radically alter the social and economic fabric of the province as both NDP partisans and opponents claimed that it would. For decades in opposition the CCF-NDP had argued for a redistribution of wealth and power from rich to poor, from the more privileged to the less so. In its platforms and campaigns it claimed to represent the underdog, the relatively deprived, in a struggle against vested interests. As a government the NDP had an opportunity to deliver on its ideology. A few of the government's programs were innovative and were not likely to be introduced by its opponents on the right, but there was no evidence that the NDP government had actually threatened the interests or welfare of the dominant classes in society. Rather, government activities were almost always within bounds that threatened no one. The NDP insisted repeatedly, just as had Conservative and Liberal governments in earlier years, that government programs were designed to serve the interests of all Manitobans and not those of particular segments of society. It was a view of society that claimed to transcend class divisions in pursuit of some ostensibly higher public, provincial, interest.

The NDP government's legislative program focused on piecemeal reform programs, particularly giving attention to income supplements, short-term public sector job creation, and social welfare. In its first fifteen months in office 193 bills were passed, an unprecedented performance by Manitoba's legislature. In the 1969 legislative session the government reduced medicare premiums by 88 per cent, established an ombudsman, expanded consumer protection laws, lowered the voting age, lowered transit fares for pensioners, established a northern task force, and provided new credit arrangements for farmers. In 1970 the government established a Human Rights Commission and a Law Reform Commission. It lowered the age of majority to eighteen, permitted both French and English to be used as languages of instruction in schools, created the office of a rentalsman, introduced public automobile insurance, and expanded public housing. In 1971 the government nationalized the scandal-ridden Churchill Forest Industries at The Pas, created a provincial employment program, established a property tax credit plan, and reorganized the City of Winnipeg and its suburbs. New legislative efforts that came later included the subsidization of prescription drug costs, a legal aid program, a new labour code, and reformed marital laws. Many projects were funded on a cost-shared basis with the federal government and parallelled programs in the other provinces. In the case of housing, for example, and in a pilot guaranteed income project that included 2500 families and which was quietly forgotten, Ottawa contributed 75 per cent of costs. By the summer of 1971 Schreyer felt that his government had discharged its 1969 election promises.[52]

The most celebrated and bitterly contested legislative act of the NDP government was public automobile insurance (known as Autopac). It was the only case where the government seriously challenged the interests of a large private industry. A massive lobbying effort was launched by the industry, thousands of insurance agents and sympathizers marched on the legislature, and the legislative gallery was packed for weeks as it never was before or after. The government carried through on its campaign pledge, but appeared frightened by the confrontation and launched no other campaigns against the private sector.

After the 1973 election, the government's imagination was spent; few new bills of substance were introduced in its second term. Most of the legislation was uncontentious and many bills represented no more than housekeeping. Government ministers read the Manitoba electorate as essentially content and cautious, suspicious of more reforms and government bureaucracy. They talked of "consolidation" and of not getting too far ahead of their constituents' thinking.

Although the Manitoba of the 1970s was certainly transformed from the Manitoba of earlier decades, the changes were not so much a result of NDP government as of broader, national, economic and social trends. Government programs in the various provinces were more notable for their similarities from one jurisdiction to the next than for their differences. Parties of different ideological stripes undertook many similar programs when in government. Such NDP initiatives in Manitoba as the Human Rights Commission and the property tax credit plan had counterparts in neighbouring Conservative Ontario. Policy differences among the parties have never offered a reliable key to explaining the traditional social bases of party support. Nor was it clear that government programs inspired by a specific ideological perspective, socialist or otherwise, necessarily achieved their philosophic objectives. For example, the NDP had greatly increased the supply of public housing, a fact ministers repeated often. But this had no appreciable dampening effect on rapidly rising rents and property values, a key part of its initial rationale.[53]

The proliferation of government programs and services during the 1970s was not unique to the NDP. Provincial governments under every party, and the Liberal federal government, were growing rapidly in size and influence. In Manitoba, as elsewhere, general economic growth produced more money for government programming: between 1961 and 1977 the GPP expanded from $1.9 billion to $8.6 billion.[54] The size of government, however, grew at a faster rate: between 1961 and 1977 the budget expanded from slightly over $100 million to over $1.5 billion. Government social programs proliferated relatively faster in the 1970s under the NDP than in the 1960s under the Conservatives, NDP supporters and opponents could argue, because of the historic tendency of social democrats to look more favourably upon a larger, active, public sector than do economic liberals. One could have as easily related this development, however, to the general inflationary conditions of the decade, conditions that boosted by leaps government revenues in all the provinces with little need for new, higher, rates of taxation. "In fact," concluded one study, "the NDP in Manitoba increased the size of the public sector to a lesser degree than had their Conservative predecessors."[55]

The government's tax changes were considered by Schreyer as his government's foremost achievement. The elimination of medicare premiums reflected the CCF-NDP's traditional concern with expanding public health and welfare. The concomitant progressive increases in personal and corporate income taxes reflected the CCF-NDP's desire for a more equitable form of taxation, based on ability to pay. This latter aim represented the basis of the NDP's property tax credit plan in 1972 and its cost of living tax credit plan in 1974. These plans aided the NDP in projecting the image that it was helping poorer people without challenging established interests. The government, for example, provided a $10,000 wage earner with a savings in taxes over his 1969, pre-NDP, tax bill; but it did not do this at the expense of those better off: a $50,000 wage earner saved in total taxes, too.[56]

Although the tax credit schemes brought an additional element of equity to the taxation system, they did not alter the relationship of rich to poor or the discrepancies in their relative conditions. Data on the tax credit schemes took up forty pages in the government's 1975 budget. No mention was made anywhere in the budget, however, of the parallel dramatic rise in the cost of milk. Milk prices (which were subject to government control and subsidy) were permitted to rise by 40 per cent in 1974 alone and had their greatest effect on the working poor.[57]

Despite the provincial economy's expansion and the steady, continuing, rise in transfer payments under the NDP government, the gap between rich and poor was not shrinking. The average incomes of Manitoba professionals, investors, and property owners grew at a slightly faster rate than the average incomes of farmers and employees. The increase in professional incomes alone between 1968 and 1976—from $17,600 to $29,600 i.e., $12,000—was greater than either the average farmer's income of $8,300 or the average employee's income of $10,100 in 1976.[58] Government transfer payments in Manitoba (and nationally) were at best keeping the relative disparities between rich and poor from growing but were certainly not reversing the pattern. The NDP government, like the federal and other provincial governments, could not reverse this pattern because it operated within self-imposed limits that did not challenge society's established property and reward structure.

On the hustings and in the legislature the government measured its performance in much the same terms that the other parties had used when they were in power. The economic indices pointed to by the NDP as measures of its performance in office were growth in the gross provincial product, growth in per-capita income, growth in industrial activity, new capital investment, and so on. To counter Conservative charges of mishandling the economy Schreyer proudly repeated, in almost every campaign speech he made in 1973, that Manitoba's GPP grew as much in four years of NDP government as it had in the previous nine years of Conservative government. (That much of this growth was inflationary and not real was ignored.) In 1977 he similarly repeated that under the NDP Manitoba had attained its highest rating ever on the New York bond market, a boast that might have drawn ridicule from CCFers in the 1930s and 1940s. Measurements such as gross provincial product and bond market ratings ignored the issue of distribution of the province's wealth and income among different segments or classes of society. And it was on this issue of distribution rather than sheer economic growth on which the parties were ideologically divided historically.

An indication of the government's hesitancy to consider redistributing wealth was its approach to provincial mineral resources. In 1960, the value of mineral production in Manitoba was $59 million; by 1968 it had grown to $210 million; and by 1977 to $564 million.[59] Although the CCF–NDP had promised throughout its history to ensure that the public as a whole would receive substantially greater benefits from the province's natural resource wealth, it collected less in mineral royalties in 1973 than the Conservative government had in 1968—less than $4 million.[60] The NDP government, like its predecessors and other provincial counterparts, relied more heavily on income and consumption taxes. In 1977, for example, the 5 per cent provincial sales tax generated $190 million, individual income taxes brought in $172 million, government liquor profits produced $67 million and the gasoline consumption tax (on an almost wholly imported resource) raised $55 million.[61] Although mineral royalty legislation was changed and mineral royalties rose to $19 million in 1977 (on annual production valued at over half a billion dollars), they still amounted to less than the cost of operating the government department that regulated mining activity. Schreyer's response to the *Report on Natural Resource Policy in Manitoba* prepared by Eric Kierans, a former federal Liberal cabinet minister and president of the Montreal Stock Exchange, was that it was "too drastic and retrospective."[62] It called for a planned, long-term, takeover of the private mining industry with full compensation. But Schreyer was not interested: "The mining industry," the premier reassured International Nickel's Manitoba general manager, when the Kierans proposals were released, "has nothing to fear."[63]

The NDP also failed to have an impact on some areas where all the provincial parties agreed on objectives. A good example was the shrinking farm population. By 1976, only 11 per cent of the province's population was still on farms (compared to 24 per cent in 1956), and only 31 per cent lived in rural areas.[64] Manitoba's movement toward increasing urbanization proceeded unabated during the NDP's tenure in office. The NDP's "stay option" policy—that is, providing programs that would prevent residents from being coerced by economic forces to leave their preferred areas of residence—was offered in theory but had little practical impact: between 1956 and 1966 the number of Manitoba farms shrunk from 49,000 to 40,000 and, by 1976, to 32,000. Family farms continued to disappear while those farms remaining became larger and less likely to be owner-operated. Moreover, land prices skyrocketed: in 1973 they rose by 30 per cent and, in the mid-1970s, the government expected "the most spectacular increase in farm land prices" in provincial history.[65]

Government programs did have a discernible effect in the north, a region particularly dependent on the legislature's goodwill. The north continued in the 1970s as a sparsely populated, economically exploited, hinterland. Although wages edged marginally ahead of southern rates, food and other prices were still substantially higher than in Winnipeg.[66] The north received more attention from the NDP than from any former administration. The government acted in a number of ways, by creating a Department of Northern Affairs, forming a Communities Economic Development Fund to funnel money into labour intensive northern projects, contracting with northern Indian bands for road and airport bush clearance, and shaping Leaf Rapids, the province's first government-planned mining community. The NDP provided an assortment of social and economic programs and grants for northern and native residents. It ingratiated itself to the northern population by generating a feeling that sustained economic growth and government largesse had come to stay. It ingratiated itself to the north's multinational mining corporations by dismissing the relevant recommendations of the Kierans Report.

An area of public policy under continual controversy was hydroelectric development. The Schreyer government, like the Roblin and Weir governments before it, was committed to exploiting the half-million square mile watersheds of the Nelson and Churchill rivers. The flooding of Southern Indian Lake was an issue in the 1969 election with environmentalists and native groups attacking the Conservative position. The NDP, which ran on a plank of more public study (unlike the Liberals who flatly promised to halt the proposed diversion), formulated a compromise proposal after its election. The NDP plan affected 300,000 acres, in contrast to the Conservative plan to flood 900,000 acres, and did not spell the end of an Indian community on the lake. The issue was a contentious one within the NDP, but the party convention voted in 1972 to support Schreyer's stand.

Schreyer's attitude to hydro development was unrestrained. His zeal was reflected in a quote he borrowed from an American admiral: "Damn the torpedoes—full steam ahead."[67] His government's enthusiasm for hydro development was evident in its spending priorities. In 1974-75 it poured $480 million of its $622 million self-sustaining capital program into Manitoba Hydro; in 1975-76, $336 million out of $482 million.[68] (In contrast, the Manitoba Housing and Renewal Corporation operated with a relatively modest $20 million capital authority in 1974-75.)

With respect to organized labour, its relations with the government were generally warm. The MFL applauded the NDP government's labour code (passed in its first term) and the philosophy behind that code: that the government's role was to act as impartial referee in disputes between labour and management. But in its last two years in office the government's amicable relationship with the labour movement came under some strain. Schreyer, with rare praise from the *Free Press*, supported the federal government's 1975 wage and price controls policy. It was a policy opposed by the CLC and the MFL, and Schreyer was booed at a meeting of unionists.

There were also strains in the relationship because of changes in the labour movement. The MFL's largest affiliate during the 1970s became the provincial government's employees association (MGEA). The MGEA and the government became embroiled in a series of disputes that led the MGEA to question the MFL's policy of endorsing the NDP. Although majority sentiment in MFL circles was that labour "had never had it so good as under the present government,"[69] MGEA delegates pointed out that the MFL had passed a resolution at its 1976 convention making continued MFL support for the government contingent on the government's passing certain labour law amendments which it had not passed. The government's stock was particularly low with a union unaffiliated with the MFL and on strike at a Winnipeg steel foundry against compulsory overtime, something the government was not willing to exempt from the labour bargaining process. It led to a number of loud and angry exchanges between party members and MLAs at party meetings in 1977.[70]

Between the 1920s and the 1970s the NDP—and before it the CCF and ILP—advanced from being a minor party to becoming a major one. It grew from being a city-based, labour-oriented party to one that had members and voting support across a much broader spectrum of Manitoba society. Despite its defeat in 1977, the NDP maintained a sufficiently large measure of public support to make it a leading contender for office in future elections. The NDP's record in government in the 1970s showed that the party had also evolved from being a perceived radical alternative to the older parties into a party that had come to accept the economic system which in earlier years it was so eager to transform. The NDP in Manitoba, as in Canada, had become an established and conventional party in the electoral arena, much like the Western European social democratic parties years earlier. Manitobans inside and outside the NDP took great pride in the appointment of Ed Schreyer as Governor General of Canada in 1979. This revealed, once again, that the outlook of the NDP and its leaders had become more and more like the outlook of the other parties and their leaders.

Epilogue

Manitoba in the twentieth century has reflected social and economic divisions between city and country, working class and dominant class, European-origin minorities and an Anglo-Saxon charter group. In Winnipeg there have been cleavages between north and south, between the working class and the economic elite, between those who identified with the Winnipeg General Strike tradition and those who did not. In the countryside, cleavages have existed between the southwest wheat belt and the marginal agricultural belt, between the part of the province that controlled the reins of government and the part that did not.

Within both the working class and the dominant class there have also been divisions. In the working class they have been between those who endorsed the politics of British-origin labourist social democracy (represented at various times by the ILP, CCF, and NDP), those few who favoured European Marxism and continental socialism (the Communist Party and the Social Democratic Party), and that still smaller group that favoured British Marxism and syndicalism (the Socialist Party of Canada and the One Big Union). In the dominant class the differences have been between varying shades of liberals; from those historically more tory-touched (generally the Conservatives), to those less so (generally the Liberals), to those who came nearest to being Manitoba's agrarian populists (the UFM Progressives).

Within both the European-origin minorities and the dominant Anglo-Saxon group there have been still deeper divisions. Within the European-origin group cleavages have existed among Ukrainians, Mennonites, Scandinavians, Jews, Germans, etc., between those who came from urban Europe to work in urban Manitoba and those who came from rural Europe to fish and farm in rural Manitoba, between those oriented to class politics (the CCF-NDP and the CP) and those oriented to the politics of national fraternal organizations (generally, the Liberals). Within the Anglo-Saxon group there have been cleavages between those who came from Ontario and those who came from Britain, between those who came as pioneers and homesteaders and those who came as proletariat, between those who led liberal and conservative parties and those who led social democratic and socialist parties.

In many respects Manitoba has been a microcosm of Canada: it is both rural and urban, with urbanization being the trend; it contains an ethnic mosaic anchored by an internally diverse Anglo-Saxon charter group; its economic life and institutions reflect a hinterland status; and its politics are perhaps best noted for their typically Canadian moderation. The analogy of microcosm applies also to the province's social democratic party. Until 1969 the Manitoba CCF-NDP, like its national counterpart, never attained office; yet it never withered. Neither party formed a large parliamentary opposition; yet both were more than merely minor parties. The CCF in the Commons at Ottawa and in the provincial legislature on Broadway Avenue was an influential minor party. Neither the national nor the provincial party underwent an impossibilist, or otherwordly, phase, where socialist doctrine overshadowed pragmatic politics. And the party's core of support, nationally as in Manitoba, has traditionally been in the working-class districts of the city.

Successive Manitoba governments in the first half of the twentieth century reflected an alliance of Anglo-Saxons in the southwestern wheat lands and in south Winnipeg. This alliance went under various labels at different times: Liberal, Conservative, United Farmers of Manitoba, Progressive, Liberal-Progressive, Brackenite, Coalition, and even Non-Partisan. What distinguished it from its main ideological opponent was class and heritage, not ethnicity. In 1919 the warring Strike Committee and Citizens Committee had one feature in common: Anglo-Saxon backgrounds. In working-class Winnipeg the European minorities lined up behind the British-led Strike Committee because the Citizens Committee gave them little choice, identifying them as alien radicals. In rural Manitoba these minorities deferred to the established, Canadian-born, anti-strike forces. These divisions carried over into the electoral arena.

The early influence of Ontarian settlers was reflected in Manitoba's early farm and political organizations and their leadership. The absorption of Manitoba's Crerars, Brackens, and other Progressives into the Liberal and Conservative parties was logical. Manitoba's farm leaders went the way of Ontario's. The United Farmers of Alberta, the United Farmers of Canada (Saskatchewan Section), and even the United Farmers of Ontario affiliated with the CCF in 1932 (although the latter disaffiliated in 1934.) The United Farmers of Manitoba, like its forerunners a half-century before, was true to the values of rural Ontario and remained aloof.

It was not until the late 1940s that agrarian politics in Manitoba began to shift somewhat. Jake Schulz organized the Manitoba Farmers Union (MFU), a new competitor for the UFM's successor, the Manitoba Federation of Agriculture (MFA). Schulz sat as a CCF rural MP for a period in the 1950s and his son-in-law, Ed Schreyer, became Manitoba's first social democratic premier. The MFU's membership came largely from more northerly, less prosperous, continental-born, and second generation Canadian farmers. By the 1950s, ethnic interaction over the course of forty years made possible the viability of such an organization. To the MFU leadership the MFA, like the UFM before, represented the richer, Anglo-Saxon, Liberal farmers.Diefenbakerism won most farmers in both the MFU and the MFA over to the federal Conservatives. But after both Diefenbaker and provincial Conservative premier Duff Roblin left their respective leadership posts in 1967, the provincial NDP capitalized, with the selection of Ed Schreyer, on gaining informal MFU support in certain rural areas. It was a breakthrough that helped make it possible for the NDP to win enough rural seats to form a government in 1969. For a combination of reasons Schreyer was the only figure in the Manitoba NDP who could attract such support.

Manitoba had enough of Ontario in it to have sustained the only provincial Conservative party west of Ontario that has never collapsed. But it also had enough of modern Britain and continental Europe to provide CCFer J.S. Woodsworth and provincial Communist leader W.A. Kardash with parliamentary seats. Manitoba also had enough of the prairies in it to produce national and provincial Progressive parties. Their Ontario-born liberal leadership, however, led both parties back into the realm of official Liberalism.

The rural forces in Manitoba dominated politics for so long because Winnipeg meant little in terms of provincial power. John Bracken's first cabinet in 1922, for example, contained only one Winnipeg minister and he was predictably from wealthy, Ontarianized, south Winnipeg. Winnipeg counted for little in the government's considerations, and central and north Winnipeg, where the British and European-born had settled, counted for less. This neglect was not penalized because a rurally biased electoral map ensured agrarian dominance. Between 1920 and 1949

Winnipeg had only ten seats in a fifty-five seat legislature. In the 1922 election, labour votes equalled those for twenty-seven non-labour MLAs, but Labour won only six seats. In 1945 the CCF received more votes than the Liberal–Progressives and double the Conservative total, but the CCF won only ten seats to the Liberals' twenty-five and the Conservatives' thirteen.

The CCF's fortunes were brighter after the Second World War because more and more of the ethnic minorities in the city, and in the country as well, began to look more favourably upon the party and to be less suspect of its ideology. Until at least 1945 much of the politics of the large Ukrainian community in north Winnipeg, for example, were still tied to the Russian Revolution. Those opposed to the Revolution generally supported the Liberals. The CCF, for many virulent anti-communists, was a socialist step in a hated communist direction. Those in sympathy with the Revolution embraced the Communist Party. The CCF, for the communists, was a naive, liberal, social democratic, reformist gang. Since the Second World War, ethnic assimilation has contributed to strengthening the CCF–NDP position within both the former Liberal and Communist Ukrainian groups. Political preferences of second and third generation Ukrainians were more likely dictated by working conditions than by the Russian Revolution. Most of the unions that Ukrainian and other Manitoba workers belong to have been sympathetic to the CCF–NDP. The imprisonment of Canada's lone Communist MP on charges of espionage in 1947 and the general tenor of the Cold War emaciated the CP. Because many Canadians defined socialism as a "foreign" ideology the CCF was also weakened. The CCF–NDP easily outlived the Cold War, however, because it had little to do with the CP or the Soviet Union. The CP withered because the older continental-born generation that supported it died and the party lost its base. In contrast, the ideology of British labourism survived and took root. Other socialist traditions among British and continental immigrants, in later generations, either accommodated themselves to this dominant influence on the left or they generally withered as did both the Socialist Party of Canada and the CP.

Pragmatic electoral politics, rather than socialist doctrine, always played a central role in the CCF–NDP's calculations. This was reflected in the party's coalition experience in the early 1940s, its expulsion of anti-NATO MLAs in the late 1940s, in the content of its campaigns, and in its legislative program in the 1970s. The CCF–NDP never "sold out" to the capitalist system, as some argued, because it was not at all clear that the party had ever "bought into" the anti-capitalism attributed to it by others.

In the context of the boom and bust economy of Canada and Manitoba in the 1920s and 1930s, the ILP–CCF was no more and no less radical than the NDP was in the context of the relatively affluent and stable 1960s and 1970s. What had not changed was where the party stood on the political spectrum. No one denied it stood somewhere on the left. The change, rather, was in its bases of support. Whereas in its earlier years the Manitoba CCF was a city-based party representing British-born workers, the party successfully broadened its appeal over the years to attract more of the province's non–Anglo-Saxon population, in the city, and the poorer areas of the country too.

In the autumn of 1981, the NDP was returned to office. The policies of Sterling Lyon's Conservative government of 1977-81 revealed how acceptable, rather than how radical, the NDP government's reforms of the 1970s had been. The Conservatives kept the NDP programs they had earlier denounced—such as public automobile insurance, tax credit schemes for poorer citizens, and limited partnership with private firms in the exploitation of the province's mineral resources. The 1981 election of the NDP was not so much a smashing popular triumph for the party as it was a rejection of the Conservative government. The Lyon government failed miserably at living up to the standards set by its own rhetoric. It had campaigned in 1977 on the pledge of balancing the budget and dramatically cutting down the size of the civil service. Once in power, however, it generated the largest deficit recorded in provincial history. And although it alienated the civil service and dismissed some bureaucrats who had been hired by the NDP, the size of the civil service did not shrink but actually grew. Furthermore, the promise of economic prosperity based on less government involvement in the economy did not bear fruit. Unemployment rose and outmigration continued unabated; so much so that by 1981 there were fewer resident Manitobans than there had been in 1977. Lyon's pugnacious style was a further liability to the Conservatives.

The elimination of the Liberals from the legislature in 1981, for the first time in the century, produced a pure two-party system with one party on the left and one on the right. Unlike the two-party systems in Atlantic Canada, however, where elections are contests of "ins" and "outs" devoid of ideological connotations, Manitoba took the path established in Saskatchewan and British Columbia where the NDP is also a major party. Whereas Atlantic Canadian politics have been the product of immigrants with a political culture rooted in the conservative and liberal eighteenth and nineteenth centuries, Western Canadian politics have been much more the product of twentieth-century immigrants steeped in a political culture that contains some socialist ideas. Thus, although in practice the policy outputs of the various Western provincial parties have not been that dissimilar, their ideological rhetoric certainly has been, as is revealed in the insults thrown back and forth between the "socialist hordes" and the "outdated laissez-faire capitalists."

The tone of Manitoba politics is different when the NDP is in power. There is a perceptible but immeasurable sense that the traditional outsiders and marginal elements of Manitoba's society—the underprivileged, the unpropertied, the poorer farmers, the wage labourers, the ethnic minorities—have defeated the traditional insiders and more powerful elements—the privileged, the propertied, the wealthier farmers, and the Anglo-Saxon business and corporate community.

Ironically, Howard Pawley, the new NDP premier, opposed the formation of the NDP in the late 1950s and early 1960s, on the grounds that the CCF's brand of socialism would be diluted and that the party would fall too much under the influence of the organized labour movement. He feared then that the NDP would become too much like the Liberals and Conservatives and no longer appear as a distinctive alternative. Although he lost the fight to save the CCF, Pawley's fears were allayed because the NDP was not all that different from the CCF. In Manitoba, as in Canada, the NDP's leaders, policies, and base of electoral support barely changed in the 1960s from the CCF experience of the 1950s.

One of the few people to emerge in the new party who had not belonged to or been identified with the CCF was labour lawyer Sid Green. Although he secured a seat in the legislature in the 1960s by virtue of his strong support from the union movement and his success in a heavily unionized north Winnipeg constituency, Green broke with the NDP before the 1981 election on the grounds that the party in his view had come too much under the influence of the trade union movement, something Howard Pawley had warned of over two decades earlier. Along with two other former Schreyer government ministers, Green formed a new Progressive Party, an odd assortment of political misfits that included a former Social Credit MLA. All of them were soundly trounced in the election. The NDP was the only viable opposition force to the Conservative government.

In 1969 the NDP could not have won with anyone but Ed Schreyer. In 1981 it could have won with anyone. Everyone, including Howard Pawley, knew this. The victory was clearly one of party rather than personality. By winning 47 per cent of the popular vote and 34 of the 57 seats in the legislature, the NDP became the province's undisputed leading party. Although the future electoral prospects of the NDP are, as always in politics, unpredictable, the party has securely established itself as a force in the mainstream, rather than on the periphery, of Manitoba politics.

Notes

INTRODUCTION

1 Morton, *Manitoba,* chap. 9.
2 For a discussion of the effects of settlers on the politics of the three prairie provinces, see Wiseman, "The Pattern of Prairie Politics."
3 Horowitz, "Conservatism, Liberalism, and Socialism in Canada: An Interpretation."
4 *Reformers, Rebels, and Revolutionaries.*
5 For a full discussion of the Winnipeg General Strike, see Bercuson, *Confrontation at Winnipeg.*

CHAPTER 1: THE TWENTIES AND THIRTIES

1 McNaught, *A Prophet in Politics.*
2 The overwhelming majority of the Citizens' League fifty-six member executive were professionals, industrialists, and businessmen. See Barber, "Class Conflict in Winnipeg Civic Politics."
3 Tipping, "Vote for the Men in Jail," p. 12.
4 ILP, Minute Book of the Centre Branch, Winnipeg, December 16, 1920.
5 *Winnipeg Free Press,* January 18, 1951.
6 CCF Papers, Provincial Archives of Manitoba; hereafter referred to as CCFP–PAM.
7 Morton, *Manitoba,* pp. 378-79.
8 Peterson, "Ethnic and Class Politics in Manitoba," p. 88.
9 *Canadian Annual Review, 1932,* vol. 31, pp. 241-42.
10 Beatrice Brigden interview.
11 Minutes of 1932 convention, Dauphin, November 1-3, 1932, United Farmers of Manitoba Papers, PAM.
12 In reply to an inquiry from the CCF regarding the size of the UFM (6,000 members in 300 branches in 1933) the UFM secretary added: "As a preponderance of nationality or race, I might say that the greatest number of members are all British Canadian origin. We have a slight scattering of Minnonites (*sic*), Icelanders and

Ukerainians (sic)." Anna Gray to N.F. Priestley, July 14, 1933, CCF Records, Public Archives of Canada; hereafter referred to as CCFR–PAC.

13 The platform's preamble noted that "In the capitalist system, human beings are merely instruments for the production of wealth; the source of necessary power — labor power — which like the coal in the furnace or the oil in the machine has its price and sole value determined in the commodity market." "Independent Farmer Party Platform," 1932, CCFP–PAM.

14 Manitoba Free Press, April 11, 1932.

15 W.J. Smith to N.F. Priestley, June 26, 1933, CCFR–PAC.

16 See the Clubs' president's statement in the minutes of meeting, Manitoba Farmers' Section, CCF, November 3, 1933, and H.G. Johnson to N.F. Priestley, March 23, 1934, ibid.

17 W.E. Gordon, Christianity, Socialism and the CCF.

18 Manitoba Commonwealth, April 26, 1935; June 29, 1935; and July 5, 1935.

19 Minutes of the National CCF Convention, August 3-5, 1936, CCFR–PAC.

20 In 1931, 5 per cent of Manitobans over ten years of age were unable to speak English. Among Ukrainian Manitobans, an important swing group in voting patterns, the level was 14 per cent. Census of Canada, 1931, vol. 4, Table 53, p.979.

21 Quoted in Peterson, "Ethnic and Class Politics in Manitoba," pp. 91-92.

22 Gray, The Winter Years, pp. 126-27.

23 S.J. Farmer to M.J. Coldwell, June 14, 1935, CCFR–PAC.

24 Hampton Hindson, MFS secretary, to M.J. Coldwell, December 13, 1934, ibid.

25 Manitoba Commonwealth, July 17, 1936.

26 Ibid., July 3, 1936.

27 Ibid., September 25 and October 2, 1936.

28 For example, Pierce, Socialism and the CCF.

29 The exchange of letters between Sam Carr and J.S. Woodsworth is reprinted in the Manitoba Commonwealth, May 3, 1935.

30 For example: F.G. Tipping's call for a minimum united program; a resolution passed by the Marquette constituency association; and a resolution proposed by Brandon delegates and defeated in convention, ibid., August 2, 1936; October 16, 1936; and October 23, 1936.

31 For example: the speech by Alex Stewart, CCF federal candidate in Churchill constituency; and the article by Charles G. Stewart, secretary of the Winnipeg and District CCF Clubs, ibid., August 2, 1936; and December 18, 1936.

32 For a discussion of the national CCF as a movement-party, see Young, Anatomy of a Party.

33 Social Credit or Social Ownership.

34 David Orlikow interview.

35 Rae, "The Politics of Class," p. 235.

36 McNaught, A Prophet in Politics, pp. 286-88.

37 Statement by ILP Executive to membership in convention, August 14, 1933, CCFR–PAC.

38 Heaps, The Rebel in the House, p. 138.

39 Manitoba Commonwealth, October 23, 1936.

40 Fred C. White, ILP secretary, to Beatrice Brigden, CCF provincial secretary, February 7, 1938, CCFR–PAC.

41 M.J. Coldwell and David Lewis to John Queen, February 9, 1938, ibid.

42 John Queen to M.J. Coldwell, February 21, 1938, ibid.
43 Alistair Stewart to David Lewis, March 17, 1942, ibid.
44 *Manitoba Commonwealth,* February 19, 1943.
45 Brigden interview.
46 Hedrick Peddie, provincial organizer, to David Lewis, February 23, 1938, CCFR-PAC.
47 He expressed his thoughts on the war: "Canada is at war. She has taken her rightful place side by side with other component parts of the British Empire. Without stint or reward we must give that assistance to the Mother Country which the situation demands." 1940 Heaps election pamphlet, "An Appeal to the Electors of North Winnipeg," CCFP-PAM.
48 Charles Biesick, CCF provincial secretary, to David Lewis, December 26, 1939, CCFR-PAC.
49 Comparative data on Manitoba, Saskatchewan, and Alberta agricultural economic conditions are in Canada, Royal Commission on Dominion-Provincial Relations, *Report,* Book 1, Table 76, p. 194.
50 *Manitoba Commonwealth,* October 29, 1937.

CHAPTER 2: THE "NON-PARTISAN" GOVERNMENT

1 Knowles, in contrast to most of the CCF leaders, was born in the United States. He could trace his ancestry to the *Mayflower.*
2 Stanley Knowles interview.
3 *Manitoba Commonwealth,* June 4, 1937; October 23, 1936.
4 S.J. Farmer to David Lewis, August 7, 1940, CCFR-PAC.
5 Such as executive member Fred Tipping, interview with author.
6 F.R. Scott to David Lewis, August 15, 1940, CCFR-PAC.
7 David Lewis to S.J. Farmer, August 14, 1940, ibid. (emphasis in original).
8 Stanley Knowles to Lloyd Stinson, March 9, 1957. Personal papers in the possession of Mr. Knowles in Ottawa; used by permission and hereafter referred to as Knowles Papers.
9 S.J. Farmer to David Lewis, August 15, 1940, CCFR-PAC.
10 David Lewis to G.H. Williams, September 24, 1940, ibid.
11 Charles Biesick interview.
12 Knowles interview.
13 Biesick interview.
14 John Bracken to S.J. Farmer, October 25, 1940, Knowles Papers.
15 Kendle, *John Bracken,* p. 176.
16 Minutes of the Fifth Annual Convention, CCF (Manitoba Section), Winnipeg, October 26, 1940, CCFP-PAM.
17 Ibid.
18 Compare "Suggested Draft Statement sent to Mr. S.J. Farmer, M.L.A." attached to David Lewis to S.J. Farmer, September 23, 1940, CCFR-PAC. and the statement attached to S.J. Farmer to John Bracken, October 29, 1940, Knowles Papers.
19 Knowles interview and Minutes of the Sixth National CCF Convention, Winnipeg, October 28-29, 1940, CCFP-PAM.
20 Two examples are in the *Manitoba Commonwealth,* November 22, 1940, and May 8, 1941.
21 Ibid., November 8, 1940.

22 Ibid., May 8, 1941.
23 *Winnipeg Free Press,* September 17, 1949.
24 Stanley Knowles to Lloyd Stinson, March 9, 1957, Knowles Papers.
25 Knowles interview.
26 CCFP-PAM (emphasis in original).
27 *Manitoba Commonwealth,* April 11, 1941.
28 Minutes of CCF National Executive Meeting, September 19-20, 1942, CCFR-PAC.
29 CCFP-PAM and *Manitoba Commonwealth,* February 14, 1941.
30 Stanley Knowles to David Lewis, March 14, 1942, Knowles Papers.
31 Minutes of the Seventh Annual Convention, CCF (Manitoba Section), Winnipeg, October 22-23, 1942, CCFP-PAM.
32 Lloyd Stinson interview.
33 S.J. Farmer to John Bracken, December 9 and December 17, 1942. John Bracken to S.J. Farmer, December 15, 1942, Knowles Papers.
34 Stinson interview.
35 Knowles interview.
36 Minutes of the Eighth Annual Convention, CCF (Manitoba Section), Winnipeg, October 22-23, 1943, CCFP-PAM.
37 Angus MacInnis to S.J. Farmer, September 21, 1940; and G.H. Williams to S.J. Farmer, October 8, 1940, CCFR-PAC.
38 Elmer E. Roper to S.J. Farmer, September 26, 1940; and E.B. Jolliffe to David Lewis, August 12, 1940, ibid.
39 Donnelly, *The Government of Manitoba,* Table 1, p. 60.
40 S.J. Farmer to David Lewis, August 15, 1940, CCFR-PAC.
41 Report of Proceedings, Tenth Annual Convention, CCF (Manitoba Section), Winnipeg, December 6-8, 1945, CCFR-PAC.

CHAPTER 3: THE COMMUNISTS AND THE EXPULSIONS

1 Undated speech or manuscript for pamphlet in 1943 by-election, signed by B.R. Richards, CCFP-PAM.
2 Stinson interview.
3 Report of Proceedings, Tenth Annual Convention, CCF (Manitoba Section), Winnipeg, December 6-8, 1945, CCFP-PAM. The number of members in The Pas was 573 in 1943.
4 Knowles, Stinson, and Biesick interviews. David Lewis also told Richards that in time he would become the provincial leader: B.R. Richards to author, January 16, 1972.
5 Report of Proceedings, Tenth Annual Convention, CCF (Manitoba Section), Winnipeg, December 6-8, 1945, CCFP-PAM.
6 McNaught, *A Prophet in Politics,* pp. 305-07.
7 Letter to a Winnipeg branch of the Canadian Legion, Provincial Council minutes, December 4, 1941, CCFP-PAM.
8 Independent Labour Party of Manitoba, "Municipal Platform," 1940, ibid.
9 *Canadian Tribune,* February 13, 1943. In 1943-44, when the Communists refused to attack the government, some CCF spokesmen argued that the CCF was the only anti-capitalist party in Canada. See, for example, David Orlikow's articles, *Manitoba Commonwealth,* January 21 and February 18, 1944.

10 Buck addressed a rally in Winnipeg estimated at being between 3,500 and 4,000. *Canadian Tribune*, July 10, 1943.
11 Letter dated October 19, 1943, ibid.; November 6, 1943.
12 Ibid., November 6, 1943. See also Report of Proceedings, Eighth Annual Convention, CCF (Manitoba Section), Winnipeg, October 22-23, 1943, CCFP-PAM; and the *Winnipeg Tribune*, October 25, 1943. In 1944, the provincial convention rejected a resolution favouring round-table discussions among CCF locals and other political organizations. Most delegates took this to mean the LPP: *Winnipeg Free Press*, October 27, 1944. The convention minutes contain no reference to this resolution and its debate.
13 D.L. Johnson to author, February 8, 1972.
14 "I remember I had a very high regard for Woodsworth and when they [the Communists] referred to Woodsworth as a social fascist I was pretty annoyed with them." Biesick interview.
15 *Canadian Tribune*, August 14, 1943.
16 Ibid., December 9, 1944.
17 David Lewis to Donovan Swailes, January 15, 1945, CCFR-PAC.
18 Lloyd Stinson to all provincial associations and units, March 29, 1945, CCFP-PAM.
19 Dated February 8, 1945, Knowles Papers.
20 D.L. Johnson and B.R. Richards to Manitoba CCF Executive Committee, February 16, 1945, CCFP-PAM.
21 "Notes on Discussion re Richards-Johnson Request," Executive Committee minutes, February 16, 1945, ibid.
22 Richards and Johnson to Swailes, February 22, 1945; and Swailes to Richards and Johnson, February 24, 1945, ibid.
23 David Lewis to Stanley Knowles, February 27, 1945, Knowles Papers.
24 "Statement by D.L. Johnson and B.R. Richards in the Manitoba Legislature," March 1, 1945, CCFR-PAC.
25 *Winnipeg Tribune*, March 2, 1945.
26 *Manitoba Commonwealth*, March 3, 1945.
27 D.L. Johnson to author, February 8, 1972.
28 *Winnipeg Free Press*, editorial, "Manitoba Bombshell," March 3, 1945.
29 Ibid., editorial, "Hewing to the C.C.F. Line," March 6, 1945. *Free Press* editor John Dafoe firmly believed David Lewis to be a communist in 1938; McNaught, *A Prophet in Politics*, p. 269.
30 *Canadian Tribune*, March 17 and March 24, 1945.
31 *Winnipeg Tribune*, editorials, March 2 and March 10, 1945.
32 *Tribune* and *Free Press*, March 9, 1945; and CCF Provincial Executive Committee minutes, March 9, 1945, CCFP-PAM.
33 The in-camera proceedings are contained in CCF Provincial Council minutes and addenda, March 10, 1945, CCFP-PAM. A general summary of the debate appears in the *Manitoba Commonwealth*, March 17, 1945.
34 B.R. Richards to author, January 16, 1972.
35 Ibid.
36 D.L. Johnson to author, February 8, 1972.
37 Provincial Council minutes, March 10, 1945, CCFP-PAM.
38 B.R. Richards to author.
39 Secretary's Report, Provincial Executive Committee minutes, July 13, 1945, CCFP-PAM.

40 Stanley Knowles to E.A. Hansford, March 23, 1945, Knowles Papers.
41 *Free Press*, May 31, 1945.
42 Ibid., May 26, 1945.
43 *Manitoba Commonwealth*, June 30, 1945.
44 Stanley Knowles to Lloyd Stinson, November 9, 1945, Knowles Papers.
45 Report of Proceedings, Tenth Annual Convention, CCF (Manitoba Section), December 6-8, 1945, Winnipeg, CCFP-PAM.
46 W.A. Kardash to the Delegates at the Manitoba CCF Convention, December 7, 1945, ibid.
47 *Free Press* and *Tribune*, December 10, 1945.
48 Provincial Executive Committee minutes, December 21, 1945, CCFP-PAM.
49 D.L. Johnson to Stanley Knowles, September 24, 1949. Knowles replied to this "Dear Stan" letter with a short "Dear Dwight" letter reaffirming his faith in socialism but refusing to enter "an interminable argument." September 29, 1949, Knowles Papers.
50 D.L. Johnson to author, February 8, 1972. Johnson's wife had been elected to the provincial LPP committee in 1947 and 1948. *Free Press*, January 27, 1947 and February 23, 1948.
51 B.R. Richards to author, January 16, 1972.
52 D.L. Johnson to author, February 8, 1972.
53 B.R. Richards to M.J. Coldwell, May 26, 1946; M.J. Coldwell to B.R. Richards, May 31, 1946, Knowles Papers.
54 Mabel Richards to M.J. Coldwell, June 8, 1946; M.J. Coldwell to Mabel Richards, June 14, 1946, ibid.
55 *Free Press*, November 1, 1946.
56 B.R. Richards to author. For a press account of this speech see *Free Press*, May 29, 1947.
57 *Free Press*, May 1, 1947.
58 Report of Proceedings, Twelfth Annual Convention, CCF (Manitoba Section), Portage la Prairie, June 26-28, 1947, Knowles Papers.
59 The complete front page of the *Western Tribune* (later *The Westerner*), June 7, 1947, was devoted to Richards, based on an interview he gave and an anti-American speech delivered at The Pas. Articles by Richards were printed in *The Westerner* on October 18, 1947, and April 24, 1948. On May 15, 1948, it reprinted, word for word, one of his radio broadcasts on behalf of the CCF.
60 For example, in his speech at the north Winnipeg LPP rally of March 28 and at the 1947 provincial convention. Report of Proceedings, Twelfth Annual Convention, CCF (Manitoba Section), Portage la Prairie, June 26-28, 1947, Knowles Papers.
61 *Canadian Tribune*, April 6, 1946.
62 "Is he a Socialist?" read the rhetorical headline, ibid., August 24, 1946.
63 *The Westerner*, February 7 and February 21, 1948.
64 Knowles interview.
65 Provincial Executive Committee minutes, November 13, 1948, CCFR-PAC.
66 Editorials, "Mr. Barry [sic] Richards and Communism," November 26, 1947; "But the Critics are Missing," March 29, 1948; and "A Matter of E.R.P.," August 21, 1948.
67 Report of Proceedings, Thirteenth Annual Convention, CCF (Manitoba Section), Winnipeg, June 24-26, 1948, CCFP-PAM.

68 *Manitoba Commonwealth,* July 17, 1948.
69 *Tribune,* August 20, 1948.
70 *Free Press,* December 11, 1948.
71 *Manitoba Commonwealth,* March 5, 1949.
72 Transcript of Radio Broadcast by W. Doneleyko, delivered over CKRC, Winnipeg, March 9, 1949, CCFP-PAM.
73 *Tribune,* March 16, 1949.
74 Provincial Executive minutes, March 12, 1949, CCFP-PAM.
75 Stanley Knowles to E.A. Hansford, March 13, 1949, Knowles Papers.
76 Stanley Knowles to E.A. Hansford, March 18, 1949, ibid.
77 Stanley Knowles to Lloyd Stinson, March 21, 1949, ibid.
78 Mabel Richards to Donovan Swailes, March 19, 1948, [*sic:* 1949], CCFP-PAM.
79 Text of letter, dated April 16, reprinted in *Free Press,* May 13, 1949.
80 *Manitoba Commonwealth,* April 30, 1949.
81 Telegram, David Lewis to Don Swailes, May 24, 1949, CCFP-PAM.
82 Stanley Knowles to David Lewis, May 25, 1949, Knowles Papers.
83 *Tribune,* May 16, 1949.
84 *Free Press,* May 6, 14, 17 and June 3, 1949.
85 *Tribune* editorials, "Berths for Fellow-Travellers," May 16, 1949; and "C.C.F. and 'Mischief Makers,'" July 8, 1949.
86 Knowles interview.
87 Report of Proceedings, Fourteenth Annual Convention, CCF (Manitoba Section), Winnipeg, July 14-16, 1949, CCFR-PAC.
88 Tipping interview.
89 B.R. Richards to author, January 16, 1972.
90 Stinson interview.
91 David Lewis to Donovan Swailes, September 16, 1949, CCFR-PAC.
92 Knowles interview.
93 *Free Press,* July 15, 1949; and *Tribune,* July 16, 1949.
94 *Free Press* editorial, "The C.C.F. and the Pact," July 19, 1949.
95 *Manitoba Commonwealth,* July 23, 1949.
96 *Free Press,* August 12, 1949.
97 *Tribune,* September 17, 1949.
98 Wilbert Doneleyko to Delegates assembled at the CCF convention in St. Clements, October 15, 1949, CCFP-PAM.
99 Don Swailes to Ed. Smee, April 29, 1953, ibid.
100 Walter Young in *The Anatomy of a Pary,* p. 277, states: "in 1949 Communists won the provincial by-election in St. Clements and St. Andrews." He is in error on a number of counts: (1) St. Clements and St. Andrews were two seats, not one; (2) there were no by-elections in 1949; by-elections were held in both seats in October 1950; (3) the Communists never contested St. Andrews; (4) the LPP ran a candidate in St. Clements, placing a poor third with only 254 votes out of over 3,500 cast.
101 Don Swailes to W.S. Duncan, September 12, 1952, CCFP-PAM.
102 Lorne Ingle to Don Swailes, June 19, 1950, CCFR-PAC.

CHAPTER 4: THE FORTIES AND FIFTIES

1 D. Swailes to L. Ingle, national CCF secretary, November 3, 1952, CCFP-PAM.
2 "What is the C.E.C.?", a pamphlet authored by Campbell Haig, CEC chairman, undated, ibid.

3 Article 5, section 5, CCF (Manitoba Section), *Constitution* (1943), ibid.
4 L. Stinson to T.C. Douglas, October 23, 1957, CCFP-PAC.
5 A Stewart to L.R. Shaw, October 4, 1943, ibid.
6 Provincial Council minutes, April 4, 1944, ibid.
7 Secretary's Report, Provincial Council minutes, January 20, 1951, CCFP-PAM.
8 D. Swailes to Mrs. E. Johnson, May 7, 1957, ibid.
9 Magnus Eliason interview; and "St. George Byelection" File, CCFP-PAM.
10 Lipset, *Agrarian Socialism*, p. 6; and Caplan, "The Failure of Canadian Socialism," p. 108.
11 Various pamphlets in CCFP-PAM.
12 Report of the Secretary-Treasurer, Report of Proceedings, Twentieth Annual Convention, CCF (Manitoba Section), Winnipeg, November 9-10, 1956, Eliason Papers, PAM.
13 Ibid.
14 D. Swailes to author, February 25, 1972.
15 *Winnipeg Tribune*, January 12, 1950.
16 Canada, *Report of the Committee on Election Expenses*, Chart 5, p. 495.
17 "Membership Records," dated December 31, 1958, Eliason Papers.
18 S. Knowles to D. Swailes, September 25, 1949, Knowles Papers.
19 D. Swailes to Dan Bachewich, March 10, 1952, CCFR-PAM.
20 *Tribune*, August 30 and September 29, 1949; *Winnipeg Free Press*, October 4, 1949.
21 "Liberal–CCF Controversy," an undated memo written by Lloyd Stinson in July 1958, Stinson Papers. This memo, along with Stinson's article in the *Free Press*, February 20, 1971, are the major sources for this account.
22 Minutes of meeting of CCF Provincial Executive and Elected Candidates, June 20, 1958, CCFP-PAM.
23 Provincial Executive Committee minutes, July 5, 1958, ibid.
24 Campaign speech by Lloyd Stinson, April 6, 1959, ibid.
25 Peter Desbarats, "Taking the Fog Out of Politics," *Tribune*, April 20, 1959.
26 Quoted in the *Free Press*, January 11, 1959.
27 Provincial Council minutes, January 17, 1959, Eliason Papers.
28 Provincial Leader's Report, Report of Proceedings, Nineteenth Annual Convention, CCF (Manitoba Section), Dauphin, July 15, 1955, Stinson Papers.
29 Represented in, among other places, Zakuta, *A Protest Movement Becalmed*.
30 The word is David Lewis's after the adoption of the Winnipeg Declaration of Principles, *Free Press*, August 4, 1956.
31 Transcript of radio broadcast, CKY, August 9, 1944, CCFP-PAM.
32 M.J. Coldwell, *Left Turn, Canada*, pp. 72-93.
33 Address of F.R. Scott to the Eleventh National Convention, CCF, Vancouver, July 26-28, 1950, CCFP-PAM.
34 Transcript of radio broadcast, CKRC, September 26, 1945; and Manitoba CCF pamphlet entitled "A New Deal for the Manitoba Farmer," (1945), ibid. (emphasis in original).
35 Fred Tipping, Report on Education, Report of Proceedings, Eleventh Annual Convention, CCF (Manitoba Section), Brandon, October 31, November 1-2, 1946, CCFR-PAC.
36 Provincial Platform adopted at the Fourteenth Annual Convention, CCF (Manitoba Section), Winnipeg, July 14-16, 1949, ibid. (emphasis in original).

37 These and other pamphlets in CCFP–PAM.
38 Report of Secretary-Treasurer, Report of Proceedings, Thirteenth Annual Convention, CCF (Manitoba Section), Winnipeg, June 24-25, 1948, ibid.
39 D. Swailes to Mrs. Hazel Allan, January 15, 1954, ibid.
40 Brandon Provincial CCF Association, Letter to Membership, September 1954, ibid.
41 David Orlikow, interview with author, April 1972.
42 Report of Proceedings, Twenty-third Annual Convention, CCF (Manitoba Section), Winnipeg, November 20-21, 1959, CCFP–PAM.
43 Excerpts from an address at an election rally, May 4, 1959, Eliason Papers.
44 "Report of A.R. Paulley, CCF House Leader, on the First Session of the Twenty-Sixth Legislature of Manitoba," ibid.
45 A speech in the Manitoba Legislature entitled "Amendment of Anti-Coalitionists," c. 1950, Stinson Papers.
46 Excerpt from letter by G.F. Fines and D. Swailes, 1953, CCFP–PAM.
47 *Free Press*, April 4, 1956.
48 Pickersgill and Forster, The *Mackenzie King Record*, Volume II, quoted on p. 409.
49 Editorial entitled "Invasion from Saskatchewan," October 10, 1945.
50 *Free Press*, October 15 and 26, 1949.
51 Editorial entitled "C.C.F. Convention," June 19, 1950.
52 Provincial Council minutes, January 9, 1954, CCFP–PAM.
53 Walter Conn (?) to D. Swailes, October 19, 1959, ibid.
54 Thomas McClure, General Secretary, OBU, to S. Knowles, December 2, 1942 and Thomas McClure to A.N. Robertson, November 18, 1942, Knowles Papers.
55 "Organization Report to National Council by National Treasurer," March 1-2, 1952, CCFR–PAC.
56 Report of Secretary-Treasurer, Report of Proceedings, Twentieth Annual Convention, CCF (Manitoba Section), Winnipeg, November 9-10, 1956, Eliason Papers.
57 Manitoba Provincial Council, CCF, to All Union Locals in Manitoba, 1953, ibid.
58 Lloyd Stinson, "Notes in Reply to the Speech from the Throne," February 3, 1956, Stinson Papers.
59 Jimmy James, interview with author.
60 Porter, *The Vertical Mosaic*, Table XXXII, p. 350.
61 D. Swailes to Dan McKinnon, April 20, 1954, CCFP–PAM.
62 Len Evans to Gordon Fines, July 10, 1952 and Provincial Council minutes, July 12, 1952, and January 10, 1953, ibid.
63 S. Lee to D. Swailes, February 25, 1955; and George Watson to D. Swailes, May 27, 1954, ibid.
64 Provincial Council minutes, November 13, 1948, CCFR–PAC.
65 Manitoba CCF pamphlet, "A New Deal for The Manitoba Farmer," 1945, CCFP–PAM.
66 Quoted in the *Free Press*, July 15, 1949.
67 Fred Tufford interview.
68 Manitoba Farmers Union, pamphlet, "M.F.U. Policy and Progress" (Winnipeg, 1957-58 issue).
69 D. Swailes to Mrs. R.S. Moore, December 12, 1952, CCFP–PAM.
70 Herb McIntosh to D. Swailes, December 21, 1952, ibid.
71 D. Swailes to Dan McKinnon, April 20, 1954, ibid.
72 D. Swailes to L. Ingle, April 21, 1954, CCFR–PAC.

73 Fred Tipping interview.
74 Orlikow interview.
75 Tufford interview.
76 Eliason interview.
77 See memo entitled "An Appeal to the Ukrainian Members and Sympathizers of the CCF," March 22, 1944, CCFR–PAC; Provincial Council minutes, March 10, 1944 and November 13, 1948, CCFP–PAM.
78 D. Swailes to Mrs. E. Lyon, January 26, 1956, CCFP–PAM.
79 *Free Press*, June 17, 1958.
80 Orlikow interview.
81 Wiseman and Taylor, "Ethnic vs Class Voting."

CHAPTER 5: THE NEW PARTY

1 Horowitz, *Canadian Labour in Politics*, pp. 172-73.
2 Knowles, *The New Party*, p. 21.
3 L. Stinson to L. Ingle, June 4, 1956, CCFR–PAC.
4 Alexander, *Canadians and Foreign Policy*, quoted on p. 59.
5 D. Swailes to C. Hamilton, September 21, 1957, CCFP–PAM.
6 Orlikow interview.
7 *Winnipeg Tribune*, October 15, 1960.
8 Stinson interview.
9 Biesick interview.
10 Brigden interview.
11 Tipping interview.
12 *Free Press*, November 19 and 21, 1960.
13 Howard Pawley interview.
14 J.A. Coulter interview.
15 *The Voice of the Farmer* (Minnedosa), November 1, 1958; July 1, 1959; February 1960; May 1961.
16 Tufford interview.
17 F. Zaplitny to C. Hamilton, May 14, 1958, Knowles Papers.
18 *Free Press*, December 4, 1958. Schulz's book was *The Rise and Fall of Canadian Farm Organizations*.
19 See letter of Rudy Usick, MFU president to Sid Ransom, MFA president, in *The Voice of The Farmer*, May 1, 1960.
20 See the statement of the MFU executive in the *Free Press*, November 28, 1960.
21 D. Swailes to E. Smee, March 5, 1955, CCFP–PAM.
22 D. Swailes to A. Roulin, December 19, 1954, ibid.
23 Provincial Council minutes, January 17, 1959, ibid.
24 *The Voice of the Farmer*, June 1, 1958, and May 1, 1959.
25 Tufford interview.
26 Report by Lloyd Stinson, New Party Organizer, March 16, 1961, and "Manitoba Delegates to Founding Convention of the New Party," n.d., CCFP–PAM.
27 *Free Press*, April 23 and 29, 1959.
28 Peter Desbarats, "Six-Week Campaign Closes," *Tribune*, May 13, 1959.
29 *Free Press*, May 29, 1958 and September 1, 1960.

30 *Free Press* editorials, December 5, 1958, July 29, 1960, and September 8, 1961; *Tribune* editorials, December 4, 1958, February 25, 1960, and May 15, 1961.
31 Tufford interview.
32 D. Swailes to author, February 25, 1972. Swailes had been elected MFL president at a convention in Room 10 of the Winnipeg Labour Temple. Room 10 had been the headquarters of the 1919 strike committee. "Minutes of the First Annual Convention, Manitoba Federation of Labour," November 19-20, 1955, CCFP-PAM.
33 Memorandum in Knowles Papers and *Free Press*, February 2, 1959.
34 "CCF Conference on New Political Party," March 14-15, 1959, CCFP-PAM and a memorandum in Knowles Papers.
35 Provincial Executive Committee minutes, February 28, 1959, CCFP-PAM.
36 Minutes of "CCF Executive meeting with Representatives of Labour," March 27, 1959, ibid.
37 *Tribune*, June 17, 1959.
38 *Free Press*, July 8, 1959.
39 "CCF Conference on New Political Party," June 20-21, 1959, CCFP-PAM.
40 "Notes on Conference on New Party," September 20, 1959, ibid.
41 Tufford interview.
42 MFL, "Report of the Committee on the New Political Party," n.d., CCFP-PAM. and Report of Proceedings, Fifth Annual Convention, October 17-18, 1959, Winnipeg, Knowles Papers.
43 *The Commonwealth*, November 4, 1959.
44 Tufford interview.
45 Provincial Council minutes, February 6, 1960, CCFP-PAM.
46 A. Mackling and H. Pawley to the National Committee, Proposed New Party, February 17, 1960, CCFP-PAM.
47 Schreyer interview.
48 L. Stinson to S. Knowles, October 5, 1960, Knowles Papers (emphasis in original).
49 D. Swailes to C. Hamilton, Aplril 18, 1960, CCFP-PAM.
50 L. Stinson to S. Knowles, November 21, 1960, Knowles Papers.
51 Stinson interview.
52 *Free Press*, November 22, 1960.
53 *Free Press*, April 7, and August 6, 1960; *Tribune*, April 12, and August 6, 1960; and Russ Paulley interview.
54 *Tribune*, October 17, 1960.
55 "Grumbler," no. 3, January 3, 1961, newsletter of Local 142 of the Canadian Brotherhood of Railway, Transport and General Workers, CCFP-PAM.
56 *The Voice of the Farmer*, December, 1960.
57 Ibid., and transcript of Schulz's comments on CKRC, January 11, 1961, CCFP-PAM.
58 *The Commonwealth*, January 11, 1961.
59 Tufford interview.
60 *Tribune*, January 4, 1961, and Report of Secretary-Treasurer, Report of Proceedings, Founding Convention, NDP (Manitoba Section), Winnipeg, November 3-4, 1961, CCFP-PAM.
61 L. Stinson to S. Knowles, July 9, 1961, Knowles Papers.
62 All figures are from membership records in CCFP-PAM.
63 *Free Press*, February 24, 1961.
64 "Manitoba Delegates to Founding Convention of the New Party," n.d., CCFP-PAM.

65 *Free Press,* August 5, 1961.
66 *The Voice of the Farmer,* editorial, "The New Party Convention," August, 1961.
67 *Tribune,* August 30, and October 30, 1961.
68 *The Voice of the Farmer,* November, 1961.
69 *The Commonwealth,* September 13, 1961 and Report of the Secretary-Treasurer, Report of Proceedings, Founding Convention, NDP (Manitoba Section), Winnipeg, November 3-4, 1961, CCFP–PAM, and *Tribune,* November 6, 1961.
70 Manitoba NDP Constitution, 1961, CCFP–PAM.
71 Eliason interview.
72 Pawley interview.
73 Coulter-James interviews.
74 Stinson interview.
75 D. Swailes to author, February 25, 1972.

CHAPTER 6: THE SIXTIES

 1 Swainson, "Ethnic Revolt."
 2 Peterson, "Ethnic and Class Politics in Manitoba"; and Peterson and Barber, "Some Factors in the 1969 NDP Victory in Manitoba."
 3 Wiseman and Taylor, "Ethnic vs. Class Voting."
 4 Reports of Proceedings of all Manitoba NDP Conventions are in Manitoba NDP Papers, Winnipeg.
 5 L.C. Stinson to S. Knowles, January 7, 1963, and A.N. Robertson to S. Knowles, September 11, 1964, Knowles Papers.
 6 S.E. Varcoe to M. Eliason, May 16, 1963, Eliason Papers.
 7 M. Eliason to A.R. Paulley, April 19, 1963, and M. Eliason, untitled, undated, memorandum written soon after the 1962 election, ibid.
 8 Provincial Executive Committee minutes, January 11, 1963, ibid.
 9 Photographs of NDP billboards and campaign literature for elections in the 1960s are in NDP Papers, Winnipeg.
10 Untitled, May 28, 1966, Knowles Papers.
11. Vol. 1, no. 4, March, 1967.
12 Sam Goodman to T.C. Douglas, February 9, 1962, NDP Papers, Winnipeg.
13 Statistics in the possession of Wally Dougherty and Dave Hall, Winnipeg.
14 Report of Provincial Secretary to Provincial Council, March 3, 1962, NDP Papers, Winnipeg.
15 "Provincial Secretary's Memorandum No. 4," n.d., ibid.
16 NDP confidential questionnaire, December, 1968, ibid.
17 "Delegates in Attendance," Fourth Annual Manitoba NDP Convention, 1965, ibid.
18 Memorandum, Arthur S. Gillman, research director, to George S. Bain, provincial president, February 2, 1963, ibid.
19 Eager, "The Paradox of Power in the Saskatchewan C.C.F., 1944-1961."
20 *Free Press,* November 5, 1962.
21 Letter to New Society participants by Harold W. Huston, December 5, 1961, Eliason Papers.
22 Financial statements attached to the Reports of Proceedings of the annual conventions, ibid.
23 Canada, *Report of the Committee on Election Expenses,* Table 5, pp. 478-79.

24 "Brief of the Manitoba New Democratic Party Presented to the Committee on Election Expenses," December 10, 1965, Eliason Papers.
25 Regenstreif, *The Diefenbaker Interlude*, pp. 98 and 143. See also Alford, "The Social Bases of Political Cleavage in 1962."
26 Horowitz, *Canadian Labour in Politics*, p. 53 (emphasis in original).
27 Orlikow interview.
28 Coulter interview.
29 NDP Table Officers Meeting minutes, March 24, 1962, Eliason Papers; and J. James, MFL executive secretary to All Affiliated Local Unions and Labour Councils, January 19, 1968, NDP Papers, Winnipeg.
30 Canada, Department of Labour, *Union Growth in Canada, 1921-1967, Table V, pp. 76-77.*
31 Horowitz, *Canadian Labour in Politics*, Table 11, p. 257. Manitoba figures and names of locals are in NDP Papers, Winnipeg.
32 Paltiel, Noble, and Whitaker, "The Finances of the Cooperative Commonwealth Federation and the New Democratic Party," Table 7, p. 345. See also Paltiel, *Political Party Financing in Canada*, Table 3-III, p. 55. For the year ending December 31, 1966, affiliation fees going to the national office totalled $74,024 while membership fee income was only $50,240. Financial Statement, 1966, Eliason Papers.
33 Paltiel et al., *Studies in Canadian Party Finance*, pp. 371, 373 and NDP Papers, Winnipeg.
34 Financial Statements, NDP Papers, Winnipeg.
35 Dennis McDermott to Secretary, Manitoba NDP, August 22, 1969, ibid.
36 Sidney Green, interview with author.
37 Schreyer interview.
38 Paulley interview. See Paulley's comments in the *Free Press*, September 3, 1968 and *Tribune*, October 5, 1968.
39 Russ Paulley letter to all convention delegates, October 26, 1968, Eliason Papers, and the *Manitoba New Democrat*, vol. 11, no. 7, October, 1968, p. 3.
40 Press release issued by eight NDP MLAs, October 4, 1969, Eliason Papers.
41 *Tribune*, November 2, 1968.
42 Ibid., August 25, 1966.
43 M. Eliason to E. Schreyer, April 28, and May 5, 1969, Eliason Papers.
44 Schreyer interview.
45 Al Finkel and Harold Chorney, "A Moderate Proposal," *Canadian Dimension*, vol. 7, nos. 1 and 2, June–July, 1970, p. M2, and *Tribune*, July 5, 1969.
46 Eliason interview.
47 "Signs of Victory" by NDP president Frank Syms in *The Commonwealth*, June 18, 1969.
48 *Free Press*, May 30, 1969.
49 Eric Wells, "Is Being Premier of Manitoba as Comfortable as Ed Schreyer Makes it Look?," *Saturday Night*, October, 1969, p. 42.
50 Orlikow interview.
51 Gad Horowitz, "The Future of the NDP," p. 23.
52 "Organizer's Report," undated, NDP Papers, Winnipeg.
53 Statutory Declaration, July 28, 1969, Manitoba, *Office of the Chief Electoral Officer*, Winnipeg.

54 Statement of Income and Expenses for September 1, 1968, to August 31, 1969, attached to Provincial Council minutes, January 24, 1970, Eliason Papers; and Memo entitled "Election Expenses, June 25, 1969," NDP Papers, Winnipeg.
55 Statutory Declaration, August 22, 1969, Manitoba, *Office of the Chief Electoral Officer.*
56 Statutory Declaration, August 29, 1969, ibid.
57 McConnell Advertising Ltd. to Progressive Conservative Party of Manitoba, June 6, 1969, Progressive Conservative 1969 Election Expenses File, ibid.
58 Peterson, "Ethnic and Class Politics in Manitoba," p. 110.

CHAPTER 7: THE SEVENTIES

1 Chandler and Chandler, *Public Policy and Provincial Politics,* Tables 3.1-3.6, pp. 43-53.
2 Goldberg, "Social Democracy: A Study of the NDP in Manitoba, p. 53".
3 Wilson, "The Decline of the Liberal Party in Manitoba," Tables IX, XVII, XIX and XX, pp. 32, 38 and 39.
4 Surich, "Leadership and the Voting Decision in Ontario and Manitoba," Tables 5 and 6, pp. 10 and 11.
5 *Winnipeg Tribune,* August 15, 1969.
6 Quoted in Donnelly, "Manitoba," p. 238.
7 Arlene Billinkoff, "Party Policies to the Fore," *Winnipeg Free Press,* September 22, 1977.
8 *Manitoba New Democrat,* vol. 7, no. 3, March 1977.
9 "Schreyer Promises Bridge" and "Transportation $$ Aid Pledged," *Free Press,* June 13, 1973.
10 "Election Promises Converted to $$," ibid., June 2, 1973.
11 Ibid., October 4, 1977.
12 *Tribune,* September 24, 1977.
13 "Report" of activities by organizer John Vershagin for September 14-26, 1970, CCFP-PAM.
14 *Manitoba New Democrat,* vol. 6, no. 6, June-July 1976.
15 Quoted in Peterson, "Manitoba," p. 185.
16 Quoted in René Chartier, special assistant to the premier, to F. Petruic, August 26, 1971, CCFP-PAM.
17 Bill Allen, Saskatchewan NDP secretary, to E. Schreyer, September 21, 1971 and Schreyer to Allen, September 23, 1971, ibid.
18 Steve Kerstetter, "Premier Running Out of Firsts at 37," *Free Press,* June 13, 1973.
19 Schreyer interview and *Free Press,* March 12, 1973.
20 J.A. McAllister, secretary, South West Manitoba NDP Regional Council to Sam Uskiw, June 29, 1970, CCFP-PAM.
21 Ken Hanly, letter to the editor, *Manitoba New Democrat,* vol. 4, no. 5, April 1974.
22 *Manitoba New Democrat,* vol. 5, no. 8, September-October 1975; and Provincial Council Minutes, May 4-5, 1975, NDP Papers, Winnipeg.
23 These data are from membership records in CCFP-PAM, and Glen McRuer, "A Membership Profile of the Manitoba New Democratic Party, 1961-1973," (mimeo: n.d.), an academic paper based on the same sources.
24 *Inter-Com* (an NDP newsletter), vol. 1, no. 5, April 19, 1973.

25 Provincial Executive Minutes, June 14, 1975, NDP Papers, Winnipeg.
26 "Report of Provincial Secretary," August 23, 1974, ibid.
27 McRuer, "A Membership Profile of the Manitoba New Democratic Party, 1961-1973," p. 10.
28 R. Taves to E. Schreyer, July 8, 1975, NDP Papers, Winnipeg.
29 ICEC pamphlet, September 1971, ibid.
30 NDP press release, undated (likely September 1971), ibid. (emphasis in original).
31 F. Petruic to members of ten Winnipeg constituencies, February 10, 1971, entitled "Urban Reorganization in Greater Winnipeg," ibid.
32 Provincial Executive Minutes, June 10, 1971, ibid.
33 Provincial Executive Minutes, October 8, 1971, ibid.
34 Provincial Table Officers Minutes, August 6, 1974, ibid.
35 "Report of the Provincial Secretary," October 6-7, 1973, ibid.
36 Sam Uskiw, NDP president, to Tage Erlander, February 13, 1969, ibid.
37 E. Schreyer to W. Brandt, May 21, 1974, ibid.
38 Gorman H. King to Al Mackling, Manitoba's Attorney-General, January 22, 1973, ibid.
39 Frank P. Zeider, party state secretary, to Magnus Eliason, August 9, 1969, and Provincial Council Minutes, August 16, 1969, ibid.
40 "Organizations affiliated with the New Democratic Party," January 1, 1969; December 31, 1972; April 1, 1974; and April 1, 1978, ibid.
41 "Attendance Sheet," Manitoba New Democratic Party, 1977 Convention Report, Winnipeg, January 28-30, 1977, ibid.
42 "Report of the Provincial Secretary," October 6-7, 1973; J.A. (Art) Coulter to F. Petruic, Septembr 26, 1973; and H.L. Stevens to H. Mitchell, party treasurer, August 23, 1973, ibid.
43 "Organization and Finance Committee Minutes," April 16, 1975 and R. Taves to NDP union affiliated locals, May 27, 1975, ibid.
44 Provincial Executive Minutes, March 1, 1974, ibid.
45 R. Taves to all NDP MLAs, April 10, 1975, ibid.
46 A.R. Micay to Ed Schreyer Election Committee, June 18, 1973, ibid.
47 Provincial Executive Minutes, January 8, 1970, and Provincial Officers Minutes, August 2, 1973, ibid.
48 Files from the *Office of the Chief Electoral Officer*, Winnipeg.
49 Leo Sutyla, president Local 144, UAW, Winnipeg, to E. Schreyer, October 22, 1970, NDP Papers, Winnipeg.
50 "NDY Winnipeg Declaration," July 1972 by Lissa Donner and four others, ibid.
51 *Free Press* and *Tribune*, May 11, 1973.
52 Provincial Executive Minutes, July 10, 1971, NDP papers, Winnipeg.
53 Saul Cherniack, *Manitoba Budget Address, 1971*, p. 10.
54 *Manitoba Budget Address, 1975*, p. 30 and Donald A. Craik, *Manitoba Budget Address, 1978*, p. 35.
55 McAllister, "The Fiscal Analysis of Policy Outputs," p. 486.
56 Saul Miller, *Manitoba Budget Address, 1977*, Table 1, p. 98.
57 "Mount Carmel Clinic Talks About Your Health," pamphlet, Winnipeg, January-February 1975.
58 *Manitoba Budget Address, 1975*, p. 45, and Revenue Canada, *Taxation Statistics*, Table 9, p. 123.

59 *Manitoba Budget Address, 1975,* p. 33, and *Manitoba Budget Address, 1979,* Table 3, p. 60.

60 Manitoba, *Main and Supplementary Estimates of Current Expenditure and Revenue, 1974,* p. 44, and *Estimates of Current Expenditure and Revenue, 1969,* p. 31.

61 Ibid., 1977-8, pp. 64-5.

62 *Free Press,* April 21, 1973.

63 *Tribune,* April 23, 1973.

64 Manitoba Department of Industry and Commerce, *The Economy of the Province of Manitoba,* p. 6; and Manitoba Department of Agriculture, *Manitoba Agriculture: 1977 Yearbook,* p. 98.

65 Manitoba Department of Agriculture, *In Search of a Land Policy for Manitoba,* Tables 22, 24, and 26; pp. 65, 67, and 73 and pp. 84 and 53.

66 Brief presented to the Manitoba Economic Development Advisory Board Conference, by Dick Martin, USWA Local 6166, Thompson, January 27-29, 1975, pp. 5-6.

67 *Free Press,* April 30, 1973.

68 *Manitoba Budget Address, 1975,* p. 63.

69 *Free Press,* September 24, 1977.

70 *Manitoba New Democrat,* vol. 7, no. 4, April 1977.

Bibliography

MANUSCRIPT COLLECTIONS

CO-OPERATIVE COMMONWEALTH FEDERATION PAPERS. Provincial Archives of Manitoba, Winnipeg.

CO-OPERATIVE COMMONWEALTH FEDERATION RECORDS. Public Archives of Canada, Ottawa.

MAGNUS ELIASON PAPERS. Provincial Archives of Manitoba, Winnipeg.

INDEPENDENT LABOR PARTY, Centre Branch. Minute Book of the Centre Branch, Winnipeg, December 1920-November 1923. Provincial Archives of Manitoba.

STANLEY KNOWLES PAPERS. Privately held, Ottawa.

LIBERAL–PROGRESSIVE PARTY OF MANITOBA PAPERS. Provincial Archives of Manitoba.

MANITOBA. Office of the Chief Electoral Officer, Winnipeg. Files on Election Expenses.

MANITOBA NEW DEMOCRATIC PARTY PAPERS. Manitoba New Democratic Party, Winnipeg.

LLOYD STINSON PAPERS. Privately held, Winnipeg.

UNITED FARMERS OF MANITOBA PAPERS. Provincial Archives of Manitoba.

The location of some of these collections has changed. The Manitoba NDP Papers to 1977 have been integrated with the CCF Papers at the Provincial Archives of Manitoba. The Knowles Papers have been transferred to the Public Archives of Canada. The Stinson Papers may have been moved to the United States.

PUBLIC DOCUMENTS

CANADA. DEPARTMENT OF THE INTERIOR. *Immigration Facts and Figures.* Ottawa, 1973.

CANADA. DEPARTMENT OF LABOUR. *Union Growth in Canada, 1921-67.* Ottawa: 1970.

CANADA. DOMINION BUREAU OF STATISTICS. "Origin, Birthplace, Nationality and Language of the Canadian People." Ottawa, 1929.

CANADA. *Report of the Committee on Election Expenses.* Ottawa: Queen's Printer, 1966.

CANADA. REVENUE CANADA. *Taxation Statistics.* Toronto, 1978.

CANADA. Royal Commission on Dominion-Provincial Relations. *Report.* Ottawa, 1940.

MANITOBA. Royal Commission to Enquire into and Report upon the Causes and Effects of the General Strike in the City of Winnipeg. *Report.* Winnipeg, 1919.

MANITOBA. DEPARTMENT OF AGRICULTURE. *In Search of a Land Policy for Manitoba.* Winnipeg, 1974.

- *Manitoba Agriculture: 1974-77 Yearbook.* Winnipeg, n.d.

MANITOBA. DEPARTMENT OF FINANCE. *Budget Address.* Winnipeg, 1958-1977.

- *Main and Supplementary Estimates of Current Expenditure and Revenue.* Winnipeg, 1970-1977.

MANITOBA. DEPARTMENT OF INDUSTRY AND COMMERCE. *The Economy of the Province of Manitoba.* Winnipeg, 1973.

MANITOBA. *Guidelines for the Seventies* (3 vols.). Winnipeg, 1973.

MANITOBA. *Public Accounts of the Province of Manitoba.* Winnipeg, 1968-1977.

INTERVIEWS

Armstrong, Frank. Winnipeg. May 1972.

Biesick, Charles. Winnipeg. June 1971.

Brigden, Beatrice. Winnipeg. December 1970.

Coulter, Art. Winnipeg. April 1972.

Eliason, Magnus. Winnipeg. May 1972.

Green, Sidney. Winnipeg. February 1973.

James, Jimmy. Winnipeg. May 1972.

Knowles, Stanley. Ottawa. October 1971.

Mackling, Al. Winnipeg. February 1972.

McDuffe, Peter. Winnipeg. May 1972.

Orlikow, David. Winnipeg. April 1972.

Paulley, Russ. Winnipeg. February 1972.

Pawley, Howard. Winnipeg. February 1972.

Schreyer, Ed. Winnipeg. February 1972.

Stinson, Lloyd. Winnipeg. June 1971.

Tipping, Fred. Winnipeg. December 1970.

Tufford, Fred. Winnipeg. March 1972.

BOOKS AND ARTICLES

ALEXANDER, FRED. *Canadians and Foreign Policy.* Toronto: University of Toronto Press, 1960.

ALFORD, ROBERT R. *Party and Society.* London: John Murray, 1964.

- "The Social Bases of Political Cleavage in 1962." In Bernard Blishen et al., eds., *Canadian Society,* 3rd ed. Toronto: Macmillan, 1968.

ALLEN, RICHARD. *The Social Passion.* Toronto: University of TorontoPress, 1971.

AVAKUMOVIC, IVAN. *Socialism in Canada.* Toronto: McClelland and Stewart, 1978.

BARBER, PAUL. "Class Conflict in Winnipeg Civic Politics: The Role of the Citizens and Civic Election Organizations." Mimeo, 1970, Provincial Archives of Manitoba.

BEAULIEU, PAUL, ed. *Ed Schreyer, Social Democrat in Power.* Winnipeg: Queenston House, 1977.

BEER, SAMUEL H. *British Politics in the Collectivist Age.* New York: Knopf, 1966.

BERCUSON, DAVID JAY. *Confrontation at Winnipeg: Labour, Industrial Relations, and the General Strike.* Montreal: McGill-Queen's, 1974.

CAPLAN, GERALD L. "The Failure of Canadian Socialism: The Ontario Experience, 1932-1945." *Canadian Historical Review* XLIV (1968): 93-121.

CARD, B.Y. *The Canadian Prairie Provinces from 1870 to 1950.* Toronto: J.M. Dent, 1960.

CHANDLER, MARSHA A. and WILLIAM M. *Public Policy and Provincial Politics.* Toronto: McGraw-Hill Ryerson, 1979.

CHRISTIAN, WILLIAM, and COLIN CAMPBELL. *Political Parties and Ideologies in Canada: Liberals, Conservatives, Socialists, Nationalists.* Toronto: McGraw-Hill Ryerson, 1974.

CLARK, S.D. *The Developing Canadian Community*, 2nd ed. Toronto: University of Toronto Press, 1968.

COLDWELL, M.J. *Left Turn, Canada.* Toronto: Duell, Sloan and Pierce, 1945.

COOK, RAMSAY, ed. *The Dafoe-Sifton Correspondence, 1919-1927.* Winnipeg: Manitoba Record Society, 1966.

– "John W. Dafoe: Conservative Progressive." *Canadian Historical Association Report* (1961): 75-85.

– *The Politics of John W. Dafoe and the Free Press.* Toronto: University of Toronto Press, 1963.

DAVIDSON, C.B. *Manufacturing in Manitoba.* Winnipeg: Manitoba Economic Survey Board, 1938.

– et al. *The Population of Manitoba.* Winnipeg: Manitoba Economic Survey Board, 1938.

DAWSON, C.A. *Group Settlement: Ethnic Communities in Western Canada.* Toronto: Macmillan, 1936.

– *Pioneering in the Prairie Provinces.* Toronto: Macmillan, 1940.

DONNELLY, MURRAY S. *Dafoe of the Free Press.* Toronto: Macmillan, 1968.

– *The Government of Manitoba.* Toronto: University of Toronto Press, 1963.

– "Manitoba," in *Canadian Annual Review of Politics and Public Affairs, 1976.* Toronto: University of Toronto Press, 1977.

EAGER, EVELYN. "The Paradox of Power in the Saskatchewan CCF, 1944-1961." In J.H. Atchison, ed., *The Political Process in Canada.* Toronto: University of Toronto Press, 1963.

ENGELMAN, FREDERICK C. "Membership Participation in Policy-Making in the CCF." *Canadian Journal of Economics and Political Science* 22 (May 1956): 161-173.

ENGLAND, ROBERT. *The Central European Immigrant in Canada.* Toronto: Macmillan, 1929.

– *The Colonization of Western Canada.* London: P.S. King and Son, 1936.

FARMER, S.J. *Social Credit or Social Ownership.* Winnipeg, 1936.

FINKEL, AL, and HAROLD CHORNEY, "A Moderate Proposal." *Canadian Dimension* 7 (June-July 1970).

GAGAN, DAVID P., ed. *Prairie Perspectives.* Toronto: Holt, Rinehart and Winston, 1970.

GOLDBERG, HARVEY. "Social Democracy: A Study of the NDP in Manitoba."
Research Essay, Department of Political Science, Carleton University, 1975.

GORDON, W.E. *Christianity, Socialism and the* CCF. N.P., N.D., CCFRecords, Public
Archives of Canada.

GRAY, JAMES.*The Winter Years*. Toronto: Macmillan, 1966.

HARTZ, LOUIS. *The Founding of New Societies*. New York: Harcourt, Brace and
World, 1964.

– *The Liberal Tradition in America*. New York: Harcourt, Brace and World, 1955.

HEAPS, LEO. *The Rebel in the House*. London: Niccolo, 1970.

HOROWITZ, GAD. *Canadian Labour in Politics*. Toronto: University of Toronto Press,
1968.

– "Conservatism, Liberalism, and Socialism in Canada: An Interpretation." *Canadian
Journal of Economics and Political Science*, 23 (May 1966).

– "The Future of the NDP." *Canadian Dimension* 3 (July-August 1966).

IRVINE, WILLIAM.*Co-operative Government*. Ottawa: Mutual Press, 1929.

– *The Farmers in Politics*. Toronto: McClelland and Stewart, 1920.

JACKSON, JAMES A. *The Centennial History of Manitoba*. Toronto: McClelland and
Stewart, 1970.

KENDLE, JOHN. *John Bracken*. Toronto: University of Toronto Press, 1979.

KNOWLES, STANLEY. *The New Party*. Toronto: McClelland and Stewart, 1961.

LAPIERRE, LAURIER et al. *Essays on the Left*. Toronto: McClelland and Stewart,
1971.

LEAGUE FOR SOCIAL RECONSTRUCTION, Winnipeg Branch. *Pioneers in Poverty*.
Winnipeg: Manitoba Co-operative Publishing, 1938.

LIPSET, SEYMOUR MARTIN. *Agrarian Socialism: The Cooperative Commonwealth
Federation in Saskatchewan*. Berkeley: University of California Press, 1950; reprint
ed., Garden City, N.Y.: Anchor Books, 1968.

– *The First New Nation*. New York: Basic Books, 1963.

MCALLISTER, JAMES A. "The Fiscal Analysis of Policy Outputs." *Canadian Public
Administration* 23 (Fall 1980): 458-86.

MCCORMACK, ROSS. *Reformers, Rebels, and Revolutionaries: The Western Canadian
Radical Movement, 1899-1919*. Toronto: University of Toronto Press, 1977.

MCCRORIE, JAMES N. *In Union is Strength*. Saskatoon: Centre for Community
Studies, 1964.

MCHENRY, DEAN E. *The Third Force in Canada*. Berkeley: University of California
Press, 1950.

MACINNIS, GRACE. *J.S. Woodsworth: A Man to Remember*. Toronto: Macmillan,
1953.

MACKINTOSH, W.A. *Economic Problems of the Prairie Provinces*. Toronto: Macmillan,
1953.

– *Prairie Settlement: The Geographical Setting*. Toronto: Macmillan, 1934.

MCNAUGHT, KENNETH. *A Prophet in Politics: A Biography of J.S. Woodsworth*.
Toronto: University of Toronto Press, 1959.

MCRUER, GLEN. "A Membership Profile of the Manitoba New Democratic Party, 1961-
1973." Mimeo, N.D., NDP Papers, Winnipeg.

MAGNEY, WILLIAM H. "The Methodist Church and the National Gospel, 1884-1914."
The Bulletin 20 (1968): 3-95.

MASTERS, D.C. *The Winnipeg General Strike*. Toronto: University of Toronto Press,
1950.

MOORHOUSE, HOPKINS. *Deep Furrows.* Toronto: George J. McLeod, 1918.

MORTON, ARTHUR S., and CHESTER MARTIN. *History of Prairie Settlement and "Dominion Lands" Policy.* Toronto: Macmillan, 1938.

MORTON, DESMOND. *NDP: The Dream of Power.* Toronto: Hakkert, 1974.

MORTON, W.L. "The Bias of Prairie Politics." *Transactions of the Royal Society of Canada,* Series III, XLIX (June 1955): 57-66.

– "A Century of Plain and Parkland." *Alberta Historical Review* 17 (Spring 1969): 1-10.

– "Direct Legislation and the Origins of the Progressive Movement." *Canadian Historical Review* XXV (September 1944): 279-88.

– *Manitoba: A History,* 2nd. ed. Toronto: University of Toronto Press, 1967.

– *The Progressive Party in Canada.* Toronto: University of Toronto Press, 1950; reprint ed., 1967.

MURCHIE, R.W. *Agricultural Progress on the Prairie Frontier.* Toronto: Macmillan, 1936.

NAYLOR, R.T. "The Ideological Foundations of Social Democracy and Social Credit." In Gary Teeple, ed., *Capitalism and the National Question in Canada.* Toronto: University of Toronto Press, 1972.

ORLIKOW, LIONEL. "The Reform Movement in Manitoba, 1910-1915." In Douglas Kemp, ed., *Papers Read Before the Historical and Scientific Society of Manitoba.* Series III, no. 16 (Winnipeg, 1961): 50-61.

PALMER, HOWARD, ed. *The Settlement of the West.* Calgary: Comprint, 1977.

PALTIEL, KHAYYAM ZEV. *Political Party Financing in Canada.* Toronto: McGraw-Hill, 1970.

– HOWARD P. NOBLE, and REGINALD A. WHITAKER. "The Finances of the Cooperative Commonwealth Federation and the New Democratic Party," in Canada, Committee on Election Expenses, *Studies in Canadian Party Finance.*

PARTRIDGE, E.A. *A War on Poverty.* Winnipeg: Wallingford Press, 1925.

PETERSON, TOM. "Manitoba," in *Canadian Annual Review of Politics and Public Affairs, 1972.* Toronto: University of Toronto Press, 1974.

– "Manitoba: Ethnic and Class Politics in Manitoba," in M. Robin, ed., *Canadian Provincial Politics.* Scarborough, Ont.: Prentice Hall, 1972.

– and P. BARBER. "Some Factors in the 1969 NDP Victory in Manitoba." *Lakehead University Review* III (Fall 1970): 120-33.

PICKERSGILL, J.W., and D.F. FORSTER. *The Mackenzie King Record,* Vol. 2. Toronto: University of Toronto Press, 1968.

PIERCE, G. *Socialism and the CCF.* Montreal: Contemporary Publishers' Assoc., 1934.

PORTER, JOHN. *The Vertical Mosaic.* Toronto: University of Toronto Press, 1965.

RAE, J.E. "The Politics of Class: Winnipeg City Council, 1914-1945." In Carl Berger and Ramsay Cook, eds., *The West and the Nation.* Toronto: McClelland and Stewart, 1976.

RASPORICH, A.W., and H.C. KLASSEN, eds., *Prairie Perspectives 2.* Toronto: Holt, Rinehart and Winston, 1973.

REGENSTREIF, PETER. *The Diefenbaker Interlude: Parties and Voting in Canada.* Toronto: Longmans, 1965.

ROBIN, MARTIN. "Determinants of Radical Labour and Socialist Politics in English-Speaking Canada between 1880 and 1930." *Journal of Canadian Studies* 2 (May 1967): 27-39.

- *Radical Politics and Canadian Labour, 1880-1930.* Kingston: Industrial Relations Centre, Queen's University, 1968.
RODNEY, WILLIAM. *Soldiers of the International: A History of the Communist Party of Canada, 1919-1929.* Toronto: University of Toronto Press, 1968.
SCARROW, HOWARD A. *Canada Votes.* New Orleans: Hauser Press, 1962.
- "Federal-Provincial Voting Patterns in Canada." *Canadian Journal of Economics and Political Science* 26 (May 1960): 289-98.
SCHULZ, JACOB. *The Rise and Fall of Canadian Farm Organizations.* Winnipeg: published by the author, 1955.
SHARP, PAUL F. *The Agrarian Revolt in Western Canada.* Minneapolis: University of Minnesota Press, 1948; reprint ed., New York: Octagon Books, 1971.
SINCLAIR, PETER R. "Class Structure and Populist Protest: The Case of Western Canada." *Canadian Journal of Sociology* I (Spring 1975): 1-17.
SISLER, W.J. *Peaceful Invasion.* Winnipeg: By the author, 1944.
SMITH, A.E. *All My Life.* Toronto: Progress Books, 1949.
STINSON, LLOYD. *Political Warriors.* Winnipeg: Queenston House, 1975.
SURICH, JO. "Leadership and the Voting Decision in Ontario and Manitoba: A Preliminary Analysis." Paper presented at the annual meeting of the Canadian Political Science Association, Edmonton, June 1975.
SWAINSON, DONALD. "Ethnic Revolt: Manitoba's Election." *Canadian Forum* XLIX (August 1969): 98-99.
- ed., *Historical Essays on the Prairie Provinces.* Toronto: McClelland and Stewart, 1970.
TAYLOR, K.W., and NELSON WISEMAN. "Class and Ethnic Voting in Winnipeg: The Case of 1941." *Canadian Review of Sociology and Anthropology* XIV (May 1977): 174-87.
THOMAS, LEWIS H. *Essays on Western History.* Edmonton: University of Alberta Press, 1976.
THORBURN, HUGH G., ed. *Party Politics in Canada.* Toronto: Prentice-Hall, 1963.
TIPPING, FRED. "Vote for the Men in Jail." *The Canadian Democrat,* 2:3 (March-April 1960).
TROFIMENKOFF, S.M., ed. *The Twenties in Western Canada.* Ottawa: Papers of the Western Canadian Studies Conference at Calgary, 1972.
TROPER, HAROLD MARTIN. *Only Farmers Need Apply.* Toronto: Griffen House, 1972.
UNDERHILL, FRANK H. *In Search of Canadian Liberalism.* Toronto: Macmillan 1960.
WILSON, JOHN. "The Decline of the Liberal Party in Manitoba." *Journal of Canadian Studies* X (February 1975): 24-41.
WISEMAN, NELSON. "The Pattern of Prairie Politics," *Queen's Quarterly,* 88 (Summer 1981): 298-315.
- and K.W. TAYLOR. "Class and Ethnic Voting in Winnipeg during the Cold War."
- *Canadian Review of Sociology and Anthropology* XVI (February 1979): 60-76.
- "Ethnic vs Class Voting: The Case of Winnipeg, 1945." *Canadian Journal of Political Science* VII (June 1974): 314-28.
WOOD, L.A. *A History of the Farmers' Movements in Canada.* Toronto: Ryerson Press, 1924.
WOODSWORTH, J.S. *Strangers Within our Gates.* Toronto: Stephenson, 1909; reprint ed. Toronto: University of Toronto Press, 1972.

YOUNG, WALTER D. *The Anatomy of a Party: The National* CCF. Toronto: University of Toronto Press, 1969.
– *Democracy and Discontent.* Toronto: Ryerson Press, 1969.
YUZYK, PAUL. *The Ukrainians in Manitoba.* Toronto: University of Toronto Press, 1953.
ZAKUTA, LEO. *A Protest Movement Becalmed: A Study of Change in the* CCF. Toronto: University of Toronto Press, 1964.
ZEIGLER, OLIVE. *Woodsworth, Social Pioneer.* Toronto: Ontario Publishing, 1934.

PERIODICALS AND NEWSPAPERS

Canadian Annual Review. 1960-77.
Canadian Annual Review of Public Affairs. 1910-38.
Canadian Parliamentary Guide. 1900-77.
Canadian Tribune. 1943-47.
The Commonwealth (Regina). 1952-70.
Labour Annual (Winnipeg). 1956-61.
Manitoba Commonwealth. 1934-52.
Manitoba Free Press.
Manitoba New Democrat. 1965-79.
The Voice of the Farmer (Minnedosa). 1958-61.
Winnipeg Free Press.
Winnipeg Tribune.

PERIODICALS AND NEWSPAPERS

Index